FORTRESS TEXTS IN

# Divine Immutability

## A Critical Reconsideration

Isaak August Dorner

Translated by
Robert R. Williams and Claude Welch

with an Introduction by
Robert R. Williams

Fortress Press Minneapolis

DIVINE IMMUTABILITY
A Critical Reconsideration

First Fortress Press edition 1994.

Translated from "Über die richtige Fassung des dogmatischen Begriffs der Unveränderlichkeit Gottes, mit besonderer Beziehung auf das gegenseitige Verhältniss zwischen Gottes übergeschichtlichem und geschichtlichem Leben," *Jahrbücher für deutsche Theologie* I/2 (1856) 361ff.; II/3 (1857) 440ff.; III/4 (1858) 479ff.



Interior design: Publishers' WorkGroup

---

Library of Congress Cataloging-in-Publication Data

Dorner, I. A. (Isaak August), 1809–1884.
[Über die richtige Fassung des dogmatischen Begriffs der Unveränderlichkeit Gottes. English]
Divine immutability : a critical reconsideration / Isak August Dorner : translated by Robert R. Williams and Claude Welch : with an introduction by Robert R. Williams.
p. cm.
Translation of: Über die richtige Fassung des dogmatischen Begriffs der Unveränderlichkeit Gottes.
Includes bibliographical references and index.
ISBN 0-8006-3213-3 (alk. paper)
1. God—Immutability. 2. Theology, Doctrinal—History—19th century. I. Williams, Robert R. II. Title.
BT153.I47D6713 1994
231'.4—dc20 94-17160
CIP

---

The paper used in this publication meets the minimum requirements of American National Standard for Information Sciences—Permanence of Paper for Printed Library Materials, ANSI Z329.48-1984.

---

Manufactured in U.S.A. AF 1–3213

98 97 96 95 94 1 2 3 4 5 6 7 8 9 10

# Divine Immutability

IN THE SERIES

Protestantism and Progress
Ernst Troeltsch

What Is Christianity?
Adolf Von Harnack

Faith and Understanding
Rudolf Bultmann

Servant of the Word: Selected Sermons of Friedrich Schleiermacher

Christian Caring: Selections from *Practical Theology*
Friedrich Schleiermacher

Confessions of an Inquiring Spirit
Samuel Taylor Coleridge

The So-called Historical Jesus and the Historic Biblical Christ
Martin Kähler

Romance and the Rock: Nineteenth-Century Catholics on Faith and Reason
Edited by Joseph Fitzer

The Christian Faith
Ernst Troeltsch

Tradition and the Critical Spirit: Catholic Modernist Writings
George Tyrrell

Religion in History
Ernst Troeltsch

Against Pure Reason: Writings on Religion, Language, and History
Johann Gottfried Herder

# Contents

# Introduction

Isaak August Dorner's monograph on divine immutability originally appeared as a three-part essay published between 1856 and 1858 in the *Jahrbücher für deutsche Theologie.*[1] Although Dorner was widely known inside and outside of Germany, and although several of his books were translated into English,[2] this essay has not received much attention even from German commentators,[3] nor has it been translated into English in its

1. Isaak August Dorner (1809–1884), "Über die richtige Fassung des dogmatischen Begriffs der Unveränderlichkeit Gottes, mit besonderer Beziehung auf das gegenseitige Verhältniss zwischen Gottes übergeschichtlichem und geschichtlichem Leben," *Jahrbücher für deutsche Theologie* I/2 (1856) 361ff.; II/3 (1857) 440ff.; III/4 (1858) 479ff. Reprinted in his *Gesammelte Schriften aus dem Gebiet der systematischen Theologie* (Berlin: Verlag Wilhelm Hertz, 1883), 188-377. Dorner was one of the co-founders and co-editors of the *Jahrbücher für deutsche Theologie.*

2. I. A. Dorner, *Entwicklungsgeschichte der Lehre von der Person Christi*, Stuttgart, 1839, 2nd ed., 4 v., Stuttgart, 1846–56. E.T. from the 2nd ed., *History of the Development of the Doctrine of the Person of Christ*, 5 v., Edinburgh, 1861–63. *Geschichte der protestantische Theologie*, Munich, 1867. E.T., *History of Protestant Theology*, 2 v., Edinburgh, 1871. *System der christlichen Glaubenslehre*, 2 v., Berlin, 1879-81, 2nd ed., 1886-87. E.T., *A System of Christian Doctrine*, 4 v., Edinburgh, 1880–82. *System der christlichen Sittenlehre*, edited by the author's son, August Dorner, Berlin, 1885, E.T., *System of Christian Ethics*, Edinburgh, 1887.

3. For example, neither Emmanuel Hirsch (*Geschichte der neuern evangelischen Theologie*, 5 v., Gerd Mohn, 1960) nor Stefan-Schmid (*Geschichte der deutschen evangelischen Theologie*, Berlin: Töpelmann, 1960) acknowledge the existence of this essay in their discussion of Dorner. More surprising is the fact that Karl Barth does not mention the essay in the chapter devoted to Dorner in *Protestant Thought in the 19th Century*, a series of lectures

entirety.[4] Moreover, Dorner never published it as a monograph, although it was reprinted with other essays in his *Gesammelte Schriften* shortly before his death. Hence, it may be asked, Why should we bother with this sometimes obscure, often rambling essay?

Dorner's essay, while occasioned by the nineteenth-century kenotic christological controversy, is not a mere period piece better left buried in an obscure nineteenth-century journal. The kenotic Christology conceived incarnation as a divine self-divestment or self-emptying, which implies that God undergoes change. Thus kenoticism raised the issue of immutability. Immutability remains a topic in current theological discussions in both theology and philosophy of religion. While these discussions tend to be more philosophically oriented, Dorner approaches the issue of immutability from the perspective of soteriology and Christology, and against the conceptual background of classical German Idealism.[5] Dorner's essay

given in 1932, but first published 15 years later in 1947 (English translation: Valley Forge: Judson Press, 1973, 577ff). Barth apparently discovered Dorner's Immutability Essay sometime after 1932 but before 1940, when he published his doctrine of God. The most recent study of Dorner by Christine Axt-Piscalar, *Der Grund des Glaubens: Eine theologiegeschichtliche Untersuchung zum Verhältnis von Glaube und Trinität in der Theologie Isaak August Dorners* (Tübingen: J.C.B. Mohr, 1990; hereafter cited as GdG), acknowledges the existence of this essay, but does not analyze it and thus continues the pattern of neglect.

4. Part Three of the essay has been translated by Claude Welch in his *God and Incarnation [A Library of Protestant Thought]* (New York: Oxford University Press, 1965) 115–180. The focal point of this volume is Christology and its implications for theology in mid-nineteenth century German Protestant theology. Welch also provides one of the few English-language discussions of Dorner's proposal for a reconstruction of the concept of divine immutability. Cf. his *Protestant Thought in the 19th Century*, v. 1 (New Haven: Yale University Press, 1972) 273-282.

5. Dorner was born June 20, 1809, and was educated at Tübingen University (1827–1832), which prescribed a four-year theological course for students in the Tübingen Stift. F. C. Baur, who was influenced by Hegel, was one of Dorner's teachers. Dorner became a tutor and then associate professor at Tübingen. Beginning with a call to Kiel (1839) he had a wide range of teaching posts, including Königsberg (1843), Bonn (1847), and Göttingen (1853) before finally being appointed at Berlin (1862) as both professor and member of the superior church council. He died July 8, 1884. The fact that Dorner's formulations are in terms drawn from his nineteenth century German Idealist predecessors does not necessarily mean that his discussion is hopelessly outdated, for there has been recent interest in exploring convergences between Hegel and Whitehead in systematic reconstruction of metaphysics. Cf. *Hegel and Whitehead: Contemporary Perspectives on Systematic Philosophy* (Ed. George Lucas, Albany: State University of New York Press, 1986). The successful demonstration of such convergences points to the continuing relevance of this nineteenth century literature for both philosophy and theology. Moreover, the recent publication of critical editions of Hegel's *Lectures on the Philosophy of Religion* (Hegel, *Lectures on the Philosophy of Religion*, 3 vols., ed. Peter C. Hodgson, Berkeley: University of California Press 1984, 1985, 1987) makes possible better understanding of and appreciation for Hegel's central concept of God as spirit, on which Dorner draws. It is also worth noting that Hegel is the first modern philosopher of religion to develop the concept of the death of God as a theological concept. This lies behind both the kenotic Christology that Dorner rejects, and Dorner's own proposals.

remains perhaps the most extensive historical, philosophical, and theological treatment of immutability to date.

Although he was initially attracted to kenoticism, Dorner ultimately rejected it, as is clear from the first essay. However, kenoticism rightly raises questions concerning divine immutability that Dorner continues to explore both historically and constructively. Part Two is an historical survey of the classical doctrine of divine immutability from the patristic period to Schleiermacher. Drawing upon his massive study, The *History of the Development of the Doctrine of the Person of Christ* (1846–56), Dorner shows that the issue of immutability did not arise for the first time in nineteenth-century discussions, but was present from the beginnings in the classical period. He identifies a soteriological interest underlying the classical formulations of divine immutability. The classical concern is to combine power and goodness in the concept of God in order to show that God's immutability is the ultimate foundation and guarantee of salvation. On classical premisses any change in God could only be a change for the worse; hence any change in God would call into question the divine goodness on which soteriology rests. To forestall this possibility, change must be unconditionally excluded from God. Thus the classical doctrine suppressed any suggestion of divine suffering and change.

The classical doctrine is by no means simply mistaken. It erred, however, in giving an extreme and one-sided formulation of immutability, claiming that God must be immutable in all respects. On such premisses any positive relation between God and time, God and history, is implausible. For this reason Dorner believes that classical metaphysical theology contradicts its own trinitarian assertions that seek to articulate the theological basis for soteriology, including incarnation.

Part Three is Dorner's reconstruction of the concept of divine immutability. His rejection of kenoticism's mutable deity does not imply a return to the classical doctrine. Drawing upon Schleiermacher, Schelling, and Hegel, Dorner rejects the traditional conception of unqualified immutability, and defends a qualified immutability against the equally unqualified assertion of change in God raised by theorists of divine self-divestment. Dorner shows that immutability must be understood in ethical rather than metaphysical terms. This means not only that metaphysical immutability is significantly qualified, but also that God cannot be absolutely immutable in all respects as the tradition claimed. As the primal ethical (*Urethische*), God's being cannot be simple, but must be internally complex, with multiple interdependent modes of being. Drawing upon Schelling and Hegel, Dorner confronts such central issues as the relation between divine simplicity and aseity, God and time, and the relation between God and world. In this essay Dorner takes more explicit positions on such issues than he does later in his *Glaubenslehre*.

Even more intriguing is Dorner's claim concerning the primacy of the ethical in God. Taking his cue from Schleiermacher, and from Theodor Liebner,[6] Dorner carries out a critique of classical metaphysics and ontology that began with Fichte and continues in such contemporary philosophers as Emmanuel Levinas.[7] Like Levinas, Dorner rejects the classical derivation of ethics from ontology. Dorner would agree that classical ontology is an ontology of power. Classical ontology conceives God's power as absolute, and regards ethics as derivative from ontology, practice as derivative from theory. This has obscured the soteriological interest in love. If love—an ethical conception—is primary, then God's power is not unqualifiedly absolute, but is ethically ordered and directed by love. Further, to be loving, God cannot be absolutely immutable in all respects, but must be able to enter into reciprocal relation with the world.

Dorner's essay establishes some important continuities between nineteenth- and twentieth-century Protestant theologies; in particular it is a mediating link between Schleiermacher and Barth. In a significant aside in *Church Dogmatics*, Barth explicitly refers to the Immutability Essay as

6. Theodor Liebner (1803–1871) was co-editor with Dorner of the *Jahrbücher für deutsche Theologie*. Dorner credited him with being the driving force behind the Journal. He started his career as a pastor. His first university position was as an associate professor and university preacher in Göttingen (1837); later he was Ordinarius at Kiel (1844), at Leipzig (1851), and eventually moved to Dresden as the high court preacher and Vice-President of the Evangelical Consistory. In 1832 he published a monograph on Hugh of St. Victor. He was also influenced by Jacob Boehme and Franz von Baader. In his *Christliche Dogmatik aus dem christologischen Prinzip dargestellt*, 1 Abt. 1 Bd: *Christologie, oder die christologische Einheit des dogmatischen Systems* (Göttingen, 1849), Liebner sought to develop the entire doctrine of God, including divine attributes, on the basis of soteriology and Trinity. In turn he derived the concept of Trinity from an analysis of love. This analysis, which draws in part upon Hegel, profoundly influenced Dorner, particularly his argument concerning love as the ethical essence of God. His position can be characterized as a theological ethical personalism. I shall return to this later. For a helpful account of Liebner's thought, cf. Axt-Piscalar, GdG 121ff.

7. Levinas writes, "We cannot obviate the language of metaphysics, and yet we cannot, ethically speaking, be satisifed with it: it is necessary but it is not enough. I disagree with Derrida's interpretation of this paradox. Whereas he tends to see the deconstruction of the Western metaphysics as an irredeemable crisis, I see it as a golden opportunity for Western philosophy to open itself to the dimension of otherness and transcendence beyond being." "Dialogue with Emmanuel Levinas," in *Face to Face with Levinas* (ed. Richard Cohen, Albany: State University of New York Press, 1986) 28. See also Levinas *Totality and Infinity* (tr. A. Lingis, Duquesne University Press, 1969).

"Dorner's great essay" and adds that "Those who know this essay will recognise . . . how much I owe to Dorner's inspiration."[8] Barth's comment indicates the importance he attached to this essay. Dorner's conception of God as triune, consisting in multiple modes of being (*Daseinsweisen*), his contention that God is ethical love, and that such love requires not only reciprocity between God and world but also a revision in the classical conception of divine immutability, are important elements that influence and even reappear in Barth's discussion of the Trinity, as well as divine freedom and its perfections. Barth's acknowledgment of Dorner's influence also suggests an historical-theological connection between Barth and Schleiermacher. It is a well-known irony that Barth kept discussing Schleiermacher—more or less respectfully—in order to disagree with him. Barth's Schleiermacher discussion was a convenient vehicle for cultivating his posture of opposition to Schleiermacher on every important theological topic. In one of his essays, Barth questioned whether Schleiermacher's distinction of three forms of dogmatic propositions does not render a doctrine of God superfluous, if not impossible, by allegedly 'confining' theology to a description of human states of mind. If, as he informs us, Barth drew heavily upon "Dorner's great essay," the "inspiration" Barth finds there is in large part a result of Dorner's carefully thinking through the implications of, and completing gaps in, Schleiermacher's doctrine of God. Dorner's affinity with Schleiermacher is manifest in his treatment of love as a divine attribute, which is a sophisticated development of Schleiermacher's claims couched in Hegelian terms!

## THE OCCASION OF DORNER'S ESSAY

Dorner's discussion of the kenotic christological controversy is perhaps the most dated part of his essay.[9] This controversy instigated his massive

8. Karl Barth, *Church Dogmatics: The Doctrine of God, II/1* (tr. Parker, Johnston, Knight, Haire, Edinburgh: T & T Clark, 1957) 493. Barth's reference to Dorner is in large part responsible for the little attention that Dorner has received in this century, including this translation. Taking his cue from Barth, Claude Welch read Dorner's essay, found that it fully merited Barth's praise, and translated Part Three.

9. The concept of *kenosis* remains an important topic in contemporary Buddhist-Christian dialogue. According to Masao Abe, the concept of *kenosis*, or divine self-emptying, is fundamental to both the Christian concept of God and the Buddhist concept of Nirvana, and constitutes a common philosopical-religious conceptuality. Cf. the recent discussion in *The Emptying God: A Buddhist-Christian-Jewish Conversation*, John B. Cobb and Christopher Ives, eds. (Maryknoll, New York: Orbis 1990). None of the Christian theologians discussing Abe's proposals in this volume seem aware of the kenotic controversy in nineteenth century German academic theology, or its ontological implications and their possibilities for Buddhist-Christian discussion.

research on the history of the doctrine of Christ, that provided Dorner with reasons for rejecting kenoticism. The kenotic movement focused on the meaning of incarnation in light of the classical two-nature Christology in its specifically Lutheran development of the *communicatio idiomatum*, according to which the divine and human natures not only formed a union, but their different attributes were imparted to each other. Traditional Lutheranism tended to understand this communication as a nonreciprocal impartation of the divine to the human, and not as a genuine exchange of attributes. Thus the tradition failed to resolve a question that, with the rise of historical consciousness in the nineteenth century, had moved to center stage, namely, How can the divine attributes (e.g., omnipotence and omnipresence) be imparted to the human nature of Christ without annulling it?[10] The specific issue, in view of the ontological difference between God and world (as formulated by classical theology), and in view of modern understandings of human finitude, the temporal-historical development of freedom and personality, was this: How can the humanity of the incarnate God-man be understood? How can true humanity—which is finite and subject to temporal-historical processes of development—be reconciled with true deity—which is infinite, eternal, and immutable?

The kenotics held that the real humanity of the person of Christ can be most plausibly maintained by means of the concept of *kenosis*, an emptying or self-divestment of divine power for the sake of, and during the period of, the incarnation. This proposal appears on its surface to be scriptural (Phil. 2:5ff, although Dorner hotly contests the kenotic interpretation of this passage[11]), but also has explicit roots in German Idealism, specifically, Hegel's oft-quoted thesis that substance must be transformed into subject. Less well known is the fact that Hegel portrayed the incarnation and death of God as the event through which substance becomes subject. Incarnation for Hegel implies a critique of abstract substance and substance metaphysics, and points to process (*Werden*) as the fundamental category and feature of all reality.[12] Hegel shows that the classical conception of immutability is subject to modification and incorporation within a broader, holistic process ontology.

10. See Claude Welch, *God and Incarnation*, op. cit., pp. 25-27. In his *Protestant Thought in the Nineteenth Century* (op. cit., pp. 233-240), Welch maintains that kenoticism sums up the classical two-nature Christology, and by its inadequacies demonstrates the necessity for theological reconstruction.

11. See Article One, note 43.

12. G. W. F. Hegel, *Phänomenologie des Geistes* (Hoffmeister ed., Hamburg: Meiner Verlag, 1952) 545ff. English translation: *The Phenomenology of Spirit* (tr. A. V. Miller, New York: Oxford Universty Press, 1977) 475ff.

To be sure, the kenotic school of Christology were no Hegelians; for the most part they thought within the framework of the traditional ontological distinction between God and world, eternity and time. Granted this distinction, what does the *kenosis* of divinity mean? Many of their proposals were fragmentary. The earliest and possibly crudest version rested upon a distinction between the *possession* of divine powers and their *use*. During incarnation the eternal Logos retained possession of the divine powers but refrained from using them, in order to appear fully human. In view of such possession of divine powers, there is no self-divestment involved.

Gottfried Thomasius (1802–1875) formulated perhaps the most sophisticated of the kenotic theories. Central to his theory is a distinction between immanent divine attributes (freedom, eternity, holiness, love) that are absolute, and relative divine attributes (omnipresence, omnipotence, omniscience) that express God's contingent relation to the world.[13] Thomasius held that a God who divests himself of the absolute or immanent attributes would cease to be. But the relative attributes can be divested, he claims, because they do not refer to God but only to God's relation to the world. Since the existence of the world is contingent, the relative attributes reflect such contingencies and are, he maintains, capable of being divested at least temporarily for the purpose of incarnation and for undergoing a natural temporal human development. The apparent contradiction of divine self-divestment is mitigated somewhat by the claim that powers surrendered for purposes of incarnation are gradually restored (i.e., actualized) during the earthly development of Christ's divine-human person. Thus, the divine powers are not simply lost, but only temporarily suspended, to be regained during the self-actualization process of the incarnate God-man. Nevertheless, Thomasius concedes that self-divestment involves a withdrawal of the divine powers to a status of potence,[14] or self-limitation, in contrast to status of actualization.

Dorner criticizes both the conception of relative and contingent divine attributes, and the diminution of the divine powers from actual to potential.

13. Thomasius' chief writings on Christology are: *Beiträge zur kirchlichen Christologie* (Erlangen 1845) and *Christi Person und Werke. Darstellung der evangelisch-lutherischen Dogmatik vom Mittelpunkt der Christologie aus* (Erlangen 1853-61, and expanded ed. 1856–1863). For a translation, commentary and discussion of Thomasius' works, see Claude Welch, *God and Incarnation*, especially pp. 49n, 94.

14. The term 'potence' is ambiguous; Dorner borrows Thomasius' term (*potentia*) but also interprets it against the background of Schelling and Aristotle. For Schelling potence means power (*Potenz*); for Aristotle potence signifies *dynamis* rather than *energeia*, i.e., the potential in contrast to the actual. Dorner's claim is that the self-divestment of the Logos, or its withdrawal to potence, signifies that it has deactualized itself. As a potential deity that has deactualized itself through self-divestment, the Logos is also an ontologically inferior deity, as in Arianism.

Concerning the so-called relative attributes, Dorner, following W. F. Gess,[15] observes that divine omniscience includes within its scope not only God's knowledge of the world, but also God's self-knowledge. Thus, if omniscience is given up, it would not be a merely relative, but an inner divine attribute that is divested, and this would, on Thomasius' own terms, violate the concept of God. On the other hand, if omniscience in the sense of God's self-knowledge is not given up, then the concept of *kenosis* is contradicted.[16]

Concerning the withdrawal or reduction of the divine powers from actual to potential, Dorner believes the deactualized[17] Logos to be a modern version of the Arian claim that the Logos is inferior and subordinate to God. A deactualized deity is a diminished deity, and this tends to undermine the very soteriology that the *kenosis* theory is supposed to articulate and defend. For this reason Dorner contends that christological theopassianism, despite its attractiveness, fails to solve the central christological problem.

Dorner believes that the Arian tendency, while exhibited by Thomasius, is most starkly represented by W. F. Gess, who held that self-divestment involves a complete transformation of the Logos into a human being. For Gess the Logos became completely human and historical. Dorner considered Gess to be the most radical and most consistent of the kenotics, who at the same time demonstrated the untenability of the kenotic hypothesis. It would appear to be but a short step conceptually from Gess to Feuerbach's reduction of theology to anthropology. The difference is that, according to Gess, the depotentiated incarnate Logos subsequently acquires divine perfections such as holiness, in the same way that any human being may do, thereby reactualizing his divine potential. But it remains unclear to Dorner whether Gess' Logos is divine—in which case his *kenosis* theory is an illusion—or a creature—in which case Gess ends in Arian subordination of the Logos to deity (75f.).

Common to all forms of kenotic theopassianism is an attack on the classical concept of divine immutability. For self-divestment, withdrawal

15. W. F. Gess, *Die Lehre von der Person Christi* (Basel, 1856) 312.

16. Dorner makes this argument succinctly in his *Glaubenslehre §98*, cited in Welch, *God and Incarnation*, p. 194. This is Dorner's response to Thomasius' essay "Against Dorner" cited in the same volume on p. 94.

17. Dorner formulates kenotic self-divestment as a reduction of actuality to mere potentiality. For the purpose of incarnation, the divine in Jesus is to be understood as withdrawing from actuality to potentiality, in order subsequently to develop or actualize divine powers in the course of Jesus' personal-historical career.

from actual to potential, and self-limitation all imply that mutability, change, and suffering must be ascribed to God. Thus the kenotics succeed in displacing, if not in undermining, the classical conception of God's immutability. Dorner rejects kenoticism on christological grounds, that is, it fails to resolve the christological problem. But at the same time, Dorner indicates that the kenotic critique of divine immutability is, apart from its Christology, basically correct: "The traditional doctrine of divine immutability fails to do justice to either the scientific or religious interests" (p. 75n.54). Dorner's critique of kenoticism therefore does not mean that he is wedded to the classical doctrine of immutability. On the contrary, Dorner contends that the traditional concept of an unqualified or absolute divine immutability stands in conflict with the fundamental interests of Christian piety. Nevertheless, the traditional doctrine is not sheer error. Both its strengths and its defects must be understood historically-critically. This leads Dorner to his central topic, namely, the doctrine of immutability itself.

## THE HISTORY OF THE CONCEPT OF IMMUTABILITY

Judaeo-Christian monotheism arose as an alternative to pagan polytheism. In Greek folk religions, not only is there a pluralistic pantheon of deities, this pantheon is itself subordinate to a higher power, namely *Moira* or fate. But fate is impersonal and blind. Although fate is not ethical, it cannot be divorced from certain ethical implications: fate functions as a kind of punitive justice that corrects *hubris* or excess. Fate is inexorable, excluding reconciliation. One simply resigns oneself to it.

The positive ethical elements of Greek folk religions are represented by the figures of the gods. The latter are conceived anthropomorphically, so that they are accessible to human entreaties. But they are too human and anthropomorphic: they are not free from passions and partialities. They are not the originators of their own being, they are merely deputies of Fate. This shows, Dorner thinks, that such folk religions failed to unite the twin conceptions of power and goodness, immutability and vitality.

### The Goal of Classical Monotheism

Such a synthesis is the goal of classical monotheism: God is conceived as an immutable being that is nevertheless personal and ethical. God's being is the primal good in itself, and such goodness and perfection are self-sufficient, and exclude change. For a change could only be a change for the worse. Only when God's perfection is utterly immutable has an absolutely trustworthy object of religious devotion been found.

Dorner makes two important observations concerning the classical concept of God. The first is that the classical conception retains "the patriarchal category of omnipotence." (86) As this conception is developed and explicated metaphysically, it depicts a God turned away from the world, a being that is in itself eternal and unchangeable. God is thus portrayed as the absolute patriarch or cosmic monarch. This is the royal or monarchical metaphor. This metaphor reinforces and supports the concept of unqualified immutability and omnipotence, as well as the suggestion that God is actual and self-sufficient apart from relation. Dorner also stresses another metaphor: God as the rock of ages. Everything earthly is caught up in temporal flux and change. As the rock of ages, God is the only enduring reality and trustworthy refuge.

Dorner's second observation is that the classical conception of immutability, despite its metaphysical form, has an ethical origin and connotation. The classical doctrine locates God's ethical perfection and righteousness in God's unchangeableness. God is faithful and constant, where humans are fickle and inconstant. This ethical unchangeableness excludes any suggestion that God comes to be ethical out of a pre-ethical condition. In other words, ethical theogony, as well as the application to God of the concept of potentiality in an ethical sense, is ruled out. God can never be potentially or possibly ethical. God can only be ethically actual. This means that God cannot be portrayed simply as an ethical law or world order. The actuality of the ethical in God implies that God must be personal. Thus the classical doctrine establishes a connection between immutability and the ethical actuality of God. As will become evident, Dorner believes this is the heart of the doctrine of divine immutability and will defend it in his reconstruction.

## Exposition and Critique of the Classical Doctrine

Dorner complains not about the doctrine of immutability per se, but about the privileged, one-sided development it has undergone. Looking at the historical development of Christian doctrine, Dorner observes that there was originally no tendency towards the assertion of God's immutable self-sameness. There were patripassians strongly impressed by the suffering of Jesus. There were apologists who interpreted creation as involving God in change. The course of doctrinal controversy and elaboration gradually suppressed such differing views as pagan influences and corruptions.

The concept of immutability is systematically connected with God's simplicity, the self-same identity of the divine in all its relations, attributes, and perfections. Augustine gave classical expression to simplicity and immutability. As the simple good, God is ontologically unique and incommunicable. Simplicity is expressed in the following way: All that God has, God is. God does not have attributes, but is his attributes. Where having an attribute is equivalent to being that attribute, the attribute in question cannot change or be lost. Any loss or change contradicts divine simplicity. Consequently there are no accidents or contingent properties in God, and the possibility of change must be entirely excluded. Conversely, whatever lacks such simplicity, namely, the identity of being and having, is capable of change and dissolution, and is the bearer of contingent or accidental features, etc. Any change in God would have to be a change for the worse. But God cannot change, for simplicity, and with it immutability, are constitutive features of God's being. God's immutability is absolute; that is, God must be immutable in all respects. Any suggestion to the contrary breaches the fundamental divine simplicity. Immutability is the negative exposition of divine simplicity.

Dorner finds that by the time of Peter Lombard and Aquinas the orthodox position had hardened on two fundamental points: 1) Change is unconditionally excluded from God, and is *ipso facto* a mundane characteristic. Thus all change in the person of Christ would have to fall on the human side. 2) Incarnation involves no change in God, and adds nothing new to God. This view Dorner terms *Nihilianism* (p. 90; cf. p. 108, 188). The classical conception culminates in a portrait of God as a majestic monarch, utterly transcendent to and unaffected by the world and change, unaffected even by the death of his son. God is eternal *actus purus*, actualized outside of and without relation to time.

After considering the classical medieval formulations, Dorner turns to the Reformation period. The Reformation advances beyond the standpoint that regards God as merely lawgiver and judge, with its legal and penal standpoint on the alienation between God and human beings. The Reformation advanced a new understanding of faith that has important implications for rethinking the relation between God and world, but it failed to develop these implications in its doctrine of God. Both main Protestant confessions are caught in a tension between the classical concept of God which they retain, and their new doctrine of faith.

Dorner contends that the traditional insistence upon simplicity and immutability contradicts the now central soteriological doctrines of Trinity and incarnation. When it is asserted that all change is mundane and belongs to the human nature of Christ, and that incarnation adds nothing new to God that God does not eternally foresee or possess, such claims are logical expressions of absolute simplicity and unqualified immutability. Dorner observes that John Gerhard really does not dare to assert that incarnation adds nothing new to God, but sticks with classical immutability anyway. (102) However, the classical doctrine of God would, if thought through consistently, lead to Deism on the one hand, and a Pelagian interpretation of Christology and redemption on the other. If these results are avoided by reformed dogmaticians, it is only at the price of inconsistency.

Dorner finds that the Reformation's appreciation of human sin and evil produced a rupture with the medieval view of the world as a realm of static and timeless Platonic ideas. This involves an acknowledgment of human freedom. This means above all recognition of the primacy of interpersonal and ethical categories. Dorner is especially critical of the tradition's subordination of freedom to nature, for example, the ethical divine attributes to the metaphysical attributes. He observes that human personality cannot be developed by omnipotence or by natural powers alone, or by 'salvation magic,' but only freely in an interpersonal ethical process. This acknowledgment also implies that human freedom has an impact on the divine decree, and that the divine-human relation is fundamentally reciprocal.[18]

Dorner believes that these positions are implicit in the Reformation understanding of faith and freedom; however, the Reformation traditions failed to think through the implications of faith for the doctrine of God, and so failed to overcome the emerging tendencies towards Deist transcendence and pantheist immanence in the traditional doctrine. He traces these tendencies in the post-Reformation period, focusing on Arminianism and Socinianism. He is sympathetic to the Socinian criticisms and pressures to acknowledge a limited mutability in God's relation to the world. He is less sympathetic to Wolffian and Kantian rationalism. But theological thinking had to await a philosophical revolution to find a more adequate conceptual scheme for theological reconstruction. The overhauling of the traditional conception of God began in earnest with Schleiermacher, Schelling, and Hegel.

## DORNER ON SCHLEIERMACHER

Dorner's treatment of Schleiermacher in the *Immutability* essay is perplexing, because it reflects somewhat contradictory assessments of

18. See Essay Two, pp. 105-110.

Schleiermacher's theology and doctrine of God.[19] On the one hand, Dorner considers Schleiermacher's doctrine of God set forth in the first part of the *Glaubenslehre* to be fundamentally a restatement of the traditional concepts of simplicity and immutability. Hence Schleiermacher is the concluding figure in Dorner's historical survey of the classical concept of divine immutability. Schleiermacher represents the culmination of the classical doctrine that exposes its incoherence with the soteriology that Schleiermacher moves to the center of the system of doctrine. On the other hand, Dorner finds that Schleiermacher's substantive theological argument in the second part of the *Glaubenslehre*, and above all his treatment of divine love, constitute an exception to the otherwise negative scheme of divine attributes. This exception is far from innocuous; it requires a revision in the traditional concepts of simplicity and immutability.[20] Schleiermacher's argument concerning the divine attributes requires a revision of divine simplicity and immutability that provides the impetus for Dorner's reconstruction. Unfortunately Dorner spends more space criticizing Schleiermacher's putative traditionalism than giving him credit for his breakthrough.

According to Schleiermacher, theology is no longer to be metaphysics or morals, but an account of Christian religious consciousness, or religious affections. Consequently divine attributes are expressions of the divine causality as apprehended through the feeling of utter dependence. According to Part One of the *Glaubenslehre*, divine attributes reflect various features and aspects of utter dependence on God. But they portray God's essence only negatively: the plurality and distinctiveness of the attributes correspond to nothing real in God. This seems to suggest that Schleiermacher adheres to the classical notion of divine simplicity. He maintains that there is no distinction in God between will and ability, or knowing and willing, or between God's willing Godself and God's willing the world (123ff.). Further, the divine attributes appear to have only subjective significance, expressing the relation of self and world to God and the divine causality, but not the divine 'in itself.'

Schleiermacher combines negative theology with positive theology; he claims that the divine attributes are paired: thus instead of divine eternity,

19. Friedrich Schleiermacher, *Der christliche Glaube* (hrsg. Martin Redeker, Berlin: Walter de Gruyter, 1960); English translation, *The Christian Faith* (tr. H.R. Mackintosh, Philadelphia: Fortress Press, 1978).

20. For a study of Schleiermacher's doctrine of God that makes explicit the necessity of revisions, see Robert R. Williams, *Schleiermacher the Theologian: The Construction of the Doctrine of God* (Philadelphia: Fortress Press, 1978) especially Chapters 5 and 7.

or omnipotence, he speaks of eternal-omnipotence. Eternity is the (negative) attribute that contrasts God with world; omnipotence tends to identify God with the world. Nevertheless, this distinction between divine attributes corresponds to nothing real in God. Moreover, Schleiermacher's discussion of eternal-omnipotence implies that God is actual apart from the world and time. But if God is actual apart from world and is simple, then God does not ground or explain mundane actuality and determinacy. Determinacy and actuality have no basis in divine simplicity. Simplicity is likewise constitutive of God's relation to the world: the divine causality admits of no distinctions or degrees, and consequently is uniformly related to the world, that is, is everywhere the same.

Dorner concludes his historical survey of the traditional concept of immutability with Schleiermacher because Dorner wants to show that Schleiermacher embraces the traditional concept and makes explicit its internal contradictions. Its incoherence is evident from the attempt to correlate the system of attributes set forth in Part One of the *Glaubenslehre* with the positive historical fact of sin, grace, and redemption set forth in Part Two. The question is, how can a simple, immutable divine being support or provide a theological foundation for the historical appearance of the redeemer and the historical-existential transition from sin to grace? To embrace the classical concept of divine immutability and simplicity here is also to embrace Pelagian and ebionite conceptions of redemption and the redeemer.[21] When change is utterly excluded from God and considered simply as pertaining to the world, this implies that, in reference

21. Dorner follows Schleiermacher's determination of the essence of Christianity and his account of its natural heresies (*Glaubenslehre* §§11 22ff.). The essence is that everything in Christian existence is related to redemption through Jesus. Redemption presupposes that human beings are capable of redemption, and that Jesus is able to provide the aid that they need. The essence can be violated in a variety of ways: the human nature can be conceived so that redemption is either impossible (Manicheanism) or unnecessary (Pelagianism), and the redeemer figure can be conceived so that either his humanity is denied (docetism), or he is regarded as a merely human exemplar (ebionitism). Schleiermacher contends there is a systematic correlation between christological and anthropological heresies. Thus the Manichean anthropological heresy construes human beings as incapable of redemption, and pairs with the docetic christological heresy that denies the redeemer's humanity. The result is a supernatural or magical conception of redemption. The Pelagian anthropological heresy undermines the corruption of sin, and makes redemption a simple human possibility. This pairs with the ebionite heresy that regards Jesus as an outstanding individual that others can and should emulate. Schleiermacher suggests that these soteriological heresies correlate with certain theological heresies: the Manichean-Docetic heresies reflect supernaturalist views that separate God from world (dualism), and the Pelagian-ebionite heresies reflect rationalism, i.e., views that identify God with world (pantheism and monism). Dorner extends these last-mentioned correlations: dualism is present in Deism, that separates God from the world, and monism is present in pantheism, that identifies God with world.

to Christology, change applies only to the human nature of Christ, and that in reference to anthropology, the change from sin to grace is merely another mundane transition. Thus redemption is a simple autonomous human possibility. To be sure, Schleiermacher himself makes this point: "We would go astray into Pelagianism, if all distinctions in the divine causality were abolished, and the divine causality were supposed to be self-identical in both the sinful flesh and in the power of the God-consciousness."[22] If, owing to its simplicity, there can be no distinctions in God's causality, then God would be present in the same way in both sin and grace. Consequently there could be no theological basis for the distinction between sin and grace, but only an anthropological basis. But if no special determinate divine act is required for the transition from sin to grace, then the autonomous development of humanity is all that is necessary, and humanity would be capable of redeeming itself. This reading ends in Pelagianism and makes Christology superfluous.

Dorner finds in Schleiermacher's thought an unresolved conflict between the Reformation conception of faith and the classical doctrine of divine simplicity. Dorner tends to portray Schleiermacher as upholding the traditional concept of simplicity and immutability and as ending in a Pelagian interpretation of redemption. This reading assumes that Schleiermacher intends the divine attributes of Part One as actual and as comprising a complete doctrine of God. Only on this assumption is Dorner justified in including Schleiermacher in his survey of the traditional doctrine of immutability. However, Schleiermacher warns his reader not to make this assumption.[23] Part One of the *Glaubenslehre* sets forth a formal ontological scheme that has been abstracted from the determinate Christian religious consciousness set forth in Part Two. The exposition of divine attributes in Part One brackets temporal determinateness. The first four divine attributes—eternal-omnipotence and omnipresent-omniscience—are intended only as an indeterminate schematism of transcendence, and for this reason they do not yet constitute a full doctrine of God. The doctrine of God is not completed until the formal scheme is set forth in its concrete determinate form in Part Two. There the attributes of Part One undergo determination and modification; for example, wisdom is a determinate, modified form of omniscience.[24]

22. Schleiermacher, Gl. §80; Dorner cites this passage, but suggests that Schleiermacher's fundamental scheme set forth in Part One, if followed consistently, would end in a Pelagian account of Christianity. Dorner subsequently acknowledges that 'fortunately' Schleiermacher is not consistent, that his *Glaubenslehre* remains a Christian theology in spite of itself.

23. Gl. §§56, 62. See Williams, *Schleiermacher the Theologian*, op. cit., Chaps. 5 and 7. For a further criticism of Dorner's reading of Schleiermacher, cf. Williams, "I. A. Dorner: The Ethical Immutability of God," JAAR LIV/4, Winter 1986, 721-738.

24. Gl. §§55.1, 168.1.

Dorner recognizes that Schleiermacher does not in fact present a Pelagian-ebionite interpretation of redemption. He correctly observes that Schleiermacher asserts that the divine causality is not everywhere the same, and that redemption rests upon a special divine act of love. Further, this special divine self-communication points to love as a distinctive divine attribute. Love is special among the divine attributes because *love alone is identical with God's essence*. This implies that love is adequate to the divine essence and communicates it, makes it known—a drastic departure from the apparent negative theology of Part One.

How should this departure be understood? Dorner claims that when Schleiermacher sets forth redemption in Part Two of the *Glaubenslehre,* he *reverses* his initial position on simplicity and immutability, as well as on the relation of the divine attributes to the divine essence. Confronted with this apparent 'reversal,' Dorner believes that Schleiermacher is simply inconsistent, and this inconsistency makes explicit the incoherence between the classical doctrines of simplicity and immutability and the distinctive positive doctrines of Christianity.

The alternative reading is that Schleiermacher, far from being inconsistent, is working out the principle of positivity central to his theological project. According to that principle, the formal generic structures of Part One are not actual by themselves, and do not persist unchanged in Part Two, but are rendered determinate and modified in their concrete realization.[25] Rather than reversing his position in Part Two, Schleiermacher articulates the modifications in the formal ontological structures of Part One that occur under the impact of the Christian fact of redemption, the transition from sin to grace.

However, while Schleiermacher exhibits some of the modifications of the divine attributes (e.g., wisdom is a determinate mode of omniscience, and love is *identical* with the divine essence, or *God is love*), he does not fully work out or make explicit all the modifications. For example, if love is unique among the divine attributes because it alone is identical with the divine essence, then there is a distinction, not merely in the way we conceive God's essence, but in the divine essence itself, namely, between love and other divine attributes. This distinction is incompatible with classical divine simplicity. Moreover, he tells us that omnipotence is directed by love, and

25. For a fuller treatment of the principle of positivity, see Williams, *Schleiermacher the Theologian*, op. cit., Edward Farley, *Ecclesial Reflection: An Anatomy of Theological Method* (Philadelphia: Fortress Press, 1982).

motivated by love. This implies a further distinction in God's being, namely, between God's ethical attributes and metaphysical attributes, or between love and omnipotence. If love directs omnipotence, then the ethical attributes are primary. This means that eternal-omnipotent divine causality is not undifferentiated and formally self-identical everywhere (the Pelagian view as reconstructed by Schleiermacher), but appears in a distinctive way in redemption.

Schleiermacher does not make explicit these determinate qualifications of divine simplicity, or how redemption and the transition from sin to grace involve a change in the exercise of omnipotence. Nevertheless, according to his own principles, if Pelagianism is to be avoided, some distinctions immanent in God's being, and an alteration in the exercise of divine omnipotence are necessary. The traditional concept of divine simplicity, along with its corollaries—for example, that God's knowing and willing are identical with God's being—must be given up. But Schleiermacher never got this far. Nor did he make up his mind concerning the precise *status* of the distinctions that he found it necessary to make, both in the divine causality and in God's being, as he thought through the implications of redemption in a way that avoided Pelagianism. Consequently, Schleiermacher's doctrine of God is incomplete, rather than incoherent. Nevertheless Schleiermacher breaks with the classical tradition when he asserts the primacy of God's ethical attributes over his metaphysical attributes: specifically, that omnipotence is directed by love.

Dorner, sensing the incompleteness in Schleiermacher's execution, addresses the immutability question in light of the gaps in Schleiermacher's argument. This leads him to think through the implications of Schleiermacher's treatment of love for the concepts of divine simplicity and immutability. In the following passage, Dorner recapitulates and extends Schleiermacher's argument concerning the primacy of love among the divine attributes:

> the love of God also contains the supreme, absolute guarantee for everything that may be designated a divine attribute. The so-called physical attributes of God do not exist for themselves as if they had in themselves the absolute necessity of being and actuality; rather there is in God the superordinate and subordinate, and the physical attributes serve the ethical essence of God which is the power over them. . . . In a word, all the divine powers and attributes do not in the last analysis exist for themselves, as if they were for themselves absolutely valuable and necessary; they exist for absolute love.[26]

26. 3rd Essay (176) below. This passage is indebted not only to Schleiermacher's discussion of love as a unique divine attribute (Gl. §167), but also to Theodor Liebner, who sought to derive the concept of Trinity from an analysis of interpersonal love (cf. Axt-Piscalar, GdG 130ff.).

If a Pelagian-ebionite interpretation of redemption is to be avoided, then there must be distinctions in the divine causality that have their basis in God's being itself. If, as Schleiermacher claims, love directs and motivates the divine causality (omnipotence) towards redemption, such that love manifests the inner being of God, then Schleiermacher's *argument* concerning the primacy of the ethical attribute of love requires distinctions in God's being that contradict the classical conception of absolute divine simplicity. Dorner puts the point in the following way:

> It became evident both in the ancient church and after Schleiermacher, that either one goes forward from this (with the ancient church) to immanent distinctions in the inner divine essence, and in particular to an eternal determination . . . that corresponds to the special and enduring being of God in Christ, or else one abandons the special being of God in Christ and goes back to a mere influence of God on the man Jesus, or to a being of God similar to that which is in other believers . . . and thus one falls back to Ebionitism. That is to say, if the distinguishing dignity of Christ . . . is really found in a peculiar being of God in the redeemer, then the return to eternal distinctions in God can be circumvented only at the price of saying that this special and peculiar being of God derives only from the world, because it is not grounded in God's being. That is, it would derive from the peculiar receptivity of the humanity of Jesus to the being of God that is everywhere utterly identical with itself . . .[27]

As Dorner thinks through the logic of Schleiermacher's argument as well as enriching it with his massive studies in the history of Christology, he finds that the traditional doctrine of God must be revised on at least two related points: its doctrine of simplicity that denies distinctions in God and requires that God be absolutely immutable in all respects, and the corollary principle that change is essentially mundane and has no basis in God's being or essence. These two traditional principles lead to a Sabellian interpretation of Trinity and to a Pelagian-ebionite interpretation of redemption; they pull Schleiermacher's theology in a Pelagian-ebionite direction that appears to displace Trinity. However, Dorner belatedly acknowledges that Schleiermacher's actual argument works against the Pelagian tendency, and requires revision of the traditional metaphysical principles. Thus Schleiermacher had already begun the process of revision. But he did not go far enough.

If Athanasius is right against Arius in claiming that the trinitarian distinctions are immanent in God's being, then Schleiermacher's "official

27. Dorner, *System of Christian Doctrine*, cited in Welch, *God and Incarnation*, op. cit., p. 212. I have altered the translation slightly.

agnosticism" concerning distinctions in God must be qualified—as he does in his account of love as a unique divine attribute. But this qualification means that some immanent distinctions and internal complexity in God's being are theologically necessary and not to be dismissed as illegitimate metaphysical speculations. Dorner turns to Schelling and Hegel for aid in formulating the inner distinctions in God that Schleiermacher's soteriological argument requires. God's unity is not sheer simplicity, but must be constituted by internal distinctions and difference. Only if God's being is internally complex is it possible to conceive a positive relation of God to temporality and history in order to explain and ground Christian positivity and determinacy, that is, to provide a theological foundation for incarnation and soteriology. Dorner's careful reflections on the immanent development of the issue of divine simplicity and immutability forge an historical link between Schleiermacher to Barth. The common theme is the primacy of love among the divine attributes. Dorner's version of this primacy reflects Schleiermacher; the conceptual vehicle that Dorner draws upon to formulate Schleiermacher's position is derived from Schelling and Hegel. In his enthusiastic appropriation of Dorner, Barth also incorporates without acknowledging it, important elements of Schleiermacher's thought, recast in Hegelian conceptuality.

## DORNER'S RECONSTRUCTION OF IMMUTABILITY

The impetus for Dorner's essay was the kenotic christological movement. Dorner's analysis of kenoticism reveals that it both fails to solve the christological problem, and errs in simply rejecting divine immutability. Although the classical conception of immutability is problematic and self-subverting, it contains an important insight into divine goodness and fidelity. However, the classical doctrine stressed God's immutability so much that it separated God from world and regarded change as a mundane imperfection. Classical immutability contradicted God's vitality, or involvement in history. On the other hand, the kenotics laid so much stress upon God's self-divestment and involvement in history that they gave up immutability. Both positions have a valid insight into religious-soteriological interests, but develop it in an exclusive, one-sided way. This mutual inadequacy sets the agenda for Part Three of Dorner's essay: a revision of the classical doctrine of immutability that is compatible with divine vitality. Accordingly, Dorner attempts to give a more adequate account of the relation between divine immutability and divine vitality. Stated in somewhat different terms, Dorner reopens and struggles with the perennial problem of divine absoluteness and relativity.[28]

Despite its rejection of the classical conception of divine immutability, kenoticism nevertheless remains within the traditional metaphysical framework that opposes divine vitality to immutability. The kenotics operate within the traditional framework to the extent that they oppose to traditional absolute immutability the idea of an involvement of God in finitude and history. They believe that to account for incarnation, the classical ahistorical absolute must be abandoned because self-divestment and incarnation imply change in God that contradicts absolute immutability.

Dorner rejects the assumption that the options are either classical immutability or kenotic mutability, and he turns to Schelling and Hegel to formulate a middle position. According to Dorner, there are three levels of articulation of the concept of God, the physical, the logical, and the ethical.[29] All involve versions of God's being as internally complex. Dorner returns to this same threefold classification in his *History of Protestant Theology* (1867), but employs it in an historical as well as systematic sense to characterize the specific contributions of classical German thinkers. Dorner tells us that Schelling articulated the physical aspect of the absolute, Hegel the logical-dialectical aspect, and Schleiermacher the ethical aspect.[30]

Dorner credits the early Schelling of the *Naturphilosophie* (1795–1799) with the conception that the roots of nature and its life lie in God, and with the conception of God as a dynamic process.[31] He credits Hegel with formulating this conception with greater logical rigor, and with identifying the absolute as pure thought dialectically thinking itself. However, Dorner believes that Hegel's logic has limitations: it gives a knowledge of possibility, but not actuality, and "etheralizes into mere notions" nature, ethics,

28. According to Cyril C. Richardson, the core problem of the doctrine of the Trinity is maintaining God as both absolute and in relation (Richardson, *The Doctrine of the Trinity*, New York: Abingdon Press, 1958). For a recent study that, like Dorner, tackles the problem of God's absoluteness and relativity by drawing upon Hegel, cf. Peter C. Hodgson, *God in History: Shapes of Freedom* (Nashville: Abingdon Press, 1989).

29. Welch, 122.

30. Dorner, I. A. *A History of Protestant Theology* (English translation by G. Robson and S. Taylor 1871; reprint AMS Press 1970) Vol. II, p.359f. We have already touched upon Dorner's relation to Schleiermacher.

31. For Dorner's relation to Schelling, cf. Robert F. Brown, "Schelling and Dorner on Divine Immutability," *Journal of the American Academy of Religion*, LIII/2, June 1985, 237-250. I am indebted to Brown's analysis.

and religion.[32] Further, Dorner believes that God's complex personality is not reducible to a purely logical dialectic of cognition. On this point he sides with both Schleiermacher (the primacy of God's ethical attributes over the physical) and Schelling. God is more than a disembodied Idea or pure knower. Schelling saw this clearly (as did Boehme and Oetinger before him); he reformulated Fichte's non-ego as the not-God (or Nature) within God, that is the basis of all possibility and self-conscious life.

After 1804, Schelling revised his earlier conceptions in light of new insights into the interrelation of freedom, creation, and evil. He developed a voluntaristic conception of the absolute, that received its most explicit formulation in his *Ages of the World*.[33] There he sets forth a bipolar concept of God consisting of the twin poles of nature and freedom. But now Schelling lays emphasis on freedom: God's being is a *voluntary* duality in unity.[34] This means everything in God is freely willed, such that God *could* refrain from giving himself being or from creating the world.[35] The various versions of this duality in unity are peripheral to our present concern. The important point is that both Schelling's bipolar conception of God and Hegel's concept of identity as identity of identity and difference[36] attack the classical conception of simplicity and set forth versions of God's being as internally complex.

Dorner draws upon this Schelling-Hegel conception in his critique of the classical doctrine of God. He points out that if God were only utterly

32. Dorner, *History of Protestant Theology II*, 362. In the Immutability Essay he tells us that "for the most consistent exponents in Hegel's school, the life of God and world shrank into thought, the life-less shadow-realm of absolute logic, which was regarded as the only thing that is real, and so one is again in acosmism, (even if it was now of a logical, and no longer of a substantial sort)." See below p. 161, n. 10.

33. Schelling wrote several drafts of the Ages from 1811 to 1815. However, since the Ages was not published until 1861, Dorner could not have made use of it in the Immutability Essay. He most likely drew on the *Naturphilosophie* and the later *Lectures on Philosophy and Mythology* (where the position of the Ages reappears in diffuse form). Cf. W 125 n10. For a study of the Ages that focuses on the influence of Boehme on Schelling, cf. Robert F. Brown, *The Later Philosophy of Schelling: The Influence of Boehme on the Works of 1809–1815* (Lewisburg, PA: Bucknell University Press, 1977).

34. Brown, "Schelling and Dorner," op. cit., p. 241.

35. Recall Schelling's question, "Why is there something? Why not nothing?" This insight into the contingency of existence points to divine freedom as the ground of the world's existence. Schelling appears to extend such contingency to at least some aspects of God's being.

36. Hegel, *Difference between Fichte's and Schelling's System of Philosophy* (tr. W. Cerf & H. S. Harris, Albany: State University of New York Press, 1977) 156. Hegel later elaborated this as a triadic structure, and conceived God's being as triune. Cf. Hegel, *Lectures on the Philosophy of Religion* (ed. & trans. Peter C. Hodgson, Berkeley: University of California Press, 1984, 1985, 1987).

simple, a unity without distinction and contrast, then he could not know or will himself.[37] Nor could God love, for love requires an other. Moreover, if God were simple, then only one attribute of a contrasting pair would be attributable to God. For example, God could only be actual, but not potential, or only universal but not particular (or vice-versa), eternal but not temporal, immutable but not mutable, etc. But if God's being is complex, then such oppositions are not absolute. God can be *both* actual and potential, universal and particular, eternal and temporal, immutable and mutable.[38]

This bipolar conception also has implications for rethinking the relation between God and world. First, time and space, excluded by classical metaphysics from God's simple being, "must lie in God, eternally posited and willed by God."[39] God's being is the prototype of creation. This lays the ground for asserting that God's relation to the world is not timelessly everywhere the same, but can vary. Moreover, God and world cannot, as in pantheism, be collapsed into each other as elements of one creative process or actuality. Dorner repeatedly criticizes abstract identity and simplicity: "Thus in one and the same divine thought whereby God thinks himself in his self-sufficiency, freedom, and blessedness, and at the same time as creator of the world, there are contained two essentially different thoughts, which may indeed go together into one, but not in one and the same *simple* thought. It is one thing that God knows and wills himself, and it is another that God knows and wills himself as world-cause. In the former the condescension of love has no place; in the latter it must enter as the motive without which God would not conceive himself as cause of an actual world."[40] This bipolar conception is the basis for Dorner's rejection of kenoticism and pantheism without, however, falling back upon the classical conception of simple divine immutability.

Such internal complexity is a solution to the problem of reconciling God's absoluteness and relatedness: "For because God is distinguished in himself he can maintain himself in self-impartation without loss, remaining in himself and also being and acting outside himself."[41] Thus Dorner can, like classical theology, reject kenotic self-divestment and nevertheless, unlike classical theology, affirm a positive relation between God and world

37. Cf. Third Article below p. 138.

38. Third Article pp. 138-142.

39. Third Article p. 138. This conception later appears in Barth, cf. *Church Dogmatics* I/2 and II/1.

40. Third Article p. 142.

41. Dorner, *Glaubenslehre*, §99, in Welch, *God and Incarnation*, p. 215.

based upon God's ethical perfection: "The point must be this: that instead of God's reducing himself to mere potence for the sake of the world and his being changed into it, it is rather the actual divine perfection itself and nothing less (and indeed as perennially and immovably affirming itself) which is to be apprehended as the potence for the world. *The whole historical life of God in the world takes place, not at the expense of the eternal perfection of God himself, but precisely by virtue of this permanent perfection.*"[42]

The above assertions concerning inner differentiation in God appeal to themes common to both Schelling and Hegel. However, Hegel and Schelling offer divergent and opposing versions of this internal complexity. Dorner is more openly critical of Hegel's logical version of triunity (*Dreieinigikeit*), because of its alleged panlogism, or reduction of existence to logical categories, the realm of shadows or bloodless abstractions. This appears to signal a tilt towards Schelling. According to Robert Brown, "The later Schelling's conception of God's complex life appeals to Dorner because, despite its ethical defects, Schelling reconceives divine immutability with less modification than does Hegel of the orthodox contention that God's eternal self-conscious life is self-sufficient and does not require the creation for its own actualization."[43] Schelling seems more compatible with the traditional or classical view of the distinction between God and world. According to Schelling's voluntarism, if there is to be either God or world, the existence of such must be willed by freedom.[44] However, as Dorner develops his concept of God's ethical essence, his thought reflects Hegel and Hegel-inspired discussions, especially those of Mehring and Liebner.[45] Brown correctly sees that Dorner develops his account of divine freedom in Hegelian terms. The question is whether, as Brown maintains, Dorner's Hegelian concept of freedom stands in tension with his own assertions concerning the primacy of the ethical in God. I shall return to this issue below.

42. Cf. Third Article below 160. Italics mine.

43. Brown 1985, p. 240.

44. According to Brown, if God is, God's existence must be freely willed. But God could refrain from giving himself actuality (Brown, 241, 246). Schelling claims that Hegel fudges this question of freedom and contingency when he speaks of the Absolute Logical Idea releasing its moment of particularity or otherness, and allowing it to be as Nature. See Hegel, *Enzyklopädie* (hrsg. Nicolin & Pöggeler, Hamburg: Meiner, 1969) §244.

45. See below note 52.

## Dorner on Love as God's Ethical Essence

Dorner contends that the traditional concept of immutability needs revision, but not total elimination. The classical tradition asserted an unqualified immutability; simplicity requires that God be immutable in all respects. We have found that Dorner follows Schelling and Hegel in treating God's being as internally complex, and thus revises simplicity. For this reason, Dorner now asserts a qualified immutability: God is immutable in some respects, but not in other respects. Dorner follows Schleiermacher and Liebner in asserting that love has primacy over the other divine attributes, and that omnipotence is directed by love. The logic of this position for incarnation and soteriology is that God's power is not immutable in reference to space and time, nor is God's knowing of the world immutable. "On the contrary in all these respects there takes place also in God change, alteration, a permitting of himself to be determined. . . ."[46] On the other hand, Dorner claims that the theological interest in immutability resides in love as God's ethical essence: "Thus the ethical concept of God leaves room for vitality and movement in God—yes it may well permit even change and alteration to be reflected into God . . . if only one thing continues to be preserved, the *ethical self-identity* and *immutability* of God. This must remain inviolate. . . ."[47]

Dorner's argument concerning love as God's ethical essence takes its point of departure in a consideration of freedom as an ethical concept. The creation of free beings is both an extension and limitation of God's power. In willing free beings, God does not merely intend freedom as a natural capacity or power, he also wills that this freedom be *ethically* developed: "In the human nature there is marked out a second world, the ethical, for which nature (human nature included) has only the significance of a conditioning presupposition. Humanity can fulfill its commission only in a history of freedom."[48] However, although free beings are absolutely dependent on God's creating and sustaining activity, "it cannot suffice to trace everything from God's side to his bare omnipotent will."[49] Dorner contends that the self-limitation and mutability of God's power is manifest specifically in the power of free beings to *resist* God by committing evil: "thus for the production and preservation of free powers the omnipotent

46. Third Article p. 165.
47. Third Article p. 176.
48. Third Article p. 146.
49. Ibid.

causality of God must have acted and must act so powerfully that through God the power of possible resistance to God and his love is also present in these, in order that their free devotion to God in self-sacrificing love *becomes also a new good, valuable for God himself, which could never be achieved by omnipotence as such.*"[50]

Consequently, the religious relation of God to humans is not simply one of merely physical or natural causality. Although religion is not reducible to ethics, the religious relation is not less than an ethical one, and this requires a recognition of freedom, mutuality, and reciprocity. Dorner follows Hegel in conceiving love as inherently reciprocal, and thus corrects Schleiermacher (according to whom the feeling of utter dependence consists in an essentially nonreciprocal relation): ". . . the relation of love between God and humans must be a reciprocal relation, as this is required by the nature of love. Consequently, it is to be taught that God *himself*, who on the side of generating power remains eternally the sole original principle, enters the realm of the ethical or love in a *reciprocal relation, yes, God enters into a relation of mutual and reciprocal influence*."[51] If God enters into reciprocal relation, then divine knowledge must likewise be conditioned by reciprocity, even receptivity: ". . . if there are free powers in the world, then there are free decisions by the creatures, which indeed have their ground of possibility in God but which have their ground of actuality only in the free beings and not in God. But from this it follows that God cannot, by his simple self-knowledge, know these acts as actual, but only as possible. Consequently God cannot have a knowledge of the actual world of free beings by 'that simple, self-same eternal act of his self-knowledge,' but only by a *different* act of knowledge, however this may be conceived. But for this there must be a receptivity in God. . . . From himself God has only the knowledge of the world of freedom as he intends it. . . ; the knowledge of the actuality for which freedom will decide comes to him from the world of free beings."[52] Dorner thus openly asserts an ethical divine-human reciprocity, and acknowledges that this implies an "impact" (*Einschlag*) of human freedom on God.

The preceding analysis brings to light Dorner's rich concept of love as constitutive of God's relation to humans. Love requires reciprocity, and

50. Ibid. p. 147. Italics mine.

51. Third Article p. 148. Italics mine. On Schleiermacher, cf. *Glaubenslehre* §§4-5. cf. p. 45.

52. Third Article p.149. Cf. Whitehead's distinction between God's primordial and consequent natures.

that God be able to take account of and respond to the changing human condition. Owing to its fundamental reciprocity, love requires that God be mutable in some respects. Dorner locates this mutability directly in God's metaphysical attributes of knowledge and power, which are not formal metaphysical abstractions, but expressions of God's vitality in history and human affairs. Consequently they are capable of change, at least with respect to their operation and exercise. To this extent it must be admitted that there is potentiality in God.

Soteriology too requires that God be immutable. But this immutability is ethical, not ontological in the traditional sense. Love, as God's ethical essence, must not only remain inviolate, it must also be eternal actuality in God: "The inner personal reality of the ethical, which is God himself, can have no intermittent existence. . . . God in himself can never be mere potence of love, nor become that nor reduce himself to it."[53] God does not come to be ethical out of any pre-ethical condition. God's ethical being is primary, not derivative. This claim takes Dorner further into a discussion of God's ethical essence that includes a critique of intellectualism and voluntarism as expressed in classical ontology.

Dorner poses the issue of the ethical sharply: Is the good good because God wills it? Or does God will it because it is good? The latter alternative is affirmed by intellectualism, whose classical representatives include Augustine, Anselm, and Thomas Aquinas. The former alternative is affirmed by voluntarism, whose classical representative is Duns Scotus. Voluntarism—the good is good because God wills it—means that the goodness of the good derives not from its intrinsic worth, but extrinsically from God's will. This denies that goodness is something that is given to God, over which he has no control—a denial that gives primacy to freedom. But the problem with voluntarism is that it risks making the good contingent and arbitrary, for God could have willed otherwise. (Text pp. 79ff) The intellectualist alternative contends that the goodness of the good is intrinsic, but it implies that God is constrained by the intrinsic nature of goodness to will as he does. Thus Thomas Aquinas held that God wills his own goodness with absolute necessity and all other things in conformity with that goodness (*Summa Theologiae Ia, A 19, A3*). This guarantees the immutability of the one and only possible standard of goodness, but it implies that God is unable to act otherwise than he does. (Text pp. 75ff) This calls divine freedom into question.

53. Third Article p. 176.

Dorner rejects both positions as they are traditionally stated, because they are one-sided, and neither has an adequate appreciation of ethical freedom. If, as in intellectualism, freedom is excluded from the actualization of the ethical, the result is that goodness is understood purely ontologically as a natural property. God's goodness is the goodness of a nature. But this goodness is simply contemplated or understood; there is no realization of goodness through free action. Hence intellectualism fails to conceive God's goodness as *ethical* goodness (i.e., a goodness that is brought about and freely accomplished). On the other hand, according to voluntarism, freedom is prior to goodness. Goodness—whatever it turns out to be—comes into being through or is determined by freedom. But since goodness is thus relative to freedom, freedom itself is not subject to goodness. Hence radical freedom is pre-ethical, or ethically neutral. In voluntarism, it is not goodness but freedom that is understood in ontological terms as sheer, pre-ethical power. Thus, intellectualism and voluntarism both lead in different ways to the same conclusion, that God is understood ontologically in terms of power, whether a constraining power of a good nature, or an arbitrary power of will. "To think of God only as ethical being or as ethical substance, and to think of God only as actualized ethical will—these lead to the same result; either way we stay in the circle of the physical instead of achieving the ethical level itself."[54] If God is understood primarily in terms of power (*Machtwesen*), this means that the ethical is not among the primordial powers in God. Hence in both cases God is understood in pre-ethical, or ethically neutral, terms. In both intellectualism and voluntarism, ethics is derivative from ontology. Moreover, Schelling's voluntarism is no alternative, because Schelling too casts divine freedom in ontological rather than ethical terms and thus continues the traditional derivation of ethics from ontology.[55]

54. Third Article p. 170.

55. This does not mean that there are no differences between intellectualism and Schelling's voluntarism. The classical ontology lying behind the intellectualist view is based on a Platonic-Aristotelian conception of being as a structural principle, to which will, as an appetitive principle, is subordinate. God's will is nonreciprocally related to God's nature, such that God does not originate, but only ratifies his own goodness. Schelling's ontology is quite different, rooted in the Kantian conception of autonomy as the ability to originate good principles. The good is still present here as a structure or principle, but is subordinate to freedom. Dorner's point is that in either view, ethics is subordinate to and derivative from ontology. Ontology subordinates ethics either to the power of a nature already complete apart from freedom, or to the pre-ethical power of radical freedom. Brown expounds Schelling in a way that appears to confirm this interpretation: "Therefore, if there is to be a standard of good at all, it is given in the structure of God's own being and cannot be other than it is. In speaking this

Consequently neither intellectualism nor voluntarism is, by itself, adequate; each has partial insight into the ethical, but expresses it in an exclusive self-subverting fashion. If freedom is excluded from goodness (intellectualism), then goodness is a nature that does not have to come to be through freedom. It simply is. Conversely, if goodness is excluded from freedom (voluntarism), then freedom is lawless, arbitrary, and this implies that ethical goodness is optional, a contingent expression of God's will to power. The truth of each view can be maintained only in a higher view. In formulating this higher mediating view, Dorner agrees with Kant, Fichte, and Hegel concerning the primacy of the ethical and practical over the ontological. Dorner, like his predecessors, is not opposed to ontology, but to the subordination of ethics to ontology. Dorner expresses the primacy of the ethical when he writes, "All proofs for the existence of God are, rightly apprehended, only preludes to the ontological, which attains its truth, however, only by the ethical."[56] Dorner has a deontic view of ontology, that sublates the physical in the ethical.

Dorner agrees with Hegel that the truth is the whole, and that the ethical involves reference to an other. Ethical necessity and ethical freedom are both constitutive and *equiprimordial* features of the ethical. "Consequently it is necessary to declare both that the good becomes eternally actual through

---

way, however, we must remember that this "standard" is primarily ontological, and is only derivatively applicable to ethics. . . . No ontological constraint prevents such a God from willing evil vis-à-vis a creature already in existence. When not self-actualizing or creating per se, such a free will need not emulate the divine essence. Schelling's God doesn't actually will evil in this way, and there is no reason to anticipate that he will; but he really is capable of doing so" (JAAR, p. 247). Dorner complains that Schelling "did but little for ethics" (*History of Protestant Theology*, II, 362).

56. Third Article p. 176. On the primacy of the practical to the theoretical, cf. Kant, *Critique of Practical Reason*; Fichte, *Wissenschaftslehre 1794*, especially part II; Hegel, *Phänomenologie des Geistes*: "In my view, which can only be justified by the presentation of the entire system, everything depends on conceiving and expressing the true not as substance, but rather as subject" (Hoffmeister, Hamburg: Meiner, 1952, p. 19). G. R. G. Mure observes that in the logic Hegel elaborates a deontic theory of judgment. Mure writes: "Goodness, or intrinsic value, cannot, *ex vi termini* and as common experience amply testifies, be demonstrated as the consequent of any ground; it must be self-demonstrating. If it is not self-demonstrating, it can only be either the inexplicable pronouncement of emotional caprice, or the content of a purely miraculous intuition. Moreover, this self-demonstration must consist in the sublation of categories which, so far as they are *reell*, do not express value. If it does not, intrinsic value, be it emotional fancy or mystic intuition, is not integral to the world but a veneer upon its surface. Such is the essence of Hegel's theory of truth . . ." (*A Study of Hegel's Logic*, Oxford: Clarendon Press, 1950, p. 193). The self-realization of the ethical that Mure stresses, its nonderivability from any prior ground, requires multiple modes of being. Thus the ethical has a triadic structure—a point repeatedly made by Hegel and accepted and elaborated further by Dorner.

the active divine will, but also that the ethical cannot have its reality in God simply through divine will; rather the ethical must be an eternal reality in God's being and essence."[57] But how can this be? How is the apparent contradiction to be resolved? Dorner's answer is that the ethical in God has multiple modes of existence (*Daseinsweisen*) that nevertheless inwardly coinhere. The ethical has an inclusive triadic structure, not a simple exclusive monopolar structure.[58] Dorner identifies the elements of this structure as 1) ethical substance, or the ethically necessary, 2) ethical freedom, and 3) love as the synthesis of 1 and 2.

The ethically necessary, as a mode of being in God, Dorner correlates with the trinitarian symbol of Father. Dorner observes that the ethically necessary is grounded in the Father, including the law of Sinai and the law of conscience; even the Son sees in the Father his ethical obligation. But just for this reason the ethically necessary is not a fate inimical to freedom, nor does it suffice by itself for an account of God as such.[59] Dorner thus breaks with the ontology of power that finds expression in patriarchalism and the royal metaphor. Ethical necessity, taken by itself apart from ethical freedom, is mere law, command, or principle of obligation. But the ethically necessary demands realization, and its very nature as *ethical* necessity requires realization through its other, namely, freedom. Ethical freedom is

57. Cf. Third Article, p. 170.

58. Dorner's discussion of love as God's ethical essence is influenced by his colleague Theodor Liebner (op. cit.), who sought to develop the concept of Trinity out of an analysis of love. Liebner's understanding of love as an interpersonal conception, was in turn shaped by an essay, "*Die immanente Wesens-Trinität*," by G. Mehring (*Zeitschrift für Philosophie und spekulative Theologie*, hrsg. von I. H. Fichte, Bd 9 Erstes Heft, Bonn 1842, 157-195). In this essay Mehring discusses Hegel's concept of Trinity in the context of the theological debates over Trinity, and philosophical debates concerning the finitude of personality and the applicability of personhood to God. Although Mehring is critical of Hegel, he nevertheless finds in Hegel's thought a solution to both aforementioned problems. Genuine, as opposed to spurious, infinity is essentially social. Mehring is one of the few theologians who realized that Hegel's concept of Spirit is fundamentally interpersonal and social. Its triadic structure provides a way to conceive God as both infinite and personal. Mehring believes the concept of person is impossible on the premisses of Cartesian idealism and solipsism, because person requires an other and is fundamentally intersubjective. Hegel's concept of the trinitarian personal God clarifies how the relation of God to world is to be understood along intersubjective interpersonal lines. Cf. Axt-Piscalar, GdG pp. 151ff. For a discussion of the question of divine personality in the aftermath of Hegel, see Walter Jaeschke, *Reason in Religion* (tr. J. Michael Stewart and Peter C. Hodgson, Berkeley: University of California Press, 1990) 365-421; see especially 365-370. For a study of Hegel's account of intersubjectivity and holism, see Robert R. Williams, *Recognition: Fichte and Hegel on the Other* (Albany: State University of New York Press, 1992).

59. Third Article p. 173.

the principle of movement on the ground of a given basis.[60] This is the principle of mediation by conscious will and insight that writes the covenant upon the heart, or that translates the moral law into practice. The ethically free corresponds to the trinitarian symbol of the Son.

## Ethical Freedom Not Subordinated to Ethical Necessity

Dorner sometimes formulates the relation of ethical necessity and ethical freedom in a way that suggests subordination of the latter to the former. For example he tells us that the ethically necessary is the primary mode of being in God, and that freedom is secondary. Further, he asserts that ethical freedom is an *instrument* for the realization of ethical necessity.[61] Finally he asserts that freedom "is nothing more than the real possibility for the eternal self-generation of the ethical into actuality."[62] These formulations suggest that freedom is subordinate to necessity. Specifically, since divine freedom is nonreciprocally related to necessity, it is not able to originate, but only ratify divine goodness.[63] This nonreciprocal relation of freedom to necessity calls into question its independence from ethical necessity as a distinct mode of God's being and invites the following criticism: "In this triad, freedom (the Son) is derivative from, and can only be as the actualization of, ethical necessity (the Father). This is the Hegelian notion of ontological freedom as uninhibited and complete actualization, and not the Schellingian notion of freedom that can choose among alternatives, or at least can either will or refrain from willing. This Hegelian ontological freedom is not the notion of freedom Dorner needs to make theological talk of God's ethical nature truly convincing."[64] Thus Brown

60. Ibid. p. 172.
61. Ibid.
62. Ibid. p. 173.
63. Robert F. Brown, "God's Ability to Will Moral Evil," *Faith and Philosophy*, Vol. 8, No. 1, January 1991, 10-11. Brown characterizes the classical position as follows: "God . . . is not good because of willing his own goodness, for God's nature cannot be other than it is. Its perfect desirability makes God's goodness a final cause ineluctably drawing God's will to it; divine goodness determines divine will and not vice-versa. . . .This nonreciprocal relation between God's good being and God's will is deeply embedded in the Platonic-Aristotelian philosophical heritage that Aquinas and other classical theists build upon."
64. Robert F. Brown, "Schelling and Dorner," op. cit., p. 247. For my own earlier criticisms along these lines, see Robert R. Williams, "I.A. Dorner: The Ethical Immutability of God," *Journal of the American Academy of Religion*, LIV/4, 1986, 721-738. It will become evident that I no longer subscribe fully to these criticisms, since they fail to appreciate the complexity of Dorner's position.

suggests that Dorner, like Hegel, ends in Thomas' intellectualism, according to which everything, including will, is governed by ontological necessity.

These criticisms are directed more to Dorner's incautious formulations than to his fundamental position. In particular, it is untrue that for Dorner ethical freedom is *derivative* from or *nonreciprocally related* to ethical necessity. In the Hegelian triadic holism that Dorner draws upon, no absolute priority can be accorded any particular element. All constitutent elements of the whole are reciprocally and mutually mediating. Consequently the assertion of an *absolute* priority of one element over the others would be symptomatic of a lapse into monopolar abstract identity and simplicity. In contrast to such simplicity, all the modes of the triad are necessary to the triad; any one requires, rather than excludes, the others. The absolute therefore is not any one of the modes, but the mutually interrelated whole. The classical conception of the absolute excludes relation, but the Hegelian absolute is relatedness itself.[65] There are no exceptions to universal reciprocal mediation, or to absolute relativity.[66] Dorner makes this point when he observes that ethical necessity is not, by itself, a complete account of God as such, and that ethical necessity requires and demands that its goodness be realized. This means that ethical necessity is not by itself wholly actual. Rather it depends on its other, namely, ethical freedom, for its actualization, that is, it is actualized only in and along with its other. In trinitarian language that nevertheless breaks with the traditional trinitarian conception, Dorner's "father" symbol requires and depends on the "son."

The fundamental principle that Dorner's holism shares with Hegel's is that each mode of being finds its realization in and through an other, and consequently each requires the other for its realization.[67] Thus the "father"

65. For a contemporary discussion that contrasts the Hegelian and classical senses of the absolute, cf. Hodgson, op. cit., pp. 62, 69, 171ff.; see also Williams, *Recognition*, op. cit. Chapters 10 and 11.

66. "There is absolutely nothing, nothing in heaven, nature, spirit, or anywhere, that does not include mediation as well as immediacy. These determinations show themselves to be inseparable, both in fact and in principle. The separation of one from the other shows it to be a nullity." G. W. F. Hegel, *Wissenschaft der Logik, Band I, Werke, Theorie Werkausgabe*, Frankfurt: Suhrkamp Verlag, 1969, p. 66. Thus for Hegel, an absolute that is transcendent to or exclusive of relation, like Parmenides' One, is impossible in principle; it can only be an element abstracted from a larger dynamic whole. Dorner draws upon Hegel's analysis, even if he criticizes Hegel's system.

67. Third Article p. 172. For an analysis of the principle of self-recognition in other, see Williams, *Recognition: Fichte and Hegel on the Other*, op. cit.

(ethical necessity) needs the "son" for his realization, and the "son" (ethical freedom) needs the "father" for his realization. Dorner's apparent "subordination" is an expression of Hegel's concept of self-recognition and self-realization in other. Freedom finds its realization in its other, ethical necessity. This looks like subordination only if the reciprocal mediation of the terms is overlooked. For ethical necessity does not issue 'automatically' into reality, drawing freedom after it as a final cause. Instead ethical necessity by itself is abstract; it requires its other, namely freedom, for its actualization. These concepts are fundamentally reciprocal. "Only when the free has found itself in the unshakable objective, so that in the depths of the ethically necessary the free is likewise something willed, is the absolute actualization of the ethically necessary achieved in freedom's own desire and love."[68]

Consequently, Dorner does not, like intellectualism, subordinate freedom to necessity; he is claiming rather that ethical necessity is realized only in and through its other, namely freedom. The modes of God's being are both relatively independent and reciprocally mediating.[69] This implies

68. Ibid., p. 173.

69. It is at this point that Axt-Piscalar claims that Dorner parts company with Liebner and Mehring, (op cit., p. 154). For the latter conceive the terms of Trinity as personal, or rather interpersonally related in love. However, Dorner maintains that if the trinitarian persons are conceived as personal in the modern sense of person, this runs the risk of tritheism, in which the three persons share a common generic divine essence. Against this view, Dorner maintains that it is not the trinitarian *personae* but God that is personal, with three moments or elements constituting his personality (Welch, *God and Incarnation*, p. 110n). Thus according to Axt-Piscalar, Dorner did not accept the relational concept of the person set forth by Mehring and Liebner (154n72). I am not so sure. Several points need mention. First, Axt-Piscalar bases her claim on Dorner's late *Glaubenslehre* (1884). She does not make a study of the earlier Immutability Essay, where, I believe, Dorner may be closer to Liebner and Mehring. For example cf. pp. 9-10 where Dorner clearly affirms that human nature is always posited along with an other. Further, the texts on love we have been considering clearly exhibit a mutual reciprocal mediation that is constitutive of love, which Dorner, following Hegel, conceives as interpersonal. Second, Axt-Piscalar observes that, far from leading to tritheism, it is precisely the relational or intersubjective concept of persons that allows Mehring to handle the issue of tritheism: "Since persons come to be and exist only in a reciprocal act of self- abandonment *Selbsthingabe*, this derivation of the trinity can get around the problem of tritheism . . ." (ibid.). She does not spell this out. However the point seems to be that the interpersonal conception of mutually mediated self-realization-in-other avoids the problem Dorner raises concerning three persons sharing a generic abstract universal essence. There is no abstract generic divine essence; rather there is only the coinhering mutually interdependent *Daseinweisen* that realize themselves in and through each other. Thus the relational conception of personhood does not necessarily lead to tritheism if applied to God. On the contrary it helps to avoid that very problem. Third, in the Immutability Essay, Dorner clearly conceives the equiprimordial *Daseinsweisen* of divine personality—ethical necessity, ethical freedom, and their joint reciprocal realization in love—as involved in a

a revision of the classical conception of divine aseity, in terms of which God's goodness is the goodness of a nature that is immediately and eternally actual. It further implies a revision of classical trinitarianism according to which aseity is appropriated exclusively to God the Father (or the ethically necessary being).[70] Dorner reconstructs divine aseity and shows that it involves reciprocal mediation among the various modes of God's being (*Daseinsweisen*). God's self-actualization is complex; it cannot be reduced to a single principle as intellectualism and voluntarism would have it. Rather aseity involves *both* necessity and freedom, and thus is conceived in trinitarian terms rather than monopolar terms.

The unity of both modes of being is love, for love is not like a self-enclosed solipsist that seeks only itself; rather love seeks what is other. Love is the unifying principle of such mutual mediation and interdependence: "the absolute union of the ethically necessary and the ethically free, in which the two confirm one another, is love; and thus the primal good is love only because in him the ethical has a threefold and yet indissolubly coherent mode of being."[71] The coinherence of the various modes of being in love involves an essential reciprocity that does not cancel, but presupposes and mediates their relative difference and independence.

Dorner responds explicitly to the objection that he allegedly subordinates the ethically free to the ethically necessary: "It is not permissible to deny that there is freedom in God because a contradiction to the ethically necessary cannot be conceived in him. The possibility of this contradiction

---

complex reciprocal mediation that is structurally similar at least to self-recognition in other. This conceptual-terminological looseness should not be surprising, for Hegel himself was quite free in his use of terminology. Although there is a distinction to be made between recognition (*Anerkennung*) as a term of *Realphilosophie*, and the abstract categories of the logic, Hegel writes concerning the logical Idea that "it is the eternal vision of itself in other" (*Encyclopedia*, §214, tr. Wallace-Miller, Oxford: Clarendon Press 1873). Reciprocal self-recognition in other is a general structure common to Hegel's concepts of freedom and truth, as well as his concept of recognition. Dorner makes use of this general conception of universal reciprocity and relativity in his reconstruction of Trinity, which, according to Axt-Piscalar, breaks with the classical tradition, but *not with Athanasius*, in conceiving the Father as relative to the Son, and thus conceives divine aseity in trinitarian fashion, as *not* restricted to or proceeding from the Father alone (ibid. p. 167). The concept of God as interpersonal, therefore, is a middle ground between conceiving God as a genus in monopolar solipsist terms on the one hand, and a mere aggregate of individuals on the other (tritheism). Dorner's conception of a continuing and developing incarnation points to some sort of social-interpersonal model. God is more complex than a person (solipsism), but more unified than a mere aggregate of individuals in a genus. God's unity is not natural but ethical, and thus interpersonal or communal. Cf. below section V. Beyond the Royal Metaphor: The Family of God.

70. See Article One, note 58.

71. Third Article p. 174.

does not belong to the concept of perfected freedom . . ."[72] The impossibility of a contradiction to ethical necessity is not ontological, as Brown suggests, but an ethical impossibility that requires freedom. Put simply, freedom finds its telos or perfection in (ethical) love, and it is the essence of love to seek what is other.

Brown claims that, given Schelling's voluntarism, no ontological constraint prevents God from willing evil towards a creature, but adds that "there is no reason to anticipate he will."[73] Dorner could reply by observing 1) that the possibility that God could will evil towards a creature, thus demonstrating his freedom, cannot be given a theological basis free from incoherence,[74] thus suggesting that radical freedom is irrational, and 2) that what prevents God from so willing is not any ontological constraint, but God's ethical perfection and character, that is, God is love itself. This means that any putative predisposition of freedom towards the good and valuable, or freedom's alleged 'inability' to will evil, is not a restriction on or limitation of freedom. For freedom has its ethical telos in loving. Since love seeks what is other, love adjusts itself to its other. God's love remains constant, while God's relation to the world or the other, must—because motivated by love—be capable of variation, but only within the limits set by love.

Brown either tacitly appeals to such divine ethical perfection when he assures us that there is no reason to think God would will evil, although he could, or else his claim that "there is no reason to anticipate that he will," is to be taken literally. Then freedom is understood ontologically as neutral or indifferent to the good and valuable, and indifferent to love. In the latter case, it just happens that God does not will evil, but he might. God's ethical perfection would thus be rendered reversible and contingent upon radical, nonrational freedom. Dorner rejects this radical voluntarism. He does not wish to follow Schelling in affirming a contingent and reversible divine goodness, because this is contrary to divine love, and is a path that

72. Ibid. p. 174n. 30.

73. Brown, "Schelling and Dorner," op. cit. p. 247.

74. For an attempt to do so, cf. Kierkegaard, *Fear and Trembling* (tr. H. V. Hong, Princeton University Press, 1983). The irrationalism of the position comes out clearly in Kierkegaard's Journal commentary: "The terrifying thing in the collision is this—that it is not a collision between God's command and man's command, but between God's command and God's command" (ibid., 248). God as the author of the ethical commands Abraham to do what is forbidden by the ethical. This locates in God the contradiction implicit in the problematic concept of a teleological suspension of the ethical. God's ability to will evil towards a creature involves a setting aside or suspending of the ethical universal that God is or wills.

may end in irrationalism and anthropomorphism. But this rejection does not signal a return to the classical conception in which God's freedom is subordinate to God's good nature. Dorner shows that God's ethical goodness involves a complex self-actualization that includes reciprocal mediation between freedom and ethical necessity. God's aseity must be understood as involving a threefold mediation, or reciprocal recognition in other.

## BEYOND THE ROYAL METAPHOR: THE FAMILY OF GOD

Classical theology finds expression in a royal or monarchical metaphor.[75] Dorner himself characterizes the classical position as patriarchal, and devotes considerable space to a discussion of the divine decrees that are elements of the royal metaphor. Dorner's critique of divine simplicity and immutability is an extended critique of one facet of this metaphor. According to the royal metaphor, God is portrayed as an absolute cosmic monarch, utterly transcendent to the world and ruling the world by absolute decree on the one hand, and by absolute causal efficacy on the other.[76] God is like a king who maintains his kingdom through the rewards and punishments of a judicial system. Yet divine justice is so shot through with the classical concept of immutability that the monarch-judge is prevented from adaptation and compromise. The fundamental relation between God and humans is the nonreciprocal relation of master and slave, that is, a relation of power and domination. Even salvation is understood in these terms: salvation is a mysterious setting aside of universally deserved punishment, and is understood in terms of the master's good pleasure.

Dorner's critique of divine immutability is an attack on the monarchical model. His open assertion of reciprocity between God and humans strikes at its heart. However, divine love requires such reciprocity, and reciprocity in turn implies that there is a creaturely impact on the divine decree.[77] This suggests an interpersonal conception, not only of love, but also of the divine-human relation. This relation is conceived by Dorner, following

75. The monarchical metaphor has been subject to discussion and criticism in contemporary theology. Cf. Edward Farley, *Ecclesial Reflection, An Anatomy of Theological Method* (Philadelphia: Fortress Press, 1982); Farley, *Good and Evil* (Minneapolis: Fortress Press, 1990); Sallie McFague, *Models of God: Theology for an Ecological, Nuclear Age* (Philadelphia: Fortress Press, 1987).

76. Farley, *Ecclesial Reflection*, op. cit., 157ff.

77. Third Article p. 150.

Hegel, as self-recognition and self-realization in other. "Without participation in God, man cannot attain the concept which God formed of him, and without the developed actualized receptivity of men for God, God cannot dwell and move in men."[78] Each member of the community depends on the others, not necessarily for its existence, but for recognition.

We have already found that, owing to internal complexity, God's self-impartation to an other is not a self-loss of love, or a giving up of God's self; rather it manifests the capacity of love to be at home with itself in the other, and to be itself in and with the other.[79] Here Dorner takes over directly one of Hegel's fundamental conceptions, namely, self-recognition in other.[80] If one grants that God exists with an other, that this other is genuine and not reducible to self-sameness, then it is necessary that God take account of or recognize others. Dorner interprets incarnation to be a divine *Mitsein*, or being-with others. The royal metaphor is to be rejected in favor of an interpersonal one.

Dorner expands the interpersonal conception of divine *Mitsein* in the third section of the third essay. Dorner speaks of a divine compassion (*Mitleid*) and an analogue of affliction. Further, Dorner develops his earlier suggestion about an impact of human freedom on the divine decree, by following up Schleiermacher's suggestion of a joint divine-human co-rule (*Mitregiment*).[81] This is far from the *decretum absolutum* of the monarchical metaphor. Finally, Dorner rejects the master/slave model of divine-human relation. God is not an utterly transcendent monarch whose counsels are hidden. "To be sure, God does not hand over the reins of government to the faithful, but neither does he want to make them automatons. . . . From the very beginning he has preferred to give his friends joint knowledge of what he intends to do."[82] This joint knowledge is a *Mitwissen*, a co-knowing. Given the interpersonal reciprocal divine-human relation, the one-sided, nonreciprocal relation of master and slave is no longer appropriate: "Here is the innermost point where servitude and sonship part. The servant does

78. Third Article p. 145.

79. Third Article p. 178.

80. Dorner's debt to Hegel's concept of recognition and Spirit is evident. For a study of Hegel's concept of Spirit as an intersubjective concept, see Williams, *Recognition: Fichte and Hegel on the Other*, op. cit. Although Dorner does not use the term recognition (*Anerkennen*), this fundamentally intersubjective concept lies behind his discussion of love as inherently reciprocal, and his adoption of intersubjective terminology in the third part of his essay.

81. Third Article p. 194.

82. Ibid. p. 194.

not know what his master is doing; at most he knows the lord's law, but neither its reason nor the result and goal which the lord wants to attain; therefore fatalism has so readily been joined with the legalistic standpoint of servitude. But those who are his, the Savior has called friends, children, and free in the Father's house."[83] Theonomy is the alternative to the heteronomy of master/slave, and theonomy is to be understood *intersubjectively* as *self-recognition in other*.

The interpersonal metaphor that Dorner seems to prefer for characterizing the divine-human relation is that of the Family of God.[84] While this metaphor is not beyond criticism, especially in view of a possible nineteenth-century patriarchal understanding of the family that Dorner might have had in mind, the family metaphor is an interpersonal one, and is compatible in principle with Dorner's analysis of love as requiring reciprocity, *Mitwissen*, *Mitregiment*, and *Mitleid*, all of which flow from his critique of metaphysical patriarchalism and assertion of a qualified divine immutability. Should Dorner's understanding of the family prove, by contemporary standards, to be one-sided and patriarchal, this would establish that, in this respect, Dorner did not escape being a child of his time. However, such a criticism of patriarchalism and domination would appeal to precisely those fundamental interpersonal conceptions of love, reciprocity, and nondomination that Dorner, following Hegel, lays down as constitutive of the Family of God.

Nowhere does Dorner express his revision of divine immutability more radically or more consistently than in this early essay. Although it is not satisfactory in all respects, it merits our attention because its serious examination of fundamental issues in systematic and philosophical theology continues to repay careful study.

## NOTES ON THE TEXT AND TRANSLATION

Dorner originally published his inquiry on Divine Immutability as three separate articles in successive yearly issues of the *Jahrbücher für deutsche Theologie (1856–58)*. Later he reprinted these essays along with others in his *Gesammelte Schriften aus dem Gebiet der systematischen Theologie, Exegese und Geschichte* (Berlin, 1883). The translation follows the text

83. Third Article p. 194.
84. Third Article p. 148.

as reprinted in the *Gesammelte Schriften*. The present volume is the first time that these articles have appeared together as a monograph on immutability.

In the *Gesammelte Schriften* Dorner revised some of his notes to take account of more recent literature and discussions. All of Dorner's notes have been translated; these appear in standard (i.e., consecutively numbered) form. Translator's notes are indicated by the standard notation (—TRANS.). I have not been able to identify all of the editions, particularly Latin editions, that Dorner cites. Most readers will probably consult the English translations of Augustine, Aquinas, and Scotus. Those familiar with the Protestant scholastics (Gerhard, Quenstedt) will necessarily have Latin skills required to track down and make use of the relevant literature.

The first and second parts of Dorner's essay were translated by Robert Williams for this volume. I wish to acknowledge the assistance of Suzanne Carter for clarifying some of Dorner's formidable German sentences, Robert Sawyer for help in translation of Latin quotations, and above all Claude Welch for reviewing and making many improvements in the translation. Robert F. Brown made many valuable suggestions that improved the project and clarified points in Schelling's argument. Garrett Green helped clarify the argument and the style of the introduction. I also wish to acknowledge a Summer Faculty Research Grant from Hiram College, a grant from the University of Chicago's Midwest Faculty Seminar program, and a summer research grant from the National Endowment for the Humanities in support of this project.

The third article of Dorner's essay was originally published by Claude Welch in *God and Incarnation* (New York: Oxford University Press, 1965); some revisions have been made in the 1965 translation. Welch deserves the credit for first spotting Barth's brief but significant reference to Dorner in *Church Dogmatics II/1*, for resurrecting Dorner's essay from obscurity, and for setting Dorner's constructive proposals before the public for the first time in English. Although Part Three cannot be fully appreciated apart from Dorner's investigations and analyses in Parts One and Two, without the stimulus of Welch's pioneering work on Part Three, the translation of the rest of the essay might never have followed.

# On the Proper Conception of the Doctrine of God's Immutability with Special Reference to the Reciprocal Relation between God's Suprahistorical and Historical Life

Greek culture, even in its heyday, nevertheless had the uneasy consciousness that it had attained its possessions and riches illegitimately, namely, through a theft from the gods, or at least at their expense. This is the meaning of the Prometheus legend.[1] The same point could be expressed differently, as a remembrance of a break with earlier religions, to which the name of Prometheus became attached. The glorious, beautiful Hellenic world was conscious of itself as entering existence not under the protective benevolence of the ancient deities, but under a cloud of disfavor from the new deities whose chief was represented as jealous of the power of the emancipated human spirit; or rather, the Greek world was conscious of

1. Cf. Preller, *Griechische Mythologie* (Leipzig, 1854, I, 61–69. 128. II, 152) Schömann, *des Aeschylos gefesselter Prometheus*, Greifsw. 1844. Schelling, *Einleitung in der Philosophie der Mythologie* 1856; Nägelsbach, *die nachhomerische Theologie des griech. Volksglaubens*, Nürnberg, 1857. Aeschylos, *Prometheus*, ed. Schömann. [Dorner cites several passages from these works; the following from Preller is representative: "Prometheus (otherwise closely akin to Hephaestus) has received the special significance of being the representative of human culture *[Bildung]* so far as it overpowers nature and provokes the gods. The promethean ingenuity of the human race leads it to force its way into all the hidden recesses of nature and render all nature's powers useful (as shown beautifully in Sophocles' *Antigone*). Its indefatigable drive and thirst for truth leads it to plumb the depths of deity. But the same promethean spirit ultimately leads to defiance and contradiction. Consequently, the myth shows not only the noble gift of Prometheus—the theft of fire from the gods—it also shows that the promethean striving is essentially contradictory and mere opportunistic cleverness. Zeus must punish Prometheus because he wanted to emulate the gods."]

itself as repressed by an accusing and yet self-excusing bad conscience. Hence Greek consciousness combined the enjoyment of a bright present with a presentiment of its own transitoriness and perishability—in which the dominion of the self-attesting divine realm of Olympus was implicated. Despite the beautiful facade of a free noble existence, a sense of unfreedom and disquiet crept in. The spirit of the Greeks manifests itself as simultaneously in bondage and yet free, and it is difficult to determine which is the dominant view.

The Greek mind has doubts about the justice of its deities. But it has no fewer doubts about the legitimacy of its free progress in politics, art, science, and about the durability of its accomplishments. The new developments of its spiritual life are not blessed by or consecrated to its old faith, and so its progress did not bring a durable advance in piety, but rather a greater alienation from the divine. These are the grounds of the deep divisions that the more perceptive minds such as Aeschylos sense and express.

The present situation—a time which is full of unrest, cooly forward looking, yet troubled and despairing at the same time—bears something Promethean within it. There is likewise a living contradiction in which a heightened sense of freedom goes hand in hand with an inescapable sense of fetters and limits. It is a time of deep discomfort, uneasiness, inner desolation, and misfortune. There is a widespread conviction that, despite our great cultural and scientific progress, things are not going well, much less rightly, and that our culture does not have a good conscience in relation to God. The faith of this modern culture is not the faith of its fathers. Rather the emancipated secular consciousness has increased to a disproportionate extent.

One of the inherited forms of the doctrine of God is Deism, which, with its dilution of content and formal spirituality, offers no offense to the spirit of the age. But it also challenges and excites so little, that it is only natural if in its latest phases the age ignores Deism and seeks a closer God in its heart or in nature. The other vital form of faith, as it has always lived in the simple and naive faith of Christians, appears as an affront to the educated. It appears as unworthy, even childlike in its belief in a providence that watches over the smallest details, and which makes God subservient to the interests of the world and, in particular, the prayers of the believers. There is bad faith at work.

Theology bears its share of responsibility for this situation, since it has not done enough to heal the deep divisions in our cultural life, or to achieve a clear, well-delineated concept of God. Faith, to be sure, does not require such a doctrine for its bare existence, but it does need a doctrine of God in order to flourish. And the cultured world needs such a doctrine lest its receptivity for Christian faith sink into spiritual apathy. The contemporary world, considered as a whole, has not entirely rid itself of the stings of a conscience admonishing it about worship of God. On the one hand, it sees itself incapable of sacrificing the great fruits of human culture to the traditional concept of God, and on the other hand, it is also incapable of affirming its culture together with its traditional belief.

What the sad outcome of such alienation from inwardness and from the highest being must be, can be seen from the modern translation of the Prometheus legend into German, namely, the Faust legend and the solution to it proposed by its great poet. This solution recalls the fate of the other Titans, who, after their wings melted, ended in misery. The moderns, even though they had wanted a proud flight to merely ideal heights, have come to a wretched conclusion. Faust, as colonizer and master of the material might of land and sea, becomes a man of public utility and social good. Thereby he fulfills one side of the human vocation, namely that the human being should become master of the earth. If belief in the reality of an ideal world becomes a substitute for belief in God, and if the human being feels itself to be lord of the earth such that there is supposedly nothing of greater worth than humankind itself—these ideas lend work (labor) its ideal glory and its higher significance. But such a cultural Gestalt is neither God-like, nor like a master, but rather like someone destitute or a castaway. The human being seeks in vain to pass off its possessions for well-being, and its beggar-stick for a royal scepter.

There is something titanic in our age; something titanically audacious, but also titanically unhappy and restless. The traditional belief in God is severely shaken, the concept of the living God has become vapor and smoke, or terrifying like a ghost. Since the human being cannot live without a god, there arise diverse forms of deification of the world: pseudo-religions that seek to fill the void left by a dying faith with superstitious projections such as deifications of matter, human nature, or the works of human culture—statesmanship, art, and science.

Although there is something in the depths of our people that undermines the foundation, not only of Christian, but also human existence, still there are hundreds in various positions who are firm believers in foundations and who have time to dispute with others over the finest points of traditional doctrine. If the undermining process is allowed to continue and run its course, it will be the ruin of us all. Yet amazingly few hands bestir themselves in thought and science to ward off or avert this decline.

Certainly science alone is insufficient to guide us through the mighty dangers that threaten us. The church must zealously redouble its efforts, love, and concern. But science (*Wissenschaft*) must not rest content if the preaching of the church is enlightened and the modern spirit of the age increases. It is obvious from our cultural situation that speculative thinking, including philosophy, is scarcely evident in the practice and in the spiritual life of our people. We live in an era of enlightenment, but not yet in an enlightened age.

The strengthened secular consciousness of our present age hungers and thirsts for realism to replace our accustomed idealism. In itself this is not to be censured but rather praised. Further, if the older metaphysical doctrine of God was demonstrably supposed to suffer from a lack of idealism[2] and so removed God into an abstract beyond, contemporary theology will perform appropriate service if it vindicates for the concept of God a powerful worldly realism that will repristinate the almost impotent representations God and fill them with life and spirit. Theology would do well to recognize phenomena such as Feuerbach and the currently resurgent materialism, as a counterblow directed against the hitherto dominant idealism. However, it should be noted that the term 'realism' by itself has no magical monopoly on truth. Its very newness requires careful consideration. We should keep in mind that error is no less possible in realism than idealism.

In what follows I want to examine carefully only one aspect of the concept of God. However, it is a central problem in contemporary philosophical theology. This problem is closely related to the religious interest. And there are so many related questions that a satisfactory answer can be viewed as a precondition for a renewal and validity of the concept of the living God for the present "world of cultured despisers." I want to explore the proper concept of the immutability of God, with special reference to the relation between the supra-historical and historical life of God. I make no pretensions to having exhausted the topic. If in the course of this essay I must oppose many views that contrast with the traditional concept of divine immutability, it will be evident in the last part of this essay that I

2. Precritical thought failed to do justice to God as subject, personal. For example, Hegel criticized classical thought for insufficient appreciation of freedom and subjectivity,—TRANS.

am far from asserting that the received traditional concept is beyond revision.[3] Rather it requires revisions that are substantial and genuine, and not merely change for change's sake.

We often hear that the interests of philosophy diverge from those of theology. We will have to test this view, since substantial conflict between philosophy and theology leads to their separation and impoverishment. In the last ten years the concept of the personality of God has been of special concern to both philosophy and theology. The objections against divine personality have come not merely from the critics who claim that it confuses the concept of personality with the concept of subjectivity or individuality (the elder Fichte was particularly influential here), but even more from an idea that modern philosophy has not so much invented as taken over, namely the concept of the divine nature as an infinite being unlimited in extension. Since self-consciousness is possible only by the reflection of the self to itself in conscious distinction from others, the personality of God seems possible only at the price of a limitation by an other which is not God. In other words, to attribute personality to God seems to require giving up the fundamental idea of an unlimited divine being.

Conversely, the infinity of God is possible only by sacrificing the concept of divine personality. For similar reasons, Origen had already entertained doubts about divine consciousness in preference for divine infinity. However, Spinoza formulated the proposition that all determination is negation, and so denied the infinity of God for the sake of personality. Theologians return to this axiom despite Hegel's rejection of it, when they do not (as in the case of Gabler and the Hegelian right) accept *Geist*, the absolute reason, and also when they do not posit Being or the world as the absolute first, as the real prius. Modern philosophical theology has denied the absolute personality of God in favor of the infinity and sublimity of God, because personality would imply imperfection and limitation in God. Moreover, the divine infinity is represented as an eternal actualization of God in the world (in agreement with Hegel) which excludes all being outside of God and thus conceives God as an all-inclusive being. But also in agreement with Hegel, the divine actualization in the world is conceived

3. Cf. the article, "Die deutsche Theologie und ihre Aufgaben in der Gegenwart." [This is the editor's introduction to the first issue of *Jahrbücher für deutsche Theologie* (1856) of which Dorner and Theodor Liebner were the editors and driving forces. Part One of Dorner's essay on divine immutability also originally appeared in this volume.—TRANS.] pp. 28ff. Cf. also Ehrenfeuchter, *theologische Principienlehre*, *Jahrbücher für deutsche Theologie* I, 1, 53ff.

as an eternal process of becoming subject in and through finite spirits. Errors are corrected by the development and extension of the knowledge that everything depends on the concept of the true infinite, the intensive rather than the extensive infinite.[4] This concept has become current among those who do not stand in awe of the domination of the object (Nature), but, for the sake of absolute indeterminacy and emptiness of the object, conceive the intensive infinite as determined in and through itself, that is, power over extensive magnitude. Thus it is not contradictory to maintain that God is both intensively infinite and nevertheless personal. God's infinity does not consist in the utter absence of determination, but rather in

4. I am happy to find that popular theology recognizes that God, as Oetinger puts it, is to be conceived as an intensive magnitude rather than as an extensive magnitude. Thus Weitbrecht, *die christliche Glaubenslehre*, Zweiter Teil, 1955, p. 53, "We cannot save the concept of the personality of God except by recourse to the representation of the self-comprehension of God in his magnitude, that now becomes something in God, since God is an intensive magnitude." This language has the defect that it represents the extensive magnitude in God as the first, the original, and only through a negation (limitation) of such magnitude does personality arise. On the contrary—if one wishes to speak metaphorically of a 'before' or 'after'—the intensive magnitude of God should be the absolute first. Further, it will not do to determine this magnitude as the other, as *Geist* in general, or as *res cogitans*. Otherwise there will again be a coordination with *res extensa* that must lead either to dualism, or to a monism of either a spiritualist or materialist sort. But rather than a lapse into Spinozism—as the history of the Hegelian system makes manifest—the preservation of truth lies in conceiving the intensive absolute *Geist* determinately as ethical *Geist*. To be sure, the concept of God includes extensive magnitude as well, including the realm of infinite powers and divine fullness of life that Martensen aptly calls the divine pleroma. But this magnitude must be derived as eternally proceeding from and determined by the ethical nature of God as the absolute reality of God. Love requires a property (*Eigentum*) that it can give in order to exhibit itself, that it can animate and to which it can apply its activity. This property love finds immediately or mediately in itself. Schleiermacher has an inkling of this when he calls love "the desire of reason to become animated" [*das Seele werden wollen der Vernunft*]. "To the process of soul-making there belongs a nature, in which reason becomes soul, and in which it wants to become embodied" (*Entwurf eines Systems der Sittenlehre*, herausgegeben von A. Schweizer, pp. 364ff., §303ff.). In reference to God—a reference that Schleiermacher does not make here—this principle is modified so that nature cannot be given to God from without, but can be given only by God's own creative action, that is, according to the nature of the absolute reason conceived as ethical. This doctrine of a nature in God is recognized by all who deal with the highest problems at the fundamental level—Martensen, Liebner, Schöberlein, Hamberger, Nocholl following Oetinger's and Böhme's precedent; and by Baader, Molitor, Schelling; by Rothe, Weisse, Chalybäus et al. The chief distinction is between those who allow the divine love to direct this eternal process of self-production of the divine life, and those who would rather allow God's personality and love to proceed out of a prior dark ground—the night of God's becoming (*ek nuktos theon gennontes*), to use Aristotle's terms, and so regard nature in God as the point of mediation for the absolute self-consciousness of God. The first group views the divine self-consciousness as the product of the most immediate self-activity of the absolute ethical spirit. This ethical nature belongs to the person of God in the widest sense, namely, it belongs to the full concept of God as that which must be, not simply in itself, but which can also reveal and communicate itself, and which finds in itself the means and instruments of its self-manifestation.

the infinitude of all determinations which, in reference to the thought and will of God, constitute his infinite self-determination or personality.

Moreover, the concept of divine personality requires self-reflection, in contrast to all that is other than God, or God's non-ego, be it possible or actual. God thinks himself only if he distinguishes himself from everything he is not, that is, from all non-ego. At this point the objection arises that if God is conceived as personal, God is limited by God's non-ego or the world, and so is rendered finite. Thus the world appears to be outside of God, and the conception becomes dualistic. But dualism would result only if the non-ego whereby God distinguishes himself from himself must be something given to God, and therefore not something grounded in God's power. Rather there is something original in God, both different from God and yet related to God, the ground of God's possibilities, such that God indeed necessarily knows himself in complete self-transparency, and at the same time as the ground of the world's possibility. All that belongs to the *scientia Dei necessaria*. In this divine self-knowledge comprehending the possibility of the world, there is also included a distinction between God and world. God is supremely actual, not merely possible, and related to the world as the actual to the merely possible. The world is only partially actual through itself, but originally and entirely dependent on God for its existence.

The genesis of human self-consciousness requires something independent to solicit it and to cooperate with it. Solicitation by the world is not an act produced by human agency, but it is nevertheless our act. The human being requires such solicitation because it belongs to human nature to be posited only along with and together with an other. The connection with an other is an essential aspect of human nature, and for this reason constitutes the full actualization of human consciousness. The human being is not self-caused, does not have existence through itself (aseity) but through God, who by virtue of his aseity exists self-sufficiently and eternally brings about his self-consciousness without needing some sort of other or a pre-existing real world. In this eternal execution of his absolute self-consciousness, the non-ego is included only as something possible. There is no need to say with Rothe that with the act of divine self-consciousness there is also bound up a real positing of a non-ego as the involuntary counter-posit of God, like a shadow is essentially connected with a body.[5]

5. Richard Rothe, *Christliche Ethik*, I, §20, p. 89, A. 1. The second edition has improved this. [Dorner is most likely referring to Richard Rothe's magnum opus, the *Theologische Ethik*, 3 vols. (1845–48); 2nd ed. revised and enlarged, 5 vols. (1867–71). Rothe (1799–1867) was on the faculty at Heidelberg. For an account of Rothe, see Karl Barth, *Protestant Thought in the 19th Century*, op. cit.; Claude Welch, *Protestant Thought in the Nineteenth Century, Vol. I*, 282–291.—TRANS.]

On the contrary, the divine self-consciousness has its clarity and determinateness precisely in the fact that it distinguishes itself from what it is not, and this not-God refers not to something already actual, but rather to all that is possible. Thus Günther[6] is right that in the process of the eternal divine self-consciousness, it is consistent to posit only the concept of a possible non-ego, not a real non-ego.[7] One could mean, it is insufficient

6. Dorner is most likely referring to Anton Günther (1783–1863), a Catholic speculative philosopher, who held no university position, but was a private ecclesiastic in Vienna from 1824 until his death. He sought to counter 'the modern pantheism' of Fichte, Schelling, and Hegel. Nevertheless he made use of the general terminology of German Idealism in formulating his own philosophical doctrine. His alternative of conceiving God as personal was a widely shared desideratum on the part of both Protestant (I. H. Fichte) and Catholic speculative philosophers (cf. Walter Jaeschke, *Reason in Religion*. Berkeley: University of California Press, 1990. Chapter XIV). The endeavor to conceive God as personal led to a renewal of speculative interest in the concept of Trinity. God has a threefold personality. Günther retains J. G. Fichte's concept of the non-ego, but interprets it as distinct from the immanent trinitarian 'persons,' namely, the world or universe. As such the non-ego is God's 'Contraposition' or counterpart. In opposition to the alleged 'pantheism' of classical German Idealism, Günther insisted upon the duality between God and world, and called his view 'creationism.' Despite such distinctions, his views were considered to be inconsistent with Catholic teaching and were placed on the Index in 1857.—TRANS.

7. Rothe and Günther share the assumption that the non-ego is conceived as the contraposition of God. But Günther allows the concept of the non-ego, which is supposed to correspond to the three positive elements in the ego, or the 'three persons' of God, to be a concept that is necessary for thought, but contingent in its actualization. The contraposition in God is the following: In God there is real identity of nature (substance) but formal difference (inequality) of persons. In human being there is likewise threeness and unity, but in such a way that there is inequality of substance (*Leib, Seele*, and *Geist*) in the formal unity of consciousness. According to Rothe on the other hand, the concept of the non-ego does not arise out of the persons of the Trinity, but rather out of the unity of the absolute ego. This is more nearly correct, because, if one wants to avoid tritheism, the concept of God's other cannot derive from a hypostasis. The idea of God's non-ego presupposes the self-conceiving and self-coincidence of the trinitarian God. Both concepts are similar in that they determine the constitution of the non-ego through the logical necessity of the divine ego-concept. The non-ego must be the direct opposite of God. According to Rothe matter is God's opposite; according to Günther the relevant opposition is the reversal of the relation of unity and triplicity in reference to form and substance. However, the concept of a direct opposition cannot be deduced as necessary for the divine self-consciousness, at least for its real aspect. On the contrary, it is more important for the clarity and determinacy of the divine self-consciousness that God be distinguished from that which is not God's direct opposite and which is not God, but God's other. God must be distinguished from God's image. This point is significant for Rothe. For the immediately contraposited non-ego (in the completed, self-realized divine self-consciousness)—this non-God or opposite to God—is for Rothe only a limit, a negation of God. Yet, in order to preserve and hold fast to God's absoluteness, it is necessary to maintain that God posits the non-ego (the other) as essentially the same as himself. God thinks and posits the non-ego as the non-God in which God himself nevertheless exists, cancels the contrast between God and non-God again, and posits it as adequate or equivalent to God. Thus in God's other, God is nevertheless utterly at home with himself (I, 86). According to Rothe, this is the process of creation. The latter would have its cause in the self-preservation of God in his absoluteness, which was negated by the nonarbitrary and

to account for divine personality by positing in God only the indeterminate possibility of an other. For God's self-consciousness must include and comprehend will and the wise love of God, which, unlike fate, nonarbitrarily thinks and wills what is actual. Consequently the absolute divine self-consciousness is constituted by the fact that the world idea is already presupposed as a real developing process. But conversely, the world idea is not possible without love and wisdom. Its conception thus depends on the fact that God is self-conscious, and self-conscious independently of the world. For love and wisdom are possible only where there is self-consciousness. Therefore the divine self-consciousness is the logical prius of the world idea. Moreover, with the divine self-consciousness there is given also the self-distinguishing of God from everything that is not God, and what therein is merely thought, or merely may be. This concept of possibility in general includes and forms the loving wisdom of God along with the world picture in God, and gives impulse to the almighty will of God for its actualization. The essential interest of piety, when it becomes necessary to deny the eternity of the world, does not mean that God is inactive, or has been idle. On the contrary, such expressions involve God in time and change in an unacceptable way. Instead, the interest of piety lies in what has been said above, namely, that God does not bring the world to actuality without the mediating point of the concept of the world. This point of mediation must be taken not as existing, but as possible.

The most significant contemporary philosophers of religion, almost without exception, maintain and defend the absolute personality of God—Ritter, Chalybäus, Weisse, Fischer, Fichte, Ulrici, Lotze.[8] They realize that the infinite is not truly conceived if it is represented as limitless *res extensa*, or as incapable of being the content of consciousness.[9] However,

---

necessary development of the non-ego. Creation would be a reaction on God's part (by means of his self-knowing and self-willing necessarily positing creation) against the negation offered by matter against him. But the creation cannot be derived from love, for love cannot apply to something that has mere self-preservation for its motive. Love seeks what is other. Love is the only guarantee for the desired preservation [*Dauer*] of the other, and this is neither secured nor grounded in an absolute that is not in itself ethical.

8. Cf. Chalybäus, *Philosophie und Christentum* (1853) 80ff.; Christian Herman Weisse, *Philosophische Dogmatik oder Philosophie des Christentums* (1855) I §329; K. Ph. Fischer, *Idee der Gottheit* (1839). Heinrich Ritter, *System der Logik und Metaphysik* (1856); Lotze *Mikrokosmos III. Grundzuge der Religionsphilosophie* 1883.

9. Weisse, op. cit., 574. There is general consensus that self-consciousness is not possible without diremption into subject and object. One party sees the Christian doctrine of Trinity foreshadowed in this diremption. Others (e.g., Rothe) allow the divine essence to open up and develop eternally into the divine nature and personality (*Ethik* I §26). Weisse seeks a middle position between Rothe and traditional church doctrine in that for him nature in God is the son (op. cit. §435ff.).

there is nothing definite said about God's concrete personality either in itself, or in relation to the world, nor is there any systematic connection with the traditional concept of a self-knowing and self-willing being. Many diverse concepts of God are compatible with the latter concept. The following all held some concept of a personal God: Deism, the old rationalism, the Socinians, and the supernatural theism of Catholic and Protestant Scholasticism. We will have more to say about this in the second part of this essay. However, in the present day a third alternative has arisen, which conceives the personality of God in human-anthropomorphic terms, while the received concept of God in the Catholic and Protestant churches is found to be abstract, dead, static, and thus not satisfactory to the religious consciousness. This new alternative does not hesitate to reject the received traditional theses concerning divine immutability and unchangeability. But for its part, it formulates its own theses anthropomorphically and theopathically.

## ARTICLE ONE

# The Kenotic Attack on Immutability

For some time we have become accustomed to hear rejections of God's immutability from those who deny God's absolute personality. For if personality is denied, then the traditional predicates seem all the more unshakable. But the traditional concept of immutability has recently been challenged from more than one quarter.

The claim that a personal God must be changeable has received adroit and open articulation by the author of *The Critique of the Concept of God in Contemporary World-Views*, a book that expresses what many have felt.[1] In a short period of time, the book has appeared in a second edition. We shall begin with a brief account of it.

The author demands that the concept of divine personality be taken seriously. Personality involves self-consciousness, and self-consciousness allows of being conceived as infinite. No one can be conscious unless there is something—whether internal or external—from which it can be reflected back to itself.[2] Thus a human being needs no other being for its own self-consciousness, but only the thought or perception of the body as something

1. *Kritik des Gottesbegriffs in den gegenwärtigen Weltansichten*, by Friedrich Rohmer, Nördlingen, 1856, was originally published anonymously.—TRANS.

2. J. G. Fichte introduced a phenomenology that establishes self-consciousness requires as its condition, an other from which to distinguish the self. Thus personality involves finitude and limitation. Self-consciousness presupposes and is founded on the contrast between self and other. The interpretive question is what is meant by the other? The other may be the

different, by means of which thought can recognize itself as self-identical. Similarly, personality depends on the opposition between constitutive elements.

Consequently, God, in order to be a self-conscious person, must intrinsically possess a duality in an infinite way, something analogous to the finite organization of spirit and body.[3] "A person without actual personal attributes, without life or movement, change, or without affects, is no person at all; it is an empty word. Either God does not exist, or the attribution of human features to God—so far as an infinite person may be inferred from the human being as a higher expression of personality—must be fully and inextricably recognized."[4] "However, since theism posits God outside of space and time, it subverts the existence of God. We know of no being that does not exist in space and time."[5]

"For theism the primal being that has created the world is already complete, self-sufficient, perfectly holy, and evil is due to the misuse of freedom. Since finite spirit is an image of the divine, the task of finite freedom can only be imitation of God. Human beings can possess such freedom only because God already possesses it. Consequently, contrast and opposition must be found in God. But this does not mean that God has a choice between good and evil. If God is necessarily good, God's self-mastery completely excludes such a contingent choice. However, if the good costs God no effort, God cannot justly punish men who are tempted

---

body (Cartesianism). However, it may also refer to another person, and in the case of God, to the Logos and/or world. Concerning the intersubjective sense of other, it should be noted that there are two senses of self-consciousness that must be distinguished. The first is that of individual personal consciousness, prior to mediation by other. This is roughly the Cartesian cogito, and is finite. It is not the full concrete sense of self-consciousness, but an abstraction. The second sense reflects self-consciousness as a result of mediation by other and overcoming conflict with other. This sense involves intersubjective recognition, and the resulting self-consciousness is a social infinite, that Hegel designates by the term spirit (*Geist*). (For an account of this theory of intersubjective recognition cf. Robert R. Williams, *Recognition: Fichte and Hegel on the Other*, op. cit.) Dorner's apparent inconsistency in calling self-consciousness both finite and infinite reflects but does not make explicit this distinction. This general theory is presented with variations by Fichte and Hegel, and is extended by Dorner to speculative theology.—TRANS.

3. Rohmer, *Kritik des Gottesbegriffs in den gegenwärtigen Weltansichten*, Zweite Auflage, 1856. This deduction of a nature or corporeality in God may have little validity. Just as it is not to be denied that self-consciousness presupposes a distinction, so it must be affirmed that spirit is able, apart from the body, to distinguish itself as thinking and willing from itself as thought and willed. Indeed, this inner diremption or self-distinguishing necessarily precedes the ability of spirit to distinguish itself from body as well as everything external.

4. Ibid. p. 87.

5. Ibid. pp. 28–29. Weiss also demands that the concepts of space and time be applied to God. *Philos. Dogm. I.* §§492–498.

and placed in a struggle between good and evil. It is said that such a struggle itself is good, for an innocence that is incapable of sinning has no moral worth. Thus, genuine ethical perfection is to be found not in innocence, but in a perfection that is the result of overcoming struggle and opposition. Consequently, this must also be affirmed in the case of God, who is the archetype of all perfection.[6] So God's perfection is not ready-made and already complete, but an increasing, self-surpassing perfection. In this latter sense God is our moral archetype that we can directly imitate."[7] God's claim on us consists in this: that we, in our sphere are to act, as God acts in his; that is, we overcome relatively what God overcomes absolutely. Thus God is the first organic personality: for self-mastery presupposes an inner opposition that is to be overcome.[8]

"According to scientific theism, God has only an apparent life, and nature has no life at all. Its representations concerning both contradict the need of the human mind. Of course God is supposed to have eternal life. But what is life? It is a development, an interchange of rest and movement, a clash of opposites, a progressive flow that can change in the blinking of an eye. Where these are lacking, there we have the opposite of what we mean by life."[9] He believes that human freedom is not conceivable if God has absolute freedom, that is, an omnipotence that has no internal presuppositions and thus is an accident without opposition; or if God, like the creation, is a mixture of freedom and necessity (ibid. 69f). The biblical God, at once spirit and living person, perfect and capable of development (i.e., with intermittent changes and passions) could alone be compatible with the contradictions ruling the world. Such a God can have created the world as a showplace of the most terrifying contrasts. It is not necessary to add that, in order to make evident what it means to take seriously the concept of God's personality, this author also demands that God also be subject to moods (64), that his anger conquer the unjust, that he restrain

6. Daumer, Blasche, and E. V. Hartmann hold similar views.

7. Rohmer, pp. 50–53. Cf. Weisse, op. cit., 531ff., §471.

8. Ibid p. 53.

9. Ibid. p. 64; the unnamed author asserts the above propositions in part hypothetically, but they contain the kernel of what he finds lacking in the prevalent concept of God. Although it often appears that he lands in contradictions (like Bayle) that he does not know how to solve, nor even desire to make the attempt (e.g., the acosmic versus the pancosmic form of pantheism, which he identifies as the oriental and western forms respectively), nevertheless he speaks rationally. But then he immediately speaks about nature and God and sounds like a pantheist of Blasche's or Daumer's ilk. Thus pp. 77ff., especially 81, passages that contradict p. 61 note. He then goes on to say that he had wanted to see in God the guarantee of the objectivity of the moral law.

his inclination towards the just, even that God choose or encourage evil, etc. (as does Jehovah in the Old Testament).

We see all too well what the author is up to. He abandons the concept of God and serves up only a pagan Zeus, decked out with a few virtues to be sure, but also full of passions, moods, his waxing and waning, and in general, changeableness.[10] God is supposed to be above and beyond the world, but in fact God is here conceived only as spatially different from the world, but in all other respects as a mundane mutable being. With such a God we have to do only with something mundane, that is a particular, opposed to the world, while no less belonging to it, a greater or a higher 'person.' The author is basically a polytheist, and we find in his book the same drama as we find in the Greeks, who, instead of worshiping some unknown nameless God that weaves in the tree tops and rustles in the ripples of a brook, reacted against the pantheism of the nature religions, and posited a divine but anthropomorphic person. In order to become close to such a deity, they outfitted it with all their own features, the good as well as the bad. The author speaks well of the infinite self-consciousness of God, but he also naively posits attributes of this God that contradict his infinity no less than the different predicates contradict the concept of Zeus. Nevertheless the book is worthy of notice because it invokes a living God in opposition to the traditional doctrine that sets forth an unmoved, lifeless God that must remain as alien to human beings as the pagan deities of antiquity, and it does this out of a predilection for the living God of the Old and New Testament.[11] This may serve as an admonition for a renewed investigation, but also as an uneasy warning not to take Scripture too literally, lest we fall into unreal and irrational representations that have already been surpassed by the higher presentiments of Greek antiquity.

But what this book sums up in flashy terms and without strict scientific discipline is by no means something isolated. Today there are important figures who hold widespread theopassian[12] and anthropopathic tendencies

10. On such a view it must not be difficult to ascribe to God an intermittent self-consciousness, even sleep, and by this means explain the contradictions found in the world.

11. Ibid. 67, 37. "When the farmer, in the spirit of the Bible, fears the wrath of God, and hopes through his prayers to mollify God's mood and through his doing good hopes to change and influence God's decree and judgment, then Peter calls the enlightened Christian beyond the superstition according to which the common people believe themselves able to reduce God to their level and with his help turn person against person.

12. Dorner uses the term *Theopaschitismus*. The closest English term is theopassianism (cf. patripassianism). This denotes the general view that God is capable of suffering. In the trinitarian framework, the term patripassianism signifies more precisely that it is God the Father that suffers.—TRANS.

in the concept of God. It comes as no surprise that, even at the price of inconsistency, they seek to avoid the changeableness, which the aforementioned book seeks to extend even to the ethical, and in general pose the idea of God as absolutely perfect personality. Nevertheless, these same figures want to allow mutability, self-diminution, passion, and suffering in God, even to the point of his losing self-consciousness, because of their concern for divine benevolence and its putative interest in the world—whether in reference to creation and providence, or the incarnation.

These figures explain their thesis of the mutability of God as a supplement to Christology, or sometimes in reference to creation, while on the other hand their doctrine of God shows no trace of such changeableness nor is it laid out in reference to changeableness (e.g., Thomasius, Hofmann, Ebrard. Only Liebner shows any rigorous systematic interests here).[13] The reason for such a haphazard procedure is that the necessity for affirming divine changeableness is probably first appreciated in reference to Christology. This should require the transformation of the God-concept in favor of mutability; otherwise Christology itself would appear to be impossible and would contradict the God-concept of traditional doctrine.

This solution does not allow us to separate their theses for or against the immutability of God from their Christology, insofar as the latter is supposed to be grounded in the former. We want to examine the probative force of these ongoing arguments for God's mutability, so that we may discover whether their theological reconstructions actually are efficacious and supportive of Christology.

In the conclusion of my *History of the Doctrine of the Person of Christ*,[14] I have already called attention to this issue, but in an abbreviated fashion, in order not to allow disproportionate consideration to the most recent developments and because the momentary needs of the present could not, in an historical work, receive their due consideration. For it is undeniable that theopassianism has become widespread in present theology in relation to Christology, and this requires more detailed consideration, especially in view of the presumption that it presents a "solution" to the christological problem. Since interest in divine immutability has already taken many

13. Theodor Liebner (Dresden) was co-editor of the *Jahrbücher für deutsche Theologie* with Dorner, and an important predecessor in the development of an ethical concept of God based on a reconstruction of Trinity.—TRANS.

14. I. A. Dorner, *Entwicklungsgeschichte der Lehre von der Person Christi* (Stuttgart, 1839), ET: *History of the Doctrine of the Person of Christ*, 5 Vols. (Edinburgh 1861–1863). —TRANS.

different forms, and since there has as yet been no overview of these, we want to provide such a survey as a piece of recent history of doctrine, in order thereafter to advance to a critical testing of the principles of these various theories. The final judgment of the value of these theories will depend on the general question, how we need to conceive the relation between the supra-historical and historical life of God in reference to the question of divine immutability.

Theopassianism has appeared in different periods. Thus in the earliest period of church history it appeared in nonebionite Jewish Christians,[15] in third-century Gnosticism, in the school of Apollinaris of Laodicea, an educated, precise thinker who is not guilty of the fantasies found in his school, and among the monks of Antioch who claimed "one of the three has suffered." In the Reformation period it appeared in the Anabaptists Hofmann, Menno Simons, Corvinus, all of whom held this view, as did Zinzendorf in the eighteenth century. Theopassianism had its own coloration and diverse tendencies. Its oldest form preceded the formation of the doctrine of the Trinity and thus attained the designation of patripassianism. It reflects a source in the religious interest that knows that in Christ, the divine work of suffering, redemptive love is accomplished. It wants to secure the significance of redemption by asserting that God participates in suffering. Similarly, it is the motive that is crudely expressed by the monks of Antioch, and in a sophisticated but also most anthropomorphizing way by Zinzendorf. (Among the moderns Bushnell and Steinmeyer—for details cf. my survey of Christology.) In other cases, in connection with the Valentinian system, theopassianism is supposed to serve a scientific interest of a cosmology, as well as Christology. The spirit imprisoned in matter is, as it were, a suffering god or divine seed, that Manicheanism with its *Christus patibilis* developed further and planted deep in the medieval period.

There is likewise a dualism, though a less pantheistic than one influenced by ethical elements, in the Anabaptists of the Reformation period. They taught that Christ could not have participated in corrupt matter. The incarnation is rather to be conceived as the Logos transforming itself into a pure human being in Mary, or rather as forming a body out of a pure heavenly substance.

The grounds of the most recent theopassianism are different, at least insofar as its representatives seem to be aware of it. Recent theopassianism

15. Cf. Schneckenburger, *das Evangelium der Aegyptier* 1834.

depends on the current discussion of the doctrine of incarnation, namely, the recognition that the unity of the divine-human person cannot be satisfactorily conceived in the older dogmatic framework. The latter allows the human conception to arise in the context of divine hypostases, nature, and its idioms. Many contemporary Lutheran and Reformed theologians remarkably agree, so that where the older dogmatics sought to resolve the christological problem of incarnation and the unity of the person by the elevation of humanity to divine majesty, in contrast the moderns hope to produce the requisite unity by means of the concept of the kenosis of God.

All agree that the truth of the human reality and process in Christ must not be surrendered at any price; they believe it is necessary to assert that the Logos, in order to be one with the temporal developing humanity, must renounce and surrender itself to process; it must give up or cancel its own absolute mode of being in order to render itself compatible with the beginning of a human life. The more consistent representatives believe that the Lutheran dogmatics allows of such an interpretation. After the unity of the person was established, the Logos no longer exists or is known apart from the flesh. If on the contrary, it is assumed that the one and indivisible Logos was only partially united with this man, but that in other respects it has not yet been united, that would lead, if not to a double Logos, at least to a doubled mode of existence of the Logos prior to the completion of the person of Christ, namely the existence of the Logos *in Christ* and *outside of Christ*.[16] Not only the developing humanity, but the *Logos itself* has given up not merely the *use*, but the *possession* of the attributes that relate God to the world, for example, omniscience, omnipotence, omnipresence are given up, and with these, divine providence itself in all its majesty. Of course, apart from the world [the Logos] has other divine attributes and eternal glory. But if the Logos wanted to become a human being, these attributes would have no place in the union with a temporally

16. There prevails today only an imprecise knowledge of the meaning of the formula, the Logos not apart from the flesh (*Logos non extra carnem*). For the chief point is only that the Logos is personal only in Christ, more precisely, that only in this place does the world have a middle point with which it is personally united. After Chemnitz, Lutheran theologians with the exception of the Tübingen critics, assumed that up until the completion of Christ's mission, all the acts of ruling the world that are excluded by the temporally developing humanity (e.g., omnipresence) are therefore not exercised by the human nature. By the way, if it should not be possible for the Logos to have a temporal mode of existence in addition to its eternal existence—although both must be willed from eternity—and if it is supposed to be inconceivable that the man Jesus, owing to his doubled will, stands in both time and eternity, how are such views to be reconciled with the dual mode of being of ordinary Christians, that have through the Holy Spirit both an eternal and a temporal life?

developing human child. Consequently the Logos has given up these attributes and the divine mode of being in an act of kenosis or self-divestment, and out of love has identified itself with a human beginning, while nevertheless preserving its essential love, holiness, wisdom, and power.[17]

The older concept of God usually conceived the attributes in vital inner connection with God's essence, so that they constituted God's vital nature. Consequently these attributes are not accidental to the concept of God, nor can they be contingently predicated of God for the sake of a work contingent or accidental to God, namely incarnation. We will have to hear from the most recent theories (insofar as they do not move into subordinationist doctrines), since they take seriously the need to transform and reconstruct the doctrine of God, and do not advance their theses as an afterthought to the doctrines of creation or Christology. This latest theory claims that there is something accidental and contingent in God's inner actuality, and that even in God's irreducible essential nature there is infinite *potential*. But we will allow the chief representatives to speak for themselves.

After Zinzendorf, Sartorius was the first to make noises of this sort.[18] Since it is undeniable that the knowledge and self-consciousness of the child Jesus were subject to temporal development, Sartorius believed that, in order to unite with him, the "Logos also has to shut his eyes."[19] Later he sought to better safeguard God's immutability. "It is false and unworthy to say that deity, that admits neither diminution nor change, has at a certain time ceased to be itself, and has given up the possession of all or at least some divine attributes and exchanged its divine nature for another, or that it has undergone modification by another. To assert this means to deny the Son true deity. The Son of God never renounced the possession and nature of unrestricted efficaciousness and joy, but only the perfect use of these as a human being . . ." Thus, during the development of the assumed humanity, the Logos no longer made *use* of his individual powers and glory, although he continued to *possess* these powers.[20] To be sure, Sartorius

17. In contrast, the old kenotics of Giessen made the person of the God-man the subject of the self-divestment (renouncing the use of divine predicates) while the Logos itself was incapable of divesting itself.

18. Cf. Plitt, Zinzendorf; Sartorius, *Dorpater Beitr. I*, 348 and later in his essay, *die heilige Liebe II*. [Ernst Wilhelm Christian Sartorius (1797–1859) was professor of theology at Dorpater University.—TRANS.]

19. Sartorius, *Die Lehre von Christi Person und Werk* 1853, pp. 26–30.

20. Ibid. p. 30: "When open, the eye of man takes in heaven and earth in an instant. But when the eyelids are lowered, the eye sees less and less, but without any change of its nature or power of vision. Similarly, deity does not change its essence or forfeit its infinite

does not tell us how it is possible to possess unlimited power without using it. It may be just as difficult to speak of the possession of omniscience without its actuality or without making use of this knowledge. We can also discern a tendency to suspend only the world-related powers of the knowledge and will of the Logos. But it is not possible to remain content with this half measure, because a temporal human seed is as incompatible with the immanent Logos and its eternal actuality in God, as with the Logos that rules the world.

Accordingly, it is only natural if others who are even less cautious go even further: namely, König, and after him, Thomasius, Hofmann, Delitzsch, Ebrard, Liebner, Gaupp, Schmieder, Steinmeyer, Hahn, Kahnis, Godet, Edm. de Pressensé, Gess et al. Thus König[21] says that kenosis, or self-divestment, is the main idea through whose scriptural manifestation and conception a genuine Christology can be realized.[22] It contains the concept of a voluntary self-finitizing, self-limitation of the Logos. Without kenosis, God would have reduced himself to a merely finite Beyond, that would have the world outside of it. Thanks to kenosis, the concept of God's omnipotent love can be conceived as constantly spreading and developing out of a single point. Kenosis is the condescension to finitude and the complete assumption of finitude into the infinity of spirituality and love. In the Logos, God submits to the laws of gradual historical development, that, since they originate from God, are nothing alien to God. This infinite love manifests a complete unconditional devotion and sacrifice for humanity and desires to hold nothing back for its own sake.

Marriage is a mundane reflection of such unqualified, loving devotion. As a third ego arises out of the doubled ego of marriage, so the God-man proceeds from the loving union of deity and humanity mediated by the

---

attributes when it lowers the curtain of the flesh before the rays of its glory." This renunciation, directed primarily to knowledge, Sartorius later seeks to justify so that it must include the Logos' renunciation of omnipotence, omnipresence, etc., as actual attributes. In his *Meditationen über die Offenbarungen der Herrlichkeit Gottes in seiner Kirche* (1855), Sartorius speaks out trenchantly against the changeableness of the Logos: In the situation of kenosis no darkening or diminution of the true and holy deity may be inferred. The point here is directed not merely to God's physical or metaphysical greatness, but to his ethical holiness. God's ethical greatness is manifest in God's divestment of majesty, the humility of God's generosity.

21. Johann Ludwig König, chaplain at Mainz.—TRANS.

22. König, *die Menschwerdung Gottes als eine in Christus geschehene und in der christliche Kirche noch geschehende* (Mainz, 1844), pp. 338–345. Cf. my *Entwicklungsgeschichte der Lehre von der Person Christi* 1839, A. 1, where the kenotic concept is found, as well as A. 2, II, pp. 811–812.

faith of the Virgin Mary. The existence-form of the divine, its *doxa*, was renounced and no longer possessed by Jesus. Nevertheless his innermost being—divine love—is both manifested and preserved. And as the incarnation was necessary for divine love (for only in incarnation did the true infinity of love become manifest) so also it was necessary for God as Spirit. The life and nature of Spirit is self-objectivation. Jesus the God-man is the self-objectivation of God, the extreme of finitude and externality, so that the latter are no longer external or alien to God's nature. In the God-man, finitude becomes a moment of the divine life itself. Kenosis implies that at the moment of incarnation and entry into finitude, the Logos freely renounces the clarity of his God-consciousness and self-consciousness, and yet attained these once again through a gradual human development. He appeared in humanity with the fullness of his divine being and life in order to achieve and possess everything once again by means of a temporal human development. This kenosis or self-emptying was voluntary; it was free in its innermost being, so far as the latter determined itself for the divine. His development proceeded from his innermost being, the external situation only provided the impetus. Thus there appeared the fullness of the Logos born within him, that illumined and spread to ever wider circles. The constantly renewed devotion to the Father was in every moment a progress in his transfiguration, the absolute glorification of his body could only be the result of the completely holy life of the Lord.

König does not want to give up the inner fullness of the Logos, but only the glory that is relative to the world, that is, the omniscience, omnipotence, and omnipresence. Still less does he want—as he has often been understood—a transformation of the Logos into a human being such that the humanity is merely the form of his appearance. Rather König allows the Logos to become finite only for the sake of an easy union with a finite creature. He allows the free human being to be determined and supported by the fullness of the immanent [trinitarian] Logos.[23] To be sure, he leaves unclear what he understands by the flesh of Christ that is assumed, and he also says that the Logos freely divested himself, in order to reconstitute himself. The latter references to the Logos appear to refer to the identity, and not simply the unity, of the divested Logos and the human soul.[24] Praiseworthy are König's efforts to ground the incarnation in God's

23. Later we shall see that Thomasius drops this influence of the Logos from his conception of the kenosis, and instead posits the influence of the Holy Spirit on Jesus.

24. His image of marriage and the resulting third ego are alien and not sufficiently thought out. Moreover, as applied to Christ this would imply another ego beside the eternal Logos. Since this contradicts his basic idea, we will give it no weight.

infinite love, and to view the development of Christ as an immanent one. Later we will have to consider whether such a self-divestment of love to the point of losing consciousness is either appropriate or helpful.

Soon after König, and surpassing him in knowledge of Christology, Thomasius propounded similar views. We will treat Thomasius' theory later, because he is one of the most zealous, if not the most consistent representatives of this view. His writings have commanded attention, particularly those in the second part of his dogmatics. Originally Thomasius' view (*Christolog. Beiträge* 1845)[25] went something like this. Granting Hofmann's doctrine of the divine Spirit as particularizing itself in the education of every human being, the divine Spirit is the ground of the Adamite personality. But in Christ the Logos doffed its glory and made its absolute life the basis of a human nature. The Logos, thus emptied and united with a human nature (taking the place of the Spirit in us) was the potential for or kernel of the entire divine-human development that proceeds according to the laws of our nature. His account provoked controversy on all sides.[26] Later Thomasius modified his theory in several respects and abandoned its Apollinarian tendencies.[27] But whether these later changes have made his doctrine more consistent remains to be seen.

Gaupp held the kenotic theory in its simplest original form, and remained faithful to kenoticism as a solution to the christological problem.[28] He trenchantly criticized the older doctrine. In the traditional concept of the unity of humanity with the Logos, the emphasis was on the elevation of the human to the divine. But the classical doctrine pays insufficient attention to its anthropological underpinnings. Among the essential attributes of humanity, rationality and freedom must be reckoned as central to the *imago dei*. Instead of these, the classical doctrine placed emphasis on secondary features, and then posited a cold, unreceptive human nature for a communication of the divine attributes. At the summit was to be placed an anthropological intuition by virtue of which human nature, through transfiguration and sanctification by God's Spirit, is capable of a heavenly expansion to the point of assuming

25. Gottfried Thomasius, *Beiträge zur kirchlichen Christologie*, Erlangen, 1845. —TRANS.

26. Schneckenburger in Tholuck's literarischen *Anzeiger* 1846, Nr. 17ff, expanded in the piece on *kirchlichen Christologie* p. 196ff. Liebner, *die christliche Dogmatik aus dem christologischen Princip*, 1849, pp. 16ff.; 292, 308ff., 340. Cf. my review of Thomasius' *Beiträge* in *Reuter's Repert*. Jan. 1846.

27. *Zeitschrift f. Prot. u. Kirche*, May 1846, Jan. 1850, *Dogmatik* II.

28. Karl Friedrich Gaupp [Professor at Breslau, trans.], *Die Union* 1847, pp. 27–38; 72–81; 96–117.

the entire fullness of divinity into itself. All this without ceasing to be a finite human nature; it remains a receptacle for the divine indwelling. But he conceives this indwelling by means of the idea of self-divestment. "Incarnation would be impossible if the continuity of the divine self-consciousness were to be interrupted." The self-divestment signifies that the Son of God constituted himself as a human spirit, assumed a soul and body through the Holy Spirit, and underwent a purely human development (114). Without embarrassment Gaupp admits a latent subordinationism. "The father is greater in respect to deity than is the son." Although the latter's begetting is unchangeable, and although he remains by nature the figure of deity, nevertheless he can for a while lay aside the personal self-creation and self-transparency that is given in the ego, and divest himself of his divine nature, in order to repose as a quiet passive being in the Father, and to allow his ego to go forth newly constituted as a human ego, clothed in a human nature and subject to a human development. Then all his majesty together with all his divine attributes are deposited with the Father and cancelled, as it were, in order that he could henceforth be entirely human (114). So we would have a divine Logos without divine attributes, because they cannot be at the same time attributes of a human being whose life is just beginning. For the same reason he conceives the Logos without its self-gathered self-presence and without self-creation; consequently the Logos ceases to be a hindrance to the full truth of humanity.

To be sure, there are questions raised by this consistent depotentiation of the Logos.[29] If the Logos has given up its nature and ego, what is left of the Logos itself? Gaupp replies, what remains is the being from which he is supposed to develop as the ego common to both natures. Everything that he lays aside in kenosis, he is supposed to achieve and earn again as a human being. The Holy Spirit must be recognized as the mediating principle, since a divine consciousness alongside of or surpassing Christ's human consciousness is absolutely rejected, but on the other hand, Christ's development is assumed to be a constant, progressive communication of the divine attributes to the humanity. In the consummation of the person, the humanity receives the divine predicate.[30]

29. The term *depotentiation* is Dorner's. He uses it to suggest that kenosis involves 1) the giving up of divine powers, but also 2) the reduction of divine actuality to mere potentiality.—TRANS.

30. He conceives omnipresence as an atmosphere of power and divine influences streaming through everything, which flows from the humanity of Christ that is limited to a particular place.

Similarly Delitzsch[31] asserts that the Logos reduced itself to the root of the nature of deity (that, in each of the three persons, is the will, the presupposition of consciousness).[32] The Logos withdrew itself to this lowest basis, this primitive potency, this ground of its entire nature and so, with the divestment of its essential unfolding, makes itself subject of a human personality, and becomes objective in a [single] consciousness. This consciousness, although it has its present double nature for its content, is nevertheless not two, but is rather a self-identical unity. He calls this the systole (like the old Sabellianism), a forfeiture of the divine nature. He thus agrees with Thomasius and Hofmann in a 'psychological solution' to the problem.[33]

According to K. Th. Hofmann,[34] the unknown divine magnitude that is called the Son (Christ) in the sphere of revelation, had already gone forth from God, that is, is God in a kenosis, in order to create the finite world. The Trinity represents a real diremption in God, but only for the sake of the world. Since God wanted to be the archetypal telos of the world, what church doctrine calls the Son is nothing other than God become finite. We know nothing of, and Scripture teaches nothing about, any intradeical being. But out of love God has gone forth and has become finite. God has thus "appeared in inequality with himself" in order to become the principle of the world, in which he wants to consummate himself as archetype.[35] To be sure, this individual is supramundane (for the self-divested one stands present as the foundation of the world), and as such is essentially identical to God. These are not essentially different as the Arians claimed. For the Arians the Logos was created and thus was finite, but not exceptional. For Hofmann, the Logos,

31. Franz Delitzsch, *System der bibl. Psychologie* 1855, pp. 204ff.

32. Franz Delitzsch (1813–1890), a Professor at Erlangen, later at Leipzig.—TRANS.

33. This is nothing new, but merely the correct consequence of the classical Christology as Thomasius shows. The history of Christology clearly demonstrates that it is nothing new. Athanasius had to oppose it. But how this was repeatedly rejected by the church, and how it may constitute the correct interpretation of classical doctrine, must be more satisfactorily demonstrated by Thomasius in historical fashion, before it could be adopted without qualification. Further, this self-reduction of the Logos is not supposed to affect the doctrine of Trinity. For despite this systole of its essential development, the divine will remains. This will reflects the original will of the Father and has the essential fullness of the Father as its impetus. Leaving all else aside, I would like to ask, has not Delitzsch, despite his claim of agreement with church doctrine, forgotten the Athanasian thesis: there are not three eternities, immensities, or omnipotences, but only one?

34. Dorner is apparently referring to Johann Christian Konrad von Hoffman (1810–1877), a leading figure of the Erlangen School. His book *Der Schriftbeweis* (2 vols. 1852–1856; 2nd ed. 1857–1860) was one of the most widely cited mid-nineteenth century German works. See Welch, *Protestant Thought in the 19th Century*, Vol. I, 218ff.—TRANS.

35. Hofmann, *Schriftbeweis*, I.

while finite, has an essential identity with God. Moreover, the alleged need of God for an instrument for the creation of the world meant that the Logos was the principal unity of the world itself. It is well known that Arianism emphasized the changeableness and variableness (*treptos*) of the Logos. It distinguished the Logos from the unchangeable and unbegotten God. For Hofmann the Logos is both finite and at the same time divine; it is changeable, but its mutability is voluntary rather than natural. God himself is involved in this changeableness to the extent that the Logos owes its independent existence outside of God to the self-contraction, self-finitizing of God. But the latter are distinguished from God's creative activity. Arianism always vacillated in the direction of making God's creative act the origin of the Logos, in order to keep God unaffected by change (*das trepton*) . . . , the *apokope*. Hofmann means no offense with this changeableness of God, nor is any confusion of God with finitude to be feared. These negative consequences can be averted, provided that God's will is primary. For then God has the power to voluntarily change and transform himself.[36]

The God that is already self-divested for the creation of the world is supposed to have made further use of the kenosis on account of sin. The Logos that was supramundane power over the world, although not identical with the inner trinitarian relation, assumed the form of a servant in the second kenosis. He exchanged the predicate of divinity for the predicate of humanity or the flesh. "He now ceases to be God in order to become a human being."[37] The incarnation is therefore the Logos' assumption of human predicates in place of divine predicates, mediated by his ceasing to be God. These expressions can appear to deny any identity between the supramundane and self-divested Logos; but naturally he seeks to establish the identity in all essentials. The question is, what is meant by the predicate humanity? There is no question about the divine substance. The Logos has given up the divine attributes and assumed humanity. The self-divested one has reduced himself to mere being, for example, to a potency.[38] But the actual shape of its being, that is, its existence, is henceforth human. To be sure, the assumption of a merely human predicate without human substance or soul seems docetic. Christology becomes a mere theophany.

36. Apparently Hofmann believed that the kenosis involved no external constraint that modifies God's nature. If kenosis is free and voluntary, God can transform himself into finitude, while remaining the same, and retaining the possession but not the use of his powers. Dorner rejects this claim as fundamentally confused.—TRANS.

37. Ibid. I. 146.

38. Dorner uses the term *Potenz*, a term he perhaps borrowed from Schelling. This could be power or potential. Here the meaning is not power as actual, but as potential.—TRANS.

But Hofmann is convinced that all formulas must be abandoned that conceive incarnation as a unification of divine and human natures.[39]

Ebrard shares this conviction.[40] He is conscious of and rejoices in his

39. Ibid. II. p. 21. It is evident that his failure to mention the soul of Christ is not entirely unintentional (II. 1. 36f). He sees in the body borne by Mary only that divine individual that is reduced to passivity and to potentiality, as well as standing in need of development, but he sees no human soul. Rather this divine individual displaces the human soul and means a human being on account of the assumed predicates of temporality and corporeity. But if the name humanity is not to be used in an abusive way, this theory means that the God who reduces his actuality to potentiality is for this reason a human, or conversely, that a human is a potential God, only waiting to become actual. These and related issues lie beyond the scope of Hofmann's explanations; indeed he seems to be not even aware of them. He never gets to the issue of the humanity of Christ, but only to a human predicate of the Logos. And this implies that this 'human' individual can never develop to independence over and against God, as reconciliation requires. The substitutionary atonement would necessarily become a mere empty game, if the Son of Man were only a disguised God and not a genuine human being with a soul. Instead of atonement (accomplished to be sure through the power of the Logos) there would be left for this developing deity only the exhibition of obedience, through which communion with God is supposed to be achieved. The defects in Hofmann's doctrine of reconciliation are closely related to those in his Christology. Against the kenotic turn whereby the Logos becomes the human soul—as held by many representatives, e.g., Ebrard, Hofmann, Liebner—I want to point out some additional problems in order to show that their apparent 'solution' of the christological problem comes at too high a cost. First of all, the kenotic Christ is not genuinely human in all respects. Rather it is a God that changes into a human body. This theory is confronted with important and basic knowledge of modern Christology—namely the full truth of the human nature, and it locates itself on the side of ancient Christologies that give the divine a one-sided prominence, and sacrifices one aspect to the other for the sake of the unity. If one assumes that God's Spirit is the actual soul in all humans (if that is permissible in Christian thought), this merely masks the defect, rather than resolving it. For there must be an essential distinction between the Spirit indwelling since Adam, and the Spirit dwelling in Christians. And the latter is founded upon a yet further distinctive indwelling of the Logos in Christ. But then the essential likeness of Christ to humanity could no longer be asserted of the human soul. But where the assumption of the general divinity of the human soul is not present, the essential difference between the humanity of Christ and our own remains significant. The ethical character of the person of Christ would be no less cancelled if he were to be viewed merely as a deity changing into a body. We can recognize in Liebner an effort to secure the ethical character for the humanity of Christ, the gradual development in freedom, etc. He thinks that the Logos has the potentiality of absolute freedom and holiness, since these are developed temporally by means of the kenosis doctrine. But the potential God or Logos can never be conceived like a human soul undergoing a process of development through freedom. As the ancient church clearly saw, the denial of the human soul deprives us of an important mediating element that unites the divine nature with the body. It complicates the conclusion of Christology. For the Logos become human spirit owes its humanity to a defect, something he freely loses. The actual humanity, apart from the body, is there only as a minus of itself. Obviously the matter cannot be left at that. If humanity is produced in the consummation of the person, the minus has ceased to be, but then it is no longer a human soul, except in the sense that the Logos would be in itself eternally human. At the conclusion we have only the absolute Logos itself with a transformed corporeality as its garment.

40. Johann Heinrich August Ebrard (1818–1888), who at this time was at Erlangen. —TRANS.

agreement with Hofmann's Christology. But like Gaupp he wants to vindicate the theory of the Reformed church as the original (with the same injustice as if he had wanted to assert the Lutheran to be the original). The self-divestment of the son is to be conceived such that in place of the divine actuality or existence-form of the Logos, there appears the Logos clothed with humanity. But he denies even more clearly a human soul in Jesus distinct from the Logos. The Logos in human form is like a king's son traveling incognito (so far as he is no longer absolute but in process). He calls this Logos a human being, because he assumed a human form of existence with a nexus of certain human predicates.

Liebner represents the kenosis doctrine in speculative form, so that kenosis itself is equivalent to incarnation.[41] But he seeks to make it plausible and avoid a change of God into an inferior being or into mere potentiality, by means of his trinitarian construction. There is a process of love in God according to which the Son eternally relinquishes his fullness to the Father, who in turn eternally reflects it back to the Son. Thus the kenosis consists in the fact that this eternal process of reciprocal love is temporarily interrupted, namely, for the period of the incarnation. It is interrupted from the side of the Father, but with the 'approval' of the Son. The reenergizing of the Son is interrupted only temporarily for the sake of incarnation; the Father holds it up as it were and allows it to appear again so that the Logos—that had been reduced to mere divine form, or to mere receptive potential for the divine, a human being—regains the divine fullness by means of religion, obedience, and the free development into which he entered. Thus the Logos attains once more the fullness he had previously, in order that the body he assumed, and through it humanity and nature, may return to the good.

According to Liebner, the immanent trinitarian process presupposes both a divine fullness and receptivity for it; and out of both he derives love's eternal reciprocity of giving and receiving. Thus he contends that there is eternally contained in God both the archetype of religion and the archetype of humanity, and only in this sense does he mean to speak of a primordial humanity in God. In contrast, the sphere of empirical and real humanity is entered by coming into time and undergoing gradual temporal development, including ethical development.[42]

41. Theodor Liebner, *Christliche Dogm.* I, 286ff.

42. I wish to make the following observations: Receptivity for God is not everywhere the same; there are several grades of it in human affairs. There is a conscious and unconscious

There have been several attempts to ground the kenotic theory exegetically, but these have met with little success.[43]

---

receptivity. To which of these is the Logos supposed to have been reduced? If the Logos only gives up his fullness, but retains his absolute vital receptivity, that is inconsistent with the origin of the human [viz., an infant] where the receptivity for God can be neither willed nor conscious. If the kenosis is extended to include receptivity for God, then the Logos would have ceased to be the archetype; moreover, it would be impossible for the trinitarian Logos to renounce voluntarily even for a brief time his receptivity for God. This could be avoided only if one regarded the act of kenosis as progressively consummated, as progressively undergone by the Logos. More about this later. Liebner seeks to avoid subordinationism in that the Father and Spirit, like the Son, are also conceived as a unity of receptivity and fullness. They are no less receptive for and conditioned by the Son, than he is receptive and conditioned by them. But if that is so, as this theory requires, then if the Son is reduced to potentiality, this would threaten the Father and Spirit, since the latter are conditioned by the Son in their actual existence. Insofar as they are so conditioned, any suspension of the actuality of the Son would likewise threaten to suspend their actuality as well.

43. It is astonishing that one completely fails to find in Hofmann any scriptural justification for his kenosis of God prior to the creation of the world. Professor Hahn (*Theologie d. N.T.* I 1855, 205ff.) has undertaken the exegetical proof of the theopassian theory of Christology, and in the form which identifies the Logos with the human soul. He finds in the NT the doctrine that Christ's Spirit does not have temporal beginning like all other humans, for according to its substance and essence it is identical with the Spirit that constitutes the being of the Son of God in his preworldly condition, and therefore is eternal. Temporal beginnings imply a limited human form of existence. Thus such passages as Hebrews 9:14, 1 Peter 1:11, are supposed to indicate a recollection of a preworldly state and his coming in the flesh. For according to the NT the incarnation of the Son of God did not consist in animating an entire human nature comprised of both body and soul, but only in the assumption by the Logos of a human body (*sarx*), such that the preexistent spirit of Christ entered a human body (naturally it was in a restricted condition). The human spirit of Christ contained in itself from the beginning the seed of the fullness of deity. It is the absolute spirit that has entered a state of limitation that constitutes the nature of the Son of God. Therefore the human spirit of Christ had an infinite power of development, by virtue of which it developed in the same degree that Jesus developed; it likewise could step forth out of its limitation and into the possession and use of the divine glory, and actually did so (1 Tim. 3:16; John 1:14; Col. 2:9). So the spirit returns to its prehuman absolute perfection, only with the difference that where it previously was without a human body, now it has one. It is well known that prior to Hahn, the new Tübingen school transformed the NT incarnation into the (mere) assumption of a body. The refutation of this position by Dr. Mau (who died too young) in his *Christology of the NT*, Hahn has either not seen or failed to pay it sufficient attention. The eternal spirit of Hebrews 9:14 does not mean what Hahn says it means. If the passage is taken as referring to the divine side, there is not a trace of any depotentiation. If it refers to the human side, then "eternal" preserves its proper meaning without any suggestion of preexistence (Heb. 7:16). 1 Peter 1:11 speaks of the spirit of Christ in the prophets, but not of any self-limitation of the Logos, nor of a preexistent humanity of Christ; the spirit of Christ may or may not be distinguished from the divine in Christ; the passage does not support any identification of the human spirit of Christ with deity. That the coming of the flesh designates the transformation of the spirit into a human soul is also scarcely demonstrated, so long as it continues to be established that *sarx* in the NT refers to what is universally human, and not simply to the body.

Turning now to the other passages on which Liebner and Thomasius et al. rely, only two are important: John 17:5 and Philippians 2:5ff. Even these contain the meaning sought for

Here is the place to treat Thomasius' theory. The basis for his view as he currently seeks to explain and justify it—not without Liebner's influence—is as follows.[44] The Son of God has not produced humanity out of itself or transformed it into itself, for the eternal Logos is neither implicitly human,

---

only if a certain interpolation [*Einschiebung*] is allowed that is not found in the text; i.e., if one begs the point at issue. The interpolation is nothing less than the main point in question, namely, that the glory (John 17:5) or the form of deity (Philippians 2) is given up, such that the Logos remains only in a state of potentiality. How can it be said that this interpolation is necessary, since only the dogmatic basis of a specific Christology occasions this deviation from what has been the standard interpretation? But could not then the God-man of John 17:5 say that the glory that he already before the foundation of the world, and of which his divine-human consciousness is prepared to learn (because Jesus, despite his personal union with the Logos, does not know of this glory until after his glorification) this glory as the God-man he does not yet already know, and must not yet know, despite his union with the Logos (because the Logos does not operate with physically irresistible force), although in the not yet absolutely realized *Unio*, he already has the capacity for such knowledge. This seems to be what Philippians 2:5ff. means, not that Christ has ceased to be in the form of deity, or has given up his equality with God, but only that he, standing in this fullness and glory, has not shirked this alienation and humiliation. The subject of the sentence is Jesus, not the Logos, as Lutheran theologians have irrefutably demonstrated (Gerhard, *loci Theol.* T. III 562–570; Schneckenburger, *Deutsche Zeitschrift*, 1855). How can Philippians be regarded as an example of an act of kenosis that falls entirely within an invisible sphere? How—without begging the question by interpolating another kenosis besides the one we know—can the Logos be raised up (v. 9)? Reuss (*die Geschichte der H. Schriften N.T.* 1853, p. 121) explains the chief point quite correctly: "The idea of kenosis underlies the portrayal of the suffering and obedience of God's son (2 Cor. 13:4; Rom. 8:32; Gal. 4:4) even if the word is otherwise lacking." *Kenoun* signifies (according to 1 Cor. 9:15, 2 Cor. 9:3, Rom. 4:14, 1 Cor. 1:17) to make something null and void, to make into something despised. Thus even the devotion or the sacrifice that is made while in the divine form is not the sacrifice of this divine form itself, or of the equality with God, but rather only the sacrifice of the form of a servant *[Knechtsgestalt]*. This stands in the sharpest possible contrast to the kenotic theory. For he did not disdain similarity to an ordinary person in his external appearance, and was obedient to the point of death on a cross. . . . The more specific and fitting meaning runs thus: that although intrinsically possessing divine form, he nevertheless regarded equality with God (that pervaded his entire person) not as violence or high-handedness; that is, he saw equality with God not in the exercise of power and authority, but in humbling himself, etc. Thomasius (*Christi Person und Werke* II 136) must concede that the subject of the sentence is the historical Christ. But he immediately refers this passage to the incarnation and believes that the contrast between the form of a servant and the form of God proves that the Logos divested himself through an exchange with a human form of existence. As if the opposition and contrast of these forms of existence did not remain when, to the abiding inner form of God, the apparently incongruent form of a servant is added. If, on the contrary, Philippians 2:5 implies the giving up of the divine existence-form of the Logos itself, I would not know how the further consequences drawn by Ernesti (*die Theorie von d. Ursprung d. Sünde aus der Sinnlichkeit*, 1855, 263) could be avoided.

44. Thomasius, *Christi Person und Werk* (1855); Liebner, *der christliche Dogmatic aus dem christologische Prinzip* (1849). By assuming a human soul, Thomasius departs from Liebner, and this is significant for the ethical character of the former's Christology. But Thomasius did not see that by this concession to classical doctrine, the gain that his theory of the self-divestment of the Logos can appear to have, namely the greater simplicity for the

nor has he transformed himself into a human. In the final analysis, he is not a member of our species, but also he is no longer God. The incarnation presupposes a difference between the divine being and human nature. The humanity is assumed. The Son of God, who is not nature but person, without cancelling himself in his divinity or the creatureliness of humanity, has posited himself in relation to humanity. Through this act of condescension a personal living unity originated. How has he attained this? Through the fact that incarnation is not simply the assumption of human nature, much less the assumption of a human individual. A further element is necessary, namely a self-limitation of the divine, both in its being and influence. If the eternal Son of God qua incarnate retains his divine mode of being and working, his supramundane status, and the infinity of his world-encompassing rule, there remains a duality. The divine surpasses the human as a wider circle surpasses a narrower one, and this surpassing is not entirely concealed by his divine-human action. Rather the surpassing divine element stands, as it were, behind or above the historical Christ. Thus there is a dual mode of being, a doubled life and consciousness. The Logos is, or retains, powers that are not exhausted by the state of kenosis. But this actuality appears to destroy the unity of the ego, or at least prevents the ego from permeating both sides of the person, and does not preserve the unitary subject in which God in his fullness has become human.

On the other hand, Docetism would be unavoidable if the Son had communicated his fullness immediately and all at once to the humanity. Thus God must have determined to have an actual participation in the human mode of being. Thomasius puts it this way: "The eternal son,

---

Christology connected to Trinity, 'how the Logos could form a living unity with humanity,' is lost. If we have a human soul and a depotentiated Logos, this depotentiation accomplishes nothing for the explanation of the unity of the two. In fact, the matter is not only made worse, it becomes impossible. For if the Logos is supposed to have completely emptied himself so that he no longer surpasses even a human child, he can give humanity nothing, nor can he guide its development. According to Thomasius the Logos is so helpless in his temporal origin, he depends on the Holy Spirit and its influence. This shows that matters are insufficiently thought out when the coincidence of the Logos with humanity is propounded today as the highest christological requirement. For an immanent development of the God-man becomes impossible by virtue of an absolute coincidence of two magnitudes at the beginning. In contrast, the initial surpassing by the [classical] Logos is the impetus for divine-human progress. The relative incompleteness of the union with the Logos is the presupposition that solicits from both sides the progressively unfolding progress of unification. The union is compatible with this process, such that the Logos is constantly united with this man, insofar as the latter is actual. The assumption is the condition of the incarnation, but what is not yet actual cannot be assumed (e.g., self-consciousness is not actual in the infant). Consequently the union in all aspects is a progressive one. It belongs to the perfection of the union not merely that the Logos, but also the human being will it and know it.

second person of Trinity has abandoned itself to the limitations of a spatio-temporal existence, in the form of human limitedness. Consequently, the assumption of humanity is at the same time a self-limitation of the Son of God. This self-limitation refers not merely to the omnipresence and omnipotence of the Logos, but to the absolute life which is deity, that now comes to exist in the narrow confines of a human life. The essential determinations of God, absolute holiness and truth, are now developed in the form of human thought; absolute love assumes a human shape; it lives as a human feeling in the heart of mankind. Absolute freedom lives in the shape of human self-determination." Since the act of union, the Son of God exists no longer outside of this human being; he has kept no powers for himself, no special consciousness, no independent existence. He has become human in the totality of his being. His existence and form of life are that of an embodied, spatially and temporally conditioned human being. The Son of God has renounced not merely the use, but also the possession of divine attributes active in the world.[45] If the divine human unity is to be thus secured, the following situations create difficulties: going to sleep, the dark night of death, and especially the beginning (birth) of a divine-human life. For the Logos is supposed to assume the life of a fetus; he is supposed to preserve for himself nothing except what a fetus can possess, and Thomasius does not doubt that this means the absence of both consciousness and self-consciousness. But instead of having doubts about the Logos going to sleep or even dying, Thomasius demands that we should submerge our own consciousness in this miracle of divine love, that his own theory so graphically portrays.

Thomasius adheres to the following thesis: the Logos has abandoned itself to the limits of a spatial temporal existence, subject to the conditions of a human development, without ceasing to be God. This sounds more cautious than Hofmann's slogan, "The Logos ceased being God in order to become man." Thomasius believes he can pass the test of the condemnations of the *Formula of Concord*. The *Formula of Concord* wanted only to reject a self-divestment of the Logos that resulted in the abandonment of the the divine nature and deity of the Logos. The *Formula of Concord*

45. Thomasius distinguishes God's immanent attributes from God's relative attributes. Immanent attributes are those that God would possess even if there were no world; these attributes are necessary and cannot be renounced or divested. Relative attributes are those that express God's activity and relativity to the world. These are contingent in some sense. Thomasius' thesis is that in kenosis God gives up the relative (contingent) but not the immanent attributes. See *God and Incarnation*, ed. & tr. by Claude Welch, New York: Oxford University Press, 1965, p. 94.—TRANS.

is not justified (in Thomasius' view) in censuring the self-divestment of a divine attribute. According to Thomasius, the Logos remains the Son of God, essentially one with the Father, the absolute life, truth, holiness, love, the same ego that was in the beginning. If the Logos gives up his absolute self-consciousness, he nevertheless remains the same subject or the same person. Moreover, the self-limitation is voluntary, motivated by love; it is not a negation, but rather the very operation of his absolute omnipotent being. For only an omnipotent being can divest itself and remain self-identical.

When the older church established that the divine nature was without conditions in its anti-Arian formula *a-treptos*, *analloiotos,* and when the *Formula of Concord* also says: "Since there is no variation with God (James 1:17), nothing was added to or detracted from the essence and properties of the divine nature in Christ through the incarnation, nor was the divine nature intrinsically diminished or augmented thereby,"[46] it has said clearly enough that the divine nature is to be conceived without the concept of self-divestment. It rejects self-divestment even if the latter might be represented as self-activity. Further it is incorrect to assume that the *Formula of Concord* rejects self-divestment only insofar as it implies a giving up the divine being and the divinity of the Logos. The *Formula of Concord* also rejects those views of the kenosis that have the deity remain as potential and have it restore itself to actuality in its own time. In a word, the *Formula of Concord* rejects nothing less than the central point of Thomasius' entire theory: "They misinterpret and blasphemously pervert the words of Christ, 'All authority has been given to me' (Matthew 28:18), to mean that in the resurrection and his ascension *all power in heaven and on earth was restored or again returned to Christ according to the divine nature, as though in the state of humiliation he had laid it aside and forsaken it even according to his deity*. This doctrine not only perverts the words of Christ's testament, but it opens a way for the accursed Arian heresy."[47]

Here a view is decisively rejected that confines the omnipotence of the Logos to heaven, while denying it on earth for a while. What sort of judgment might be anticipated about a theory that denies self-consciousness to the Logos for a while, and does not shy away from ascribing to the eternal Logos insensibility, sleep, or even death? Or conceives it identical

46. Solid Declaration Sec VIII, *The Book of Concord*, tr. and ed. T.G. Tappert, Philadelphia: Fortress Press, 1959, p. 600.

47. Epitome of the Formula of Concord, op. cit., p. 491. Dorner's emphasis.

with a fetus in the body of its mother? We do not believe the *Formula of Concord* to be infallible. But Thomasius will have to concede that the yardstick with which he proposes to measure must itself be subject to measurement. In vain does he appeal to the distinction between attributes that can be given up in kenosis, and the unchangeable divine essence. Elsewhere he defends zealously and more than correctly the *communicatio idiomatum* against the suspicion of teaching a separation of the divine attributes from the divine being and essence. Later in our examination of the history of the doctrine of divine immutability, we shall consider whether the early church fathers were wrong in refusing to recognize a Logos that is no longer omniscient and omnipotent as the co-equal Son of God, regarding it instead as a mere intermediate being.[48]

Here we only want to consider what this self-divested Logos is. In my view he is a potential deity (*deus potentialis*), a spatial-temporal finite individual being that is only implicitly infinite. The same can be said about any human being. Under the conditions of human development he has lost himself to such an extent that he requires the help of the Holy Spirit to transform his potential divinity into a divine actuality. His miraculous deeds should not be ascribed to the Logos immanent in him. The Holy Spirit has equipped the God-man with extraordinary powers for his office. The entire development of the God-man is not determined or directed by the immanent Logos, but rather is externally directed by the Holy Spirit like any other human being. In other words, Jesus is conceived in ebionite fashion for his entire earthly period—a view for which Liebner was rightly censured. Liebner claims that in this person there exists the depotentiated Logos. But then Liebner must be asked, how does the depotentiated Logos manifest his presence so that it is recognizable? In fact, the conscious-less depotentiated Logos is not fundamentally different from any creaturely individual, any actual human being created in the image of God.

But is such a kenosis of any help in understanding the incarnation? Kenosis promises at least the transformation of the Logos into a human soul; thus the unity of the person would be beyond question, for the divine would be implicitly human. But Thomasius, instead of carrying out his investigation (like Liebner) consistently to the end, only goes half way, and reminds us of the ecclesiastical rejection of Apollinaris. His theory of kenosis was originally determined for something quite different than a

48. Dorner is referring to the Arian position and controversy.—TRANS.

simple equation with a human soul alongside the Logos, namely the absolutely finished, complete unity of the divine-human person. But he now wants to establish, in agreement with church doctrine, a place for the particular human soul in Christ. As though it were illuminating and helpful for the union of both natures to take the Logos in its absoluteness! On the contrary, it is far more difficult to conceive how the Logos that is a limited Spirit united with a human soul remains the absolute Logos, as Arianism discovered. For Arianism necessarily denies the human soul, because for it the person can never be a unity constituted by two finite spirits. What Thomasius achieves with the kenosis—a duality of two similar finite individuals—is so little a solution to the problem that it creates superfluous new problems, namely, how co-equal individuals, that stand in a wooden relation next to each other, should nevertheless be capable of forming a personal unity.

To be sure, Thomasius protests that his theory does not reduce the Logos to a finite individual. Holiness, wisdom, and omnipotence are essential to and inseparable from the Logos. Further, kenosis should be taken as active rather than passive, that is, as an act of the Logos. Moreover, self-divestment should be conceived as progressive. Finally Thomasius claims that what he says about the redeemer falls completely within the sphere of the economic Trinity; consequently the immanent Trinity remains completely unaffected by it. The incarnation is a voluntary act, and *eo ipso* conscious; it is an act of the eternal Son that, coinciding with incarnation and from that point on, becomes a progressive, continuous act of the God-man.[49]

As for the distinction between the external Logos of the economic Trinity and the immanent Logos, he gains nothing but might well end up losing a great deal. For the Logos of the incarnation must be the Logos of the immanent Trinity, no less and no other. Otherwise the incarnation would be neither an incarnation of God nor an absolute revelation. A double Logos, the immanent alongside of the economic, is untenable. It would lead to an inadmissible duality in God, and introduce a separation in the concept of incarnation that would subvert its very meaning. Why? What motivates such a conception? The objective is to make the unity of the divine-human person complete from the outset in order to avoid Nestorianism. But there is yet another possible twist to this distinction. It might be said that in incarnation we see only an act, but not the being of the

49. Dogm. II, 187, 273ff.—TRANS.

eternal Logos. The God-man is only an effect, or act of disclosure, but not a mode of being of the Logos. In this way the loss of self owing to the entry into time would be avoided by the eternal Logos, but at the price of adopting a Sabellian Christology. Thomasius, on the other hand, wants the Logos in the flesh, not merely an effect of such. He wants its kenosis. And thus the matter rests: insofar as he really wants an actual incarnation of the eternal Logos and deems the kenosis as an indispensable condition for this, he must implicate the immanent or trinitarian Logos in unconsciousness, in the loss of its ego and hypostasis, also in the loss of the absolute actuality of its love to the father and towards the world. Moreover, without a consciousness of its object, love is inconceivable. And since he separates the economic Trinity from the inner being of God, it is not the immanent eternal Son of God, but only another, naturally subordinate 'great man' that becomes incarnate. On this assumption the immanent Trinity itself might become, christologically speaking, a matter of indifference[50] if it has any place at all in the kenotic theory.[51]

Rather the immanent Logos appears to remain free from kenosis through the further instance, that his self-emptying is, on the one hand, to be conceived as progressive, but on the other hand, the Logos is suspended eternally above his kenosis or its results, that is, he stands 'above the line' (II 187). But it must be asked whether the will of this Logos ever actually wills or not? Does the Logos actually succeed in emptying itself? If not, why does he will this end? If he accomplishes his end, then this reflective act has so emptied him that he cannot at the same time be a passive, completely divested Logos, and an active Logos standing in its fullness and actively divesting itself. Stated otherwise, this talk of a progressive

50. Thomasius scarcely considers the Trinity, since he first establishes his christological position by the kenosis theory.

51. This doubt finds a hold in the following: If the hypostasis of the Son reduces itself to unconsciousness, it ceases to exist as an actual hypostasis. At most it is merely possible. But it cannot be an indifferent matter whether one of the trinitarian hypostases is actual or not. For however one may conceive Trinity, it must not be represented as tri-theism, for which it would be indifferent for the other two if one were actual or merely possible, or if one is or is not. The trinitarian hypostases reciprocally constitute a single deity through and by means of each other. In traditional language, how is the Holy Spirit supposed to proceed from the Son, if the latter exists only in potentiality? It would follow that the Spirit would have to be merely potential as well. The same considerations apply to the Father. For God is Father only through and by means of the Son. If the latter is merely potential, so the Father is merely a potential father. Thus we would have the Sabellian *monas*, if only in form. The potencies of Father, Son, and Spirit become successively actual again in time. Hofmann's Trinity on the other hand appears to view the trinitarian distinctions only as potencies in God, for the sake of whose actuality God wanted the world.

self-divestiture of the Logos appears to be merely a euphemism for an emptying that is not an emptying. In short, it is a merely empty concept, like the idea of a species that can only be conceived by thinking immediately of its opposite.

Similar problems attend the current version of Thomasius' theory. He is so confident in his opinion that the self-divestment of the Logos to equivalence with humanity, to unconsciousness, sleep, death, is the means to make visible the unity of the person and to establish the miracle of love, that he believes it fully agrees with the christological formula: 'neither the word apart from the flesh, nor the flesh apart from the word.' But how does the matter actually stand? He claims that the totality and fullness of the Logos is already present from the beginning of incarnation. But since the kenosis to which he previously wanted to subject the Logos simply does not allow the humanity to appropriate the fullness of the Logos, but only the self-divested Logos, Thomasius must change the above formula into another: 'neither the Logos entirely within the flesh, nor the flesh totally in the word.' He would like to regard everything that transcends the embryonic beginning of a human child—which is incapable of receiving the fullness of the Logos—as something detrimental to the divine being and the concept of the word. Similar problems attend the ascription of world-governance to the depotentiated Logos while in Mary's womb.[52]

Let us now formulate the tensions in Thomasius' views. There is a finitized Logos side by side with a finite human soul, and this duality is supposed to make clear the unity of the person; there is a giving up of absolute self-consciousness and the actual divine fullness, side by side with the opinion that Jesus from the beginning possessed and manifested the Logos in its entirety; there is the claim of complete kenosis together with the claim that the immanent Logos and Trinity itself remain unaffected by

52. We have already found that Thomasius denies the divested Logos not simply the use, but also the possession of divine omnipotence (as does Hofmann). But Thomasius also asserts: consider that the incarnation is the central act of divine world-rule to which all others are related. All others are determined such that even while in the womb the Logos through his incarnation co-directs the world. Philosophy had already spoken of a blind, effective, and plastic power of the Idea. Here we find a world-ruling Providence that is asleep and without consciousness! The cleverness of this interpretation should not be denied. . . . But if one considers the seriousness with which the older theologians defended this theory, doesn't it make a mockery out of Thomasius' and Hofmann's interpretation? And this is not without danger for Thomasius. As is well known, he strives to view incarnation as something not connected with creation or with providence, but rather as something contingent, which has nevertheless become necessary owing to the fact of sin. But here we read another incompatible thesis of his that is justified only in another theological mode of thinking, that all actions of the Logos in the world have the incarnation as their determining point of mediation.

kenosis; there is the claim that the Logos by emptying itself gives up consciousness, together with the claim that the Logos continuously and consciously directs the process of self-emptying; there is the claim of a Logos that covers itself completely with the human and no longer surpasses it, together with the claim that the Logos, as loving and progressively self-divesting, nevertheless stands above the line of divine-human development, or in the center directing the world. What are we to make of all this? It is difficult to see any advance worth mentioning on the christological problem. Rather we find only a well-intentioned eclectic endeavor that is insufficiently modest in the face of incomprehensibility, even contradiction.

A basic assumption made by the defenders of kenosis is that it is necessary for Christology to conceive the unity of the God-man as complete at the very beginning. But such a completed unity excludes movement and stages of ethical and physical development.[53] This presupposition is the reason why they focus rigidly and solely on the question how the unity of the person is attainable, like a wrestler who desperately grasps one limb and allows every other consideration to be devoured as it were by this single aspect of the problem. But the various aspects of this problem are systematically related.

The kenoticists reduce the unity of the person in more than one respect. Some identify the self-divested Logos with the human soul, or derive the latter from the former; others posit a static homogeneous duality that undermines the unity of the person or exists alongside it or even in it. But all posit a fixed unity already complete at the outset and make it the goal to be attained, instead of thinking of a self-developing and self-explicating humanity. These kenotic theories unconsciously depend on the very error they otherwise dispute, namely, the immutability that excludes genuine development from the person of Christ. I have already discussed this point sufficiently in my *History of the Doctrine of the Person of Christ* (1839).

The last significant kenotic writing confirms in its own way our previous objections against modern christological theopassianism. It allows itself to be drawn into the theopassian tendency of Christology, but it surpasses all

53. Thomasius speaks in a striking way about a personal unity present from the beginning, while according to him not merely the humanity but also the Logos has no self-consciousness at the beginning. On both sides the ego is not supposed to be actual in any sense. Clearly those have more clear right to such a conception who conceive the Logos as personally enduring, but also correspondingly posit in a continuing personal will that which can be actual on the human side, and therefore has on its [the Logos] side continuously a *Unio personalis*.

previous efforts in the acuity, consistency, and the seriousness with which it seeks to agree with Scripture.[54] The importance of this work lies in the careful and consistent thought that is not content with half measures that fail to advance the discipline and only obscure the issue. The author ventures honestly and out of concern for truth, to think the principle consistently through to the end and makes explicit its consequences. He touches on a series of objections to the theories of Thomasius, Hofmann, and Delitzsch, but nonetheless believes himself obliged to remain with the only consistent form of theopassianism. I must agree with him on the latter point: he is the most consistent of the kenotics.

He successfully shows that theory of the Logos' self-reduction to potentiality becomes unfruitful and illusory if one assumes a human soul in Christ that is distinct from the Logos (§65). He prefers to say that the Logos metamorphoses itself into a developing, purely human soul that must be ascribed freedom of choice and decision (§68). Since an immature human soul cannot at the outset possess omniscience, omnipotence, or ethical perfection, he rightly demands that we give up the artificialities of an omniscience, wisdom, holiness, and omnipotence that are still possessed after the renunciation of their actuality, as well as talk about the child Jesus participating in the governance of the world. He equally rejects as artificial those interpretations of the self-divestment that want it to apply only to the use but not the possession of the divine attributes. Rather Gess believes that the incarnate Logos must acquire holiness in the same way any other human being does. The same principle applies to the every other predicate.

No less praiseworthy is the fact that he finds it inconsistent with the depotentiation theory to say that nevertheless the Logos remains as it were 'above the line' of human development, or to say that while the Logos is completely emptied in Jesus, he remains, in his eternal aspect, completely the same. The latter would lead to a double Logos and not merely to a doubled life of the Logos, or else subvert the truth of the incarnation of the trinitarian Logos. The latter assertion is devised in order that the Trinity itself not be affected by kenosis. He openly rejects as misleading and as beating around the bush all the fruitless attempts to conceive the immanent Trinity by itself as unmoved and unchanged by kenosis—as Delitzsch and Thomasius sought to do. He openly admits that through the voluntary

54. Cf. Wolfg. Friedrich Gess (1819–1891), *die Lehre von der Person Christi*, Basel 1856. Although I cannot concur with the author, the rest of my essay will show that I recognize the rightness of the motive that inspires his work and am equally convinced that the traditional doctrine of divine immutability fails to do justice to either the scientific or religious interests.

kenosis of the Logos, his own personal life was stilled and that the necessary consequence is that for the thirty-four years of the earthly life of Jesus, the Trinity was changed: the Father no longer poured forth his fullness into the son, and the latter no longer co-originated the Spirit with the Father. Finally, the actuality and ruling of the world were for a time no longer mediated by the Logos. Rather the Father ceased for a while to beget the Son and allowed the Holy Spirit to proceed exclusively from the Father who, together with the Spirit, ruled the world.

The contribution of this work is that by a consistent execution and development of the kenotic hypothesis, it puts the latter to the test. In this execution the hypothesis confirms itself to be open to a change in God, not merely in general, but in respect to God's eternal holiness. According to Gess, God can alter the form of his existence without prejudice to this essence. He can assume a form of existence in which not only holiness has ceased to be fully actual, but in which he opens himself to the possibility of sin and evil. Gess rightly demands the latter possibility for genuine human freedom and shows that Thomasius and Hofmann, since they failed to admit this freedom for Christ, also failed to show the actual humanity of the God-man. Liebner strives for this end, but fails to get beyond the *non potuit peccare* [namely Jesus is not able to sin].

In contrast, Gess, who wants nothing of a predetermination of the God-man to sinlessness, regards it only as the free (albeit foreseen by God) work of the God-man himself on the basis of the unique nobility of his human nature. Whether the possibility of sin may be ascribed to God in his actuality will be discussed later, when we will have to investigate the limits within which alone mutability may be affirmed of God. Here we want merely to suggest that if the inadmissibility of the possibility of sin in God should become apparent, we would have a strong proof of such inadmissibility in the fact that since the actual freedom of the God-man is a condition of genuine human development and the work of redemption, a human soul—distinct from the Logos—must be ascribed to the God-man.

Leaving this point aside, it is nevertheless possible to show that even this clear-headed execution of the kenosis (the one closest to Liebner) nevertheless has no sure grasp of the matter and holds out only the appearance of being useful for the solution of the christological problem. For Gess also believes that the participation of God in suffering is necessary for the work of Christ. But he cannot mean this in the sense that the reconciliation would be conceivable without the true humanity of Christ by virtue of which he is essentially like us.[55] Gess does not assert an actual human nature essentially like ours for the God-man since the Logos—according to classical doctrine—has not transformed itself into a human soul. Thus the interests of the doctrine of reconciliation dispute a hypothesis that fails to produce a humanity different from the Logos.[56] Other elements that contradict this assumption have already been mentioned above, and in this point I must agree with Thomasius' opposition to Gess, even if the latter is the most consistent exponent of the doctrine.

Up to this point the argument has presupposed that Gess ascribes true deity to the Logos and does not make him the first creature, and as such only God's likeness. We were obliged to make this assumption for the sake of his opposition to Arianism and because he acknowledges an eternal immanent Trinity. But this acknowledgment flies in the face of a series of other assertions that are scarcely compatible with that assumption, since these lead to an inadmissible subordination. So here is the place to examine this tension in Gess' thought. For there remains here unclarity and ambiguity on his part that implies either the Logos is merely a creature—albeit preexistent, essentially like God and even eternal after a fashion—or the opposite of the Arian subordinationism, in which case it is incompatible with his kenotic theory.

In order to win a genuine human soul for the God-man, in spite of the fact that the metamorphosed Logos is supposed to be this soul, he describes the image of this Logos—in itself and in relation to the Father—in a very peculiar way. It is calculated to show that the change that is introduced into the Trinity by the putative kenosis of the Son touches the Father and Spirit as little as possible. Rather their existence and the absolute perfection of their mode of being remains intact. To be sure, during the period of the

55. Otherwise a merely illusory accomplishment of God would result. The believer considers himself as a debtor, and thus sin is censured, and so from this perception the only consistent doctrine of reconciliation would be Schleiermacher's or Hofmann's. If Gess supports his position by citing Luther's assertion "It would be a poor Christ in which only a human being suffered for me," it is well known that Luther often rejected theopassianism and so this assertion is to be understood in the sense that the God-man, by means of the accomplished union of the divine with human nature, has suffered for us. Consequently in the passion we have to regard Christ as a pure unalloyed human being that has been abandoned by God. See Thomasius II 204, 230ff. [Editor's note: Cf. Hegel's discussion of the death of God as a radical interpretation of Christology that involves God in becoming. Hegel affirms that there is tragic negativity and suffering in God. Cf. LPR III.]

56. This consideration is not laid to rest by Gess' later treatise on the doctrine of reconciliation.

kenosis the Father's begetting of the Son comes to a halt, as does the receptivity of the Son for the divine fullness of the Father. Further, the Father brings forth the Spirit alone and rules the world without the Son. But since Gess believes that the Father is in no sense conditioned by the Son, but produces the Son freely, it could be that this procreation might cease, if love requires it, just as the Son could freely give up his own life. The Father does not first become self-conscious through the Son, or only through him, but is conscious without him, as in the time when he did not have a Son.[57] The Son is only conditioned by the Father, but, although created in his image, does not condition the Father. He identifies a fundamental error in trinitarian doctrine that fails to preserve aseity for the Father alone.[58] If one but acknowledges that aseity belongs to the Father alone, then the kenosis of the Logos will be nothing terrifying or disturbing for the concept of God. Gess posits his hypothesis favoring the Son prior to and outside of God, that is, outside of the sphere through whose vital elements the true Christian God is realized. Gess has a concept of God for which it is indifferent, not to mention contingent, whether the hypostasis of the Son is present or absent.

For Gess, the Father alone is God in the eminent sense, that is, the divine *monas*, although he also calls the Spirit divine. This threefold is also a unity and not three gods. But Gess cares not a whit for this issue, as if the monotheistic principle of Scripture and Christian faith need not

57. The whole point of the introduction of subjectivity into substance (to use Hegel's expression) and the introduction of the Son into the God-head, is to develop a concept of God as a personal conscious subject. However, God cannot depend upon an other, and so the other that God requires to become self-conscious must also be God. In other words, if Dorner's exposition is accurate, Gess has insufficient grounding in the historical sources of classical German idealism. Further, the last formulation above suggests there was a time when the Son did not exist. This is the Arian (subordinationist) position, that ill accords with the inner logic of Hegelian thought, i.e., that substance becomes subject.—TRANS.

58. Thomasius agrees. But Gess fails to understand that this is the doctrine of the church that cannot be revoked if he actually wants a single triune God. Gess thinks this is merely a new speculative discovery. But Calvin's dispute with his anti-trinitarian opponents, who attacked the aseity of the Son in particular, as well as the classical doctrine itself, could have taught him otherwise. The Arminian subordinationism took its point of departure the assertion that the Son could have no aseity. The concept of the eternal true God constituted by three persons is the specific contribution of Christian faith. This concept implies that the Trinity as such is immutable, and cannot lose a member "for a while," because otherwise God would cease to be triune. Conversely, a being that is supposed to be capable of missing a member without experiencing any disturbance cannot be part of the triune conception. Consequently, Gess' endeavor to remove such contingency from the Son and to ascribe true deity to him is in vain. In aseity alone is to be found what distinguishes God from everything that is not God, because all divine attributes are communicable, but aseity is not—as the Swabian theologians of the Reformation period correctly saw.

be confirmed by the Trinity, instead of being excluded by it. For Gess, the Trinity is, as it were, a divine family whose head is the Father, but whose number and constitution are alterable if love requires, that nevertheless, taken as an intradeical determination, can be posited absolutely in and with the trinitarian hypostases.[59] Gess' exegetical grounding for this theory is superficial, for he appeals without qualification to passages that speak of a subordination of the God-man (e.g., John 5:26) to the Logos. But since this would be correct only from the standpoint of kenosis, it begs the question. Further, he has not investigated the question whether polytheism, particularly one that has a noble harmonious structure, is compatible with Scripture or with Christian faith. For with a plurality of gods we would approximate his concept of three divine egos, of which two would be relatively accidental and contingent in relation to the nature of God that is absolutely actualized by the Father. The necessity that Gess holds out for the Son and Spirit alongside the freedom of the Father is not essentially different from the necessity that can be ascribed to the world insofar as it stems from God's free love rather than sheer arbitrariness. The Son and Spirit, that are supposed to dispense with aseity while the world also has receptivity for the divine fullness, are merely quantitatively different from the world. However, Gess regards Trinity as not merely accidental and contingent—as though it could be increased—rather he sees it as grounded in the law of divine life, in the very nature of God. This vacillation is sufficient to raise questions concerning his position.

If this 'law of divine life' itself requires a threefold and not more, it must also require nothing less than this threefold; consequently the divine life itself would lack integrity—to say nothing of divine love—so long as the essential threefold is missing. Thus when Gess says that the willing receptivity of the Son is the ground of his life (and his self-consciousness

59. I say mutable because according to his theory, kenosis affects only the essence of the Logos; the result is that the Son, who is supposed to be a hypostasis through the influence of the Spirit, now proceeds from the Father and the Spirit, instead of the other way around. There is an uncanny resemblance to the Logos concept of the ancient Jewish Christians, as well as their emphasis on the Spirit rather than the Logos. The Father is supposed to have produced the Son through the Spirit. The doctrine of the Logos or eternal Son is treated as a hindrance to the incarnation, and so this Logos is set aside in kenosis, or transformed into a human created by the Spirit, in which form he is supposed to receive the Spirit and live again. Here the unhistorical misreading of the essential distinction between the wider and narrower trinitarian senses of the scriptural concept of *pneuma* exacts its price. According to the first (wider) sense, pneuma is an indeterminate archaic designation that later comes to stand for the Logos. For these reasons Gess makes the Trinity mutable, in that it is either indifferent or utterly contingent whether the Spirit proceeds from both the Father and the Son, or during kenosis, proceeds from the Father alone.

is his own act), when he derives from that ground the power and freedom over his life manifest in kenosis that distinguishes the Son from creatures, he appears to overlook the fact that he has himself thereby essentially ascribed aseity to the Son. For if his will is the ground of his life, even if it is receptive, his will must be present even apart from the fulfillment of his receptivity by the Father; his will must be rooted in the common ground of the divine nature. The receptivity and dependence of the Son's will do not touch or qualify this fundamental point. Besides, if there is supposed to be reciprocity in the inner divine life, receptivity cannot pertain merely or exclusively to the Son, as Liebner has correctly pointed out.[60]

We could easily multiply with further examples these suggestions for an inadmissible changeableness of God, namely, mutability is required to make sense of creation, providence, and incarnation. However, enough has been said.

Only one more observation. Similar theopassian expressions can also be found on the Catholic side. Apart from earlier representatives like Petav, Froschammer also deserves mention.[61] In the Fall of the primal pair, he says, all humanity also fell. The divine idea of creation realized from God's side could, after creation, have only been completed by freedom itself (e.g., spiritual humanity could have been brought forth by freedom! Cf. 1 Cor. 15:45ff.). This idea of creation realized in humanity is "the word of creation that attained to humanity. Now since no part of the divine substance has fallen under the power of evil, nevertheless humanity is the fallen creator Logos, and it can be said that the divine wisdom of creation, given actuality through the creative word, is fallen into a state of suffering."

60. In regards to exegesis I note that Gess' explanation of Philippians 2:5ff. would not at all set an example to be emulated by the Philippians as the text plainly says. For a depotentiation cannot on Gess' grounds be our own task. Indeed, according to Gess, only the Logos through his divine being has the power and ability for a self-depotentiation. This would make even more inexplicable why the apostle should have spoken in this passage about self-emptying humility and wanted to recommend Christ as an accessible and illuminating example. When Gess regards the procession from the Father into the world spatially as an abandoning of the Father, so must his abandoning of the world and return to the Father exclude his presence with us until the end of the world. But if the latter is not the case, then neither is the former (John 3:13). Gess knows the necessity of an enduring humanity and says that in all aeons his effects must be divine and human, but he acknowledges that he knows not how to demonstrate this satisfactorily. But he does not see that these difficulties are created by his own theory according to which the Logos is transformed into a human soul, but that they do not arise at all if one ascribes to Jesus an actual human soul and not merely a human body.

61. *Über den Ursprung der menschlichen Seele. Rechtfertigung des Generatianismus*, 1855, p. 175.

Here it would seem clear that humanity is regarded as the realization of the Logos itself. The Logos has passed over into change and suffering, but in such a way that Froschammer assumes, beyond the suffering Logos, a nonsuffering, redeeming Logos. Thus he comes back to a double Logos theory.

The foregoing analysis has shown the inner contradiction in the various forms of the widespread kenotic theory of the Logos. It shows that at least with respect to Christology, theopassianism in all of its forms is no gain and can prove nothing. But the fundamental question itself has not yet been decided. We must ask, How is the Christian concept of God related to the assumption of change in God? Does it absolutely exclude change? Does not the living communion of God with the world require divine mutability in some sense? Are not those who stand firm by the concept of an unqualified absolute divine immutability in conflict with the fundamental interests of Christian piety? Don't they lapse into a static and wooden relationship between God and world? The rest of this monograph will be concerned with this issue. If this question is answered in the affirmative, the situation is not improved by christological theopassianism. But the latter gives an important impetus to the task of gaining a foundation for understanding better the relation of God to the world, in reference to Christology, to individual believers, and to the church.

The timeliness of such an undertaking is beyond dispute. The traditional axiomatic immutability of God is nowadays in dispute by a majority of contemporary thinkers and from a variety of perspectives. Thus there must be a renewed theological investigation of this question in order to prepare a more satisfactory doctrine of God that is both clear and well founded.

## ARTICLE TWO

# The History of the Doctrine of the Immutability of God from the Patristic Period to Schleiermacher Set Forth Historically-critically according to Its Main Tendencies

The concept of paganism, that was earlier the rule, has without doubt some truth. For it is not the strength, but the impotence of the God-consciousness that drives toward the deification of nature (Rom. 1:23ff.). In paganism there is not merely an as yet unstrengthened consciousness of God; there is also a beginning of an abnormal development, which cannot be explained as a mere deficiency. This is essentially a moment of arbitrariness which was not denied to the beginnings even by Schelling, who aptly called it 'religion gone wild.' This view is quite compatible with another interpretation, according to which there was also in paganism [an authentic] piety. For also in paganism, the younger generation accepted the religious representations of its fathers in good faith, and we may well assume that when its piety turned to a particular god, in such moments of devotion this god could not help becoming for it the one true God.[1] The living God hears

1. That is, the genuine piety Dorner finds in paganism is treated as an anticipation of or approximation to Christian piety. This might be regarded as collapsing the very distinction between two conceptions of pagan piety that Dorner draws. However, Dorner suggests that in such moments of genuine devotion and piety, whether in paganism or in Christianity, there is no way to distinguish between the particular god (as represented, or *Vorstellung*) and the reality intended, namely the unconditional reality of God. In this conception Dorner is close to Kierkegaard's analysis of subjectivity as the truth (*Concluding Unscientific Postscript*). I am indebted to Susanna Carter and Claude Welch for help in clarifying this passage.—TRANS.

and grants many prayers that are directed to idols. Although such idols are creations of the sinful will, nevertheless God has not permitted later generations to suffer for these sins, nor has he left humanity without a trace of his presence, but is always present somehow among us.

It is the tragic power of a firmly rooted paganism that in numerous cases its polytheism cannot be surpassed without injury to piety or to worthy authorities. And where such surpassing occurs through philosophy or enlightenment, instead of through a higher form of religion, the replacement may be better only from a purely intellectual point of view, but not from a religious perspective. Often it is something worse. We can hazard the following generalization: in paganism the false is always bound up with some truth. Paganism is not a systematically worked out overthrow of a consummate religion (for the latter did not yet exist); rather folk religions are a mixture of pious and nonpious elements that stand in internal opposition. The irreligious and the abnormal are found in deifications of the powers of nature in their plurality and singularity. The religious element consists in the fact that these are not meant as merely natural powers, but rather as higher powers, for which the natural are their visible manifestations, forms of appearance, or symbols.

On the other hand, if we examine the religious representation of the most developed folk religions of the classical world, for example, the Greek, what their deities lack is not merely the fixed ethical predicates of holiness and love, but also omnipotence and omniscience.[2] We must not deny the pious Hellenes the truth of the feeling of absolute dependence.[3] Nevertheless this was not so strong or constant that it was capable of transforming the spiritual world of ideas and representations. What prevented any one of the gods from achieving primacy—not simply as the highest and most powerful of all, but as the absolute God—was not merely the splintered plurality of the gods, but Fate (*Moira*). Fate, a power outside of and superior to the divine realm, to which the gods are subordinate, prevents anything more than a distant approximation to monotheism.

Even when it becomes mythologically personified, Fate is nevertheless an immovable and inexorable law. To be sure, it may be portrayed as will, but the content of this will is merely what must inevitably occur. It leaves no room for freedom—the possibility of averting the inevitable—or for

2. Nägelsbach, *die nachomer. Theologie des griech. Volksglaubens*, 1857, p. 93.

3. Dorner makes use of Schleiermacher's term, feeling of absolute dependence, that is the generic element in religious consciousness. See Schleiermacher, *The Christian Faith* (Fortress Press, 1978) §§3–5, §10.—TRANS.

tender mercy that makes Fate endurable. There is no further appeal when matters are already concluded and simply are what they are. The fates are the daughters of the night. What appears as fatalistic necessity to human beings and the gods is, in the final analysis, mere chance. There is no self-determination in *Moira* as is the case for the other deities. Although *Moira* in itself is passive,[4] it is conceived as active in reference to men and gods. *Moira* lacks the essential conditions of personality. The portrayal of *Moira* in personal terms is metaphorical and this is true even if *Moira* is spoken of in the plural. The fact that *Moira* signifies a mere blind law makes comprehensible why it could assume no important position in the cultus.[5]

Although the unqualified unity of all things in absolute dependence on a higher power in fate is represented as certain and fixed only in popular belief, the pagan religions are not religious simply because of their belief in fate. *Moira* in the strict sense is the iron fate. Utterly lacking in feeling and immutable, it is not such that a human heart yields to it out of a sense of devotion. Rather, for the powerless and inexperienced, it is something dark and repellent, without heart, unrelenting. Also the belief in the loosening of fate through mantic and astrology can, at the most, recommend resignation as the most advisable course of action. But resignation does not make one a believer in fate. On the other hand, the Greeks were never able to separate fate from certain ethical connotations. It represents punitive justice that measures precisely and finely. Fate is the inexorability of a punishing correction of all *hubris*. It operates like a natural law and excludes all reconciliation. Consequently *Moira* makes the sinner fearful, and it makes hostile the god Apollo who might have expiated the guilt.[6] This shows that the God of light is strictly interwoven with belief in fate, and how little fate is ethically determined in itself, how far fate is from a just world order.

The positively ethical, the good, and friendliness towards human beings are therefore to be sought only in the realm of the anthropomorphic deities.

4. Cf. Nägelsbach, op. cit., p. 144.

5. Fr. Hermann (*Lehrbuch der Gottesdienstl. Altertums*, 1846) has passed over it completely. Where mention of *Moira* occurs in the cultus (vgl. Preller *Mythol I*. 330) it expresses only resignation, and not the hope that the fates would be favorably disposed.

6. If the fates (*Moirai*) sometimes appear as guardians, not merely of the natural law (the younger fates are the daughters of Themis) but of the ethical law and justice, they signify the character of pitiless inexorability, rigid, inflexible lawfulness—as in the cases in which they stand for the justice of punishment and become akin to Aisa, Nemesis, Adrasteia, etc. On the other hand, when their will is conceived as pliable and changeable, then the authentic faith in fate has been given up.

Although the latter are conceived anthropomorphically, they thereby gain in accessibility and receptivity to entreaties and favors. But on the other hand, unconditional trust has no place in reference to such kinds of deities. They are not free from passions, partiality, egoism. Since they are not originators of their own being, their dominion is not secure; they are mere deputies of fate. Only fate—which supports no religious devotion—is immutable. But the anthropomorphic deities are involved in temporal process even though they are immortal and by virtue of this stand above humans in wisdom and power. In a word, they are, in respect to their being, powers, and doings, no self-same unchanging, but thoroughly mutable beings. The result is that a piety shaped by these representations of the gods and that never gets beyond these cannot be a genuine piety, particularly if a feeling of absolute dependence is an essential feature of piety. For there can be no feeling of free and yet utter dependence in reference to a fate that is not itself ethical. To be sure, fate is immutable, but it is not spiritual or personal. In contrast, the realm of anthropomorphic deities is personal and open to fellowship. However, this realm lacks immutability and absoluteness.

Consequently, the two essential elements on whose vital connection in God religion depends and in which it lives, namely personal vitality and immutability, have disintegrated in paganism. In such disintegration they hinder, each in its own way, religious devotion and trust. For as trust denies itself to fate and in despondency or in defiance changes into sympathy for itself—what in the Adonis cult becomes a kind of self-idolizing and self-deification, a celebration of the suffering world—so the legacy of a god to whom justice is alien, a god who is changeable and not free from particularity or egoism, is to plant and nourish self-seeking egoism in human beings. Such deities are objects of worship primarily for the sake of their gifts, or their utility. Such religion is fundamentally a speculation on egoism—human and divine. But a religion that is nothing but a cultivation of egoism undermines itself.

The foregoing analysis can make clear what immense progress in religion there is when God is posited as an absolute immutable being that has no beginning and nevertheless is personal. Both the absolute and the personal elements are presented by the fundamental divine self-disclosure in Exodus 3:14. God appears as a living person, but also as the unconditional self-identical being that is free from contradictions. "I am who I am" signifies that this absolute being is who he is and has always been, without beginning.

But it also implies that he will remain what he is and therefore will never change or cease to be what and who he is. He is the being that rests utterly upon himself and as self-sufficient depends on nothing else. He is the being that is absolutely steadfast and personal. The patriarchal category of omnipotence is retained, but it has been explicated from the side of God turned away from the world, and developed into the concept of a being that is *in itself* eternal, free from contradiction and unchangeable. God is not outside of himself in the world, but primarily in himself. For example, God is in himself self-knowing and self-manifesting. All that God is, he is as self-reflected and personal.[7] And this 'in itselfness,' that is, having self and asserting self in eternal self-identity and immutability, is the immediate presupposition of conceiving God as truly and genuinely ethical or holy.[8] Divine righteousness or justice is nothing other than immutability of God elevated to ethical significance.

The books of the Old Testament have often been praised for such a noble and fundamental concept of the immutability of God in respect to both being and essence. Thus Psalm 90:2: "Before the mountains were brought forth, or ever you had formed the earth and the world, from everlasting to everlasting you are God." "Heaven and earth will pass away, but you will remain. You remain as you are, and your years know no end." The same point is made in the formula, "I am the first and the last." It is also made in reference to the divine decrees. While Plato pointed out characteristics of the gods that he rejected, namely their alleged capacity to transform and change, because they are incompatible with God's truth and perfection,[9] the Scriptures speak similarly from the beginning of the period of the Law and through the prophets "change and variability are foreign to me . . ." This same point is made in the New Testament that represents God as the Father of lights in whom there is no variation or shadow due to change (James 1:17).

We may gather from these and similar passages what great significance the immutability of God has for the religion of the Old Testament. It differs

7. It is neither textual, nor does it correspond to the matter of establishing of true faith, when the plain meaning of these passages as it stands in the texts is now blithely passed over, and, without this infinitely important but by no means self-evident historical-religious foundation, one advances to the promise of historical deeds corresponding to the covenant.

8. With personality we do not yet have the full ethical concept of God, but rather its form and possibility. Conversely, while the merely physical absoluteness appears to be in continual collision with the life-form of personality, it gains its adequate actualization in the true ethical absoluteness.

9. Plato, *Republic* Book II, 380d–382.

fundamentally from pagan religion, which propounds a realm of mutable deities. Everything earthly is necessarily caught up in flux and struggle, and the waves of this flowing world break incessantly on the human consciousness, drawing it into the whirlpool of time. The human consciousness appears as a rock on which these waves break without consequence, provided that the human consciousness is itself anchored to the rock that is God. Only then does the self-consciousness that is directed toward God attain its highest level, clarity, and stability. Only when God is discovered to be immutable has an absolutely trustworthy object been found. Only such an object makes possible and requires unconditional devotion. The immutability of God is a necessary presupposition for the unchangeableness that the human being, created in the image of God, is supposed to make its own, and whose central point is the constancy of trust and faith that has the power to make the human being secure.

For this reason the Old Testament narrations praise God as a rock, a rock of ages. To be sure, a rock is in itself hard, unmoving, impermeable, and lacking in feeling. But the religious person can say that God is my rock and my strength. His vitality and goodness, which in pagan religions degenerated into changeableness and contingency, do no harm to God's unchangeableness. On the contrary, it is precisely in such unchangeableness that the perfection and absoluteness of God's ethical nature are found. So asserts the above-cited passage of James 1:17, which discusses the human locus of evil and guilt, and that refers above all to God's inner ethical essence. For it is only because God is intrinsically righteous in himself, as well as in his deed, that he is righteous and absolutely identical with himself. God's being, the primal good in itself, is self-identical and thus unchangeable. Again, it is only through the fact that God is pure goodness, seeking nothing outside of himself for the completion of his being or blessedness, that God is eternally self-sufficient in himself and needs no other. Thus God is eternally self-identical and unchangeable.

An important corollary of this principle is that any ethical theogony—whereby God would come to be ethical out of a primal, preethical condition—is excluded. Unless God is personal, the ethical can have no actuality. But God can never be a mere ethical possibility that would need subsequently to attain realization, ethical existence, and actuality. The nonactual ethical can only be an absolute law. But there can be no law above God, and any subject to which the predicate of obedience applies would be a creature. Further, the ethical law as such is not by itself actual, but contains a tendency towards actualization, such that in its realization the absolutely highest is posited. However, the assumption that there is a process whereby God would come to be ethical—however it might come about—would contradict the very concept of an absolute supreme that proceeds from a nature already ethical in itself. Since within God's being there is no basis for ethical development (from a less perfect to a more perfect state), and no basis for any development from potential to actual, it would be necessary to assume some hostile power that restricts the ethical actualization of God to mere potentiality and is the reason for the gradual step-by-step nature of the ethical process.

Such assumptions are ruled out by James: In the Father of light there is no shadow of change or variation between darkness and light, imperfection and perfection. If therefore we wish to avoid dualism, we must say that God as conscious bearer of the divine law requires unconditional reality and therefore exists necessarily. As eternal absolute ethical actuality, God excludes contingency and ethical possibility or potentiality. If God were somehow potential, God would cease to be. As his ethical actuality cannot be limited—whether for a longer or shorter period of time—by anything outside of God, neither can it be inhibited by God himself. An inhibition of him whose actuality—not potentiality—is unconditionally the highest and most valuable cannot be admitted.[10] For God would thereby be subject to some putatively higher interest, and so would cease to be, or would be regarded as something merely mundane.

Consequently there is an indissoluble connection between immutability and the ethical nature of God. God's absolute perfection does not consist in mere ethical potentiality. The very idea of the ethical depends on its actuality. We are not speaking of an actuality that is subject to varying degrees of realization, but rather of an actuality that, instead of varying, is eternally self-same and unchangeable. Conversely, immutability gains its absolute worth, content, and personal character in the ethical nature of God. For this reason Scripture is full of expressions in which this unity is expressed. Above all, God's truth and steadfastness belong among these expressions.[11]

Truth designates a genuine being that is not deceptive—like idols—and has no trace of negation, for example, mere seeming, imperfection, or

10. Not even for the sake of the christological interest.

11. For example: Psalmss 96:3; 100:5; 92:3; 117:2; 86:9; 111:7; 119:90; 25:10.—Steadfastness: 85:11–12; 138:2; 86:15; Exodus 34:6.

self-contradiction (Jer. 10:10; 16:24). God's truth consists in his remaining ethically self-identical. In the revelation of the law God is truthful. God does not command one good for humans while regarding something entirely different as the good in itself (Pss. 19:8-10; 33:4-5). Fidelity refers to God's promises and denotes his honesty, the fundamental virtue of God in relation to his covenant. Consequently fidelity is often mentioned in reference to the fulfillment of God's promises.[12] As a sign that it is the image of divine unchangeableness in man, the same term is used in Scripture as faith or trust. Similarly, the word 'just' (*dikaios*) is the basic designation for divine honesty as for the right relation of the human being to God. The right creaturely orientation is found in faith, through which we are justified, because faith is manifested in the place that God makes possible. God is not merely just in himself, but also shows his justice in justifying the sinner. God is true, 2 Timothy 2:13 shows, because in being true for us, he is true in himself; he is not able to deny himself (*arnésasthai gàr 'eauton oú dúnatai)*. God cannot negate himself; he is purely self-affirmation and in no way negation, for there is nothing in God that is not good and the negation of which would not constitute an evil. Therefore there can be nothing in God that would hinder or diminish goodness, nor anything that must be negated in order for goodness to result. Again, there can be nothing actually good outside of God that would have to be negated for goodness in God to be. Such a good could only be an apparent good, not a necessary good, because it would require a negation of the good in God, without whose changeless actuality we would lack the norm and every criterion of goodness.

Certainly the highest element in God cannot be anything less than the ethical. This highest principle requires immutability and self-sameness and excludes change and variation from God.

The church has not only taken over the immutability of God from the Old Testament and asserted it irrevocably as an unassailable dogma, an elementary concept of all genuine religion. It has also given this dogma a privileged, one-sided development. This has provoked a necessary reaction, at least since the beginning of the nineteenth century, a reaction that has not yet run its course, much less confronted what is of fundamental significance in the traditional doctrine.

12. Romans 3:3; 1 Cor. 1:9; 10:13; 2 Cor. 1:18; 1 Tim. 5:24; 2 Tim. 3:3; 2:13; Heb. 10:23; 11:11; 1 Pet. 4:19; 1 John 1:9; 2 Cor. 1:20.

Moreover, even in the first centuries of Christian thought the tendency towards God's immutable self-sameness was by no means universal. Apart from the Trinity, there are two dogmatic *loci* where various parties desired to leave open the possibility of a process or even a change in God, namely creation and incarnation. These parties were not merely Gnostics and Manicheans. As previously pointed out, there were patripassians on whom Jesus' sufferings made a deep impression. There were also apologists like Justin, Tertullian, Hippolytus, who saw creation as a procession of the Logos from God that developed into a distinctive hypostasis, namely sonship, where it had previously existed only in God. Since the Logos is a divine being, creation implies a change in God's being itself. In reference to the Son, there is a transition from potency to act; this transition in turn implies that time is in God and is connected with a pre-Origenist representation of the generation of the Son that had occurred once and afterward is a settled fact.

Ecclesiastical development gradually suppressed all of this as a pagan corruption, and the Old Testament conceptions performed exceptional service in this suppression. But serious questioning must be undertaken by contemporary theology, whether the tradition did not go too far, whether it did not come too close to the Jewish conception of God for which the incarnation of God is an offense, and thereby emptied the basic Christian fact of all significance. In my work on Christology[13] I have attempted to show that the concept of God in classical Christology (particularly in Peter Lombard and Thomas Aquinas) had reached the point of asserting that all change in the person of Christ falls on its human side, but that incarnation involves no change in God (Nihilianism). This has the consequence of making the basic Christian fact into something merely subjective.[14] So the question arises whether we must not turn to positions that the church has previously rejected as ethnic, and whether the time is not ripe for a revision of the dominant patriarchal elements in the concept of God. As John of Damascus once said of the Trinity, since Christianity is the higher unity of Judaism and paganism, this higher unity must be worked out in the idea of God. Perhaps theology might have more success if it were steered toward

13 I. A. Dorner, *Entwicklungsgeschichte der Lehre von der Person Christi* (Stuttgart, 1839), ET: *History of the Doctrine of the Person of Christ*, 5 Vols. (Edinburgh 1861–1863). —TRANS.

14. The other christological possibility that was still cultivated in the Middle Ages was adoptianism, which, by the permanent duality of the person of Christ, denied the basic Christian fact in a different way.

those 'pagan' and 'untrustworthy' conceptions of God that were rejected by the tradition. A more certain judgment will result from a closer, more precise consideration of the facts that a historical survey of the concept will provide.

Traditional theology indisputably mastered and overcame the pagan elements that spoke of changes and variation in God. Such mastery is evident in the writings of Augustine and Pseudo-Dionysius the Areopagite. These two theologians have exerted the most decisive influence on the entire ecclesiastical doctrine of God.

Augustine[15] opened his work on the nature of good (*De Natura Boni*) against the Manicheans, in the following way: *Summum bonum, quo superius non est, Deus, ac per hoc incommutabile bonum est, ideo vere aeternum et vere immortale.* (The highest good, than which nothing is greater, is God, who is incommunicable goodness, therefore truly eternal and immortal). This God alone is. Everything else exists through God, but is not God and consequently is mutable. God alone is immutable spirit.[16] Augustine expresses this as follows: God is the only simple good and therefore is incommunicable.[17] God simply is his attributes: All that God has, God is. Where having becomes equivalent to being, the property in question cannot change or be lost. Whatever lacks such simplicity has the possibility of change and dissolution. In God, however, there are no properties that are not God's substance. It follows not only that God cannot be part of another being but that God is all his attributes, for example, God does not *have* omnipotence, God *is* omnipotence. It likewise follows that none of his attributes are different from the others.[18] In God there are no accidents, but only substance. Therefore God alone is immutable being, and existence belongs absolutely to his essence. Any change would be a change for the worse, a loss, diminution, or dying away from simple perfection.[19] God not only does not change, God cannot change. From this it follows that God transcends time and space. "In the nature of God there is nothing that does not yet exist, or has not existed, nor anything new

15. Cf. Dr. August Dorner's Essay on Augustine's Philosophy of Religion. [August Dorner was I. A. Dorner's son.—TRANS.]

16. Dorner makes several references to Augustine's works. However, I am unable to track down the editions he cites. I shall therefore omit his citations, frequently with extensive Latin quotations, and indicate only the titles, and where possible, the chapters of Augustine's writings to which Dorner refers.—TRANS.

17. Augustine, *City of God*, L. XI. 10.

18. *De Trinitate* VI, 7.

19. Ibid. V. 2.

that might exist, but only that which is in itself eternity." (*In Dei natura non est aliquid quasi nondum sit, aut fuit, quasijam non sit, sed est tantum id quod est et est ipsa aeternitas.)*[20] God is whole, complete, he is not distended or diminished by diversions; his nature is never divided nor does it have any parts.

To be sure, God does not dwell equally in all saints, but nevertheless God is everywhere the same and self-abiding (ipseity). Differences and composition pertain to the world.[21] For this reason it is said that change does not occur in the divine will itself, but only in things that are moved by God. God wills and knows everything in an unchanging way, from which it follows that there is no difference, according to Augustine, between God's will and his wisdom. "In Thou stand the causes of all mutable things; Thou art the unchangeable cause of all changeable things, and in Thou live the eternal reasons of all irrational and transient things." (*Apud Te rerum omnium instabilium stant causae et rerum omnium mutabilium immutabiles manent origines et omnium irrationabilium et temporalium sempiternae vivunt rationes.*)[22] No one needs to be reminded how closely this doctrine of the immutability of God is connected with Augustine's doctrine of predestination through which God has eternally bound both himself and the world.

Although the Greek church scarcely cultivated the doctrine of predestination, it has made its own contributions to traditional theology. For in the influential writings of the Areopagite, all divine predicates are submerged in the absolute identity and simplicity of the hyperessential One. The result is that there is no determinate representation of God; only a holy darkness remains. The negative (kataphatic) theology denies even existence to God, because it is too determinate a predicate. It worries lest God's infinity be compromised and lest the infinite be confused with what is simply indefinite. As Scotus Eriugena says, "God does not know his nature because he has no nature" (*Deus nescit se quid est, quia non est*

20. Boethius' influential and oft repeated definition that eternity is the entire and perfect possession of interminable life is consistent with Augustine's conception of eternity.

21. *De praesentia Dei*, Ep. 187.

22. Augustine *Confessions*, I, 6. p. 253. There remains some sort of passing in this, but how it is possible, Augustine does not say. Nevertheless he admits (*de Gen. ad lit.* I. c. 9) the difficulty of keeping God's creation of time separate from time itself. To what extent God has already created what is future—here he passes quickly to divine predestination (John XIV), and then jumps from that topic to assert that God has simultaneously created everything real (*de Geni. ad lit.* L, V, 23), since he has already placed a seed in the powers of creation—like a hidden treasure—from which everything is supposed to develop in its proper order under his influence.

*quid*). On the same grounds Origen denied any self-consciousness to God, in favor of omnipotence. Origen believed that omnipotence must be conceived as utterly indeterminate, because it is infinite. In such negative theology God's immutability and superiority over finitude are made clear, but these occur at the expense of sound piety.

The thought of Dionysius the Areopagite is imbued with medieval mysticism. But if God is utterly transcendent and without genuine revelation in the world, there is nothing left for the mystic longing after union with God than the submergence and annihilation of the creature in God that mystics of all times have striven for. The union with God can only occur through ecstasy—a spring over oneself, a cessation of the subject, a metamorphosis in God. The extreme tension of elevation, separation, transcendence, and immutability of God has as its consequence—so far as religion is supposed to signify a union with God—the false doctrine of identity that posits a transformation of the human into God. But it must be noted that this extreme mystic flight from pagan essences, from the ascription of creaturely determinations to God, from the defilement of God's pure essence with finite physical categories that underlie pagan anthropomorphisms, all contribute to making God into a self-enclosed, egoistic being. Consequently the whole enterprise is far from being a fundamental alternative paganism. On the contrary. The pagan philosophy of the later Neoplatonic Alexandrians lives and flourishes in these traditional concepts, which in turn easily lead to the further representation of a mediating realm that is necessary for the nonmystical natures. The concept of a mediating realm is present in both the church and in Neoplatonism.

Augustine's position is restated by Anselm. Since God is not composite, all attributes exist in God not discretely as a multiplicity, but as an absolute unity. Each of God's attributes is identical with the absolute. God does not *have*, but *is* his attributes.[23] According to Anselm, only God's essence, not any particular attribute, can be expressed, or only the 'that' but not the quality or quantity. There are no accidents at all in God, because this would imply the possibility of change.[24] Therefore God is eternal and omnipresent. This signifies on the one hand that God does not exist in any particular part of time or space—for such implies confinement and limitation—but transcends every part.

On the other hand, God is the creative principle that exists without change in all parts of time and space. Anselm does not want to conceive

23. Anselm, *Monologium*. Cf. Hasse, *Anselm von Canterbury*, 2, 132ff.
24. Ibid.

this immanence of God in respect to time as duration, for that would imply that God has present, past, and future. God would no longer be absolute. For what is past, for that very reason, is no more. It does not remain the same, but undergoes change. It becomes other and so has an other. Consequently, it can only be affirmed that God is, not that God was or that God will be. Space and time are in no way determinations of God's being in itself. God is truth. What has truth to do with space and time? One cannot speak of a place or period of truth. If one says that God is here, this is true only in the sense that God is also there and everywhere. If one says that God has been, or that God will be, or does not yet exist, this must not imply that God no longer exists, or does not yet exist, but might possibly exist in the future. More precisely put, God is not in but with space and time in a nonfleeting present *(non labile presens)*. In eternity there is no future and no past, but only an Is, and this 'is' should not be conceived as a temporal presence, for the latter is only one moment of time. But the eternal comprehends continually all time. It is the *simul* of all time relating to all times as the temporal living present. Eternity has its 'since' [*Zumal*] in which all exists simultaneously but without motion.[25] In the eternity of divine knowledge, everything is eternal, even what on earth is changeable. It is eternally in God's knowledge as what it is, namely as something temporal and changeable.

Also knowing and willing, willing and its effect cannot, according to Anselm, be distinct in God, but must coincide. This must lead to questionable consequences in reference to the problem of evil. For evil can be neither willed nor caused by God. Hence there arises for Anselm the necessity of admitting that God has no knowledge of evil. God grasps evil only negatively as nothing. But this is not consistent with his view that human freedom, corrupted by this 'nothing,' is nevertheless something positive.[26]

The main view of Thomas Aquinas is likewise that the absolute simplicity of God denies real and objective significance to the multiplicity of divine attributes. Such simplicity does not merely not allow any passivity or any matter in God, but also does not allow any potentiality or change in God.[27]

25. Hasse, op. cit., 134ff.; 621ff.

26. Hasse, op. cit., 625, 659, 419, 440. Anselm, possibly with reference to the authorities of Origen, Athanasius, and Augustine, often designates the doctrine of the negativity of evil as an article of faith.

27. Cf. H. Ritter, *Geschichte der christliche Philosophie IV*, 273ff. Besides the *Summa Theologiae*, the *Summa Contra Gentiles* should be considered.

From this it follows for Thomas that with one and the same act, God wills himself and all other beings.[28] Understanding and will are in God not as powers, but only as actions. God himself is pure act; this means there is no potentiality in God. Also, the distinction between understanding and will cannot correspond to anything real in God, although he comes back to this problem again in his doctrine of Trinity. From all of this it would seem to follow that there can be nothing accidental, or past, or any final end in God, that God acts and causes eternally in the same way. Moreover, it cannot be said, as Thomas nevertheless wants to say, that in God there is no potential to be, but there is potential to act. For according to his principles it rather follows that as God is eternal actuality and not merely the possibility or ability to be, he exists in eternal absolute actuality, the actuality of his effects. In eternity these are identical.[29] As in the case of Augustine and Anselm, these consequences follow from the rigorous conception of divine immutability.

In the world there is plurality, process, change, contingency, and without all these, that is, if these features had no reality, the world would be mere illusion. However, all these features are absolutely and in every respect excluded from God. But on the other hand, it must nevertheless be required that in some way these must be included in the ultimate ground, that is, in God. Otherwise the world would not be what it in fact is, namely something established and grounded in God. Consequently, the absolute exclusion of plurality, process, and changeableness from God leads to acosmism.[30] For whatever the world has of being, it has necessarily from God, in whose being it participates in varying degrees.

28. Ritter, op. cit., 278. He wants to establish a distinction between the habit of God towards himself, which is necessary and natural, and the habit of God towards others, which is voluntary, despite the fact that the divine will is determined by intellectual cognition. [Dorner is highly critical of Thomas' position, as will become evident in the third part of his essay.—TRANS.]

29. A feeling that such propositions from his doctrine of God are unsatisfactory betrays itself in manifold inconsistencies. According to Thomas, God is the principle of the universe, but the latter is not eternal. God is also the principle of individual parts of the universe, whose being derives from God; and since many parts of the universe have not always existed, creativity is predicated of God in a temporal rather than an eternal sense. Since Thomas derives the idea of the world from God's own self-reflection, and the idea of the world in turn is arranged for a graduated (*stufenweise*) communicability of the being of God, he departs from the concept of divine simplicity that excludes all differences from God. Moreover, God's understanding, with reference to the world, comprehends more than the being that has proceeded from his will. God is supposed to know what is present, but the latter remains for his power only something possible. Moreover, prior to Leibniz, Thomas attained the idea of the plurality of possible worlds from which God selects and chooses one.

30. Acosmism denies independent reality to the world or to certain cosmological features, e.g., plurality. Since the world has no reality independent of God, the reality of the world is identified with God, thus resulting in pantheism rather than panentheism.—TRANS.

We have surely gone beyond the pagan modes of thought, which dissolve the sacred in the world and for which the divine disintegrates pandemoniously into plurality, process, and changeableness. But since God has nothing to do with plurality and changeableness as such, we have only arrived at a different form of pantheism with those who submerge these and the actual world in God. Theoretically the semblance of reality that these categories have is broken and dissolved. But if these categories are merely illusory or have no application to God, then the difference between God and world—the limit or negation—is likewise cancelled, and the final end of man becomes whatever constitutes his existence qua particular as an end in itself. Thus one can say that the telos is represented as lying outside of one's particular existence and is attainable only through an ecstatic leaping over one's existence. This is the inevitable result when such a doctrine of God is the starting point. Whatever considerations may dominate the middle of a system, its view of the world, or its mode of thought, in the end, consistency will out. Such a concept of God will never arrive at a doctrine of creation. To be sure, the world will be assumed on empirical grounds, but there is no basis in God that explains the world in its concrete determinate existence and particularity. The world will finally appear as a mere illusion alongside such an apparently refined concept of God. The consummation of the world is physically, christologically, and soteriologically a taking back of the creation that merely seems to be an independent reality.

But even if the world only seems to have its own being distinct from God, in fact it is only an infinite multiplicity of limitations of the being of God in which it participates. The riddle remains, where does such a pluralistic world come from, if all plurality and change are excluded from God? If the world is simply an illusion, whence cometh this illusion? What sort of sublimity is it that compels God to remain in solitary transcendence? What sort of grandeur is it that leaves no place for a world of independent personal spirits that are nevertheless images of God and thus totalities or microcosms in their own right? In paganism the divine lacked the righteousness that constitutes its majesty, and so, in its living commerce with the world, the divine loses its majestic righteousness. In the pagan gods, the divine righteousness is, as it were, alienated from itself for the sake of communion with human beings, and so it was transformed into something finite. Now to be sure, the divine asserts itself; only now if communion with God is supposed to come about, the ecstasy must shift to the human side. A transformation of the finite into the divine is expressed in the medieval doctrine of communion.

Of course there were many other elements in medieval theology besides this acosmic magical theory whose time was running out. Thomas Aquinas, whose thought shaped the basic themes of the system and for whom God's will is determined simply by his knowledge (but his knowledge in turn is shaped by the various grades of created substances in nature), sought to avoid the proscription of this point of view, but it was too late. A few, like Bernhard of Clairveaux, wanted to assert to a greater independence of the world from God. The ancient thesis that God is the being of all beings and the life of all living beings was interpreted to mean that God is not the material essence, but the [formal] cause of the world.[31] In this there can be seen the striving to advance to a more definite distinction between the being of God and the being of the world. The advance is from the category of substance—in which the world is accorded no independent being of its own, but remains essentially suspended in God's being—to the category of causality, according to which cause and effect are distinct so that they no longer have in common the same kind of being.[32] (260)

But it was Duns Scotus[33] who first adopted the perspective of the world in its independence and formulated the concept of God according to this standpoint. To be sure, Scotus also says that God is absolutely simple. Only he finds the sublimity and uniqueness of God not merely in the fact that God alone is and everything else exists by participation in God, but rather in the fact that God wills and his free will is not determined by his knowledge or his nature. God must necessarily will himself, but he also has the freedom to will something other than himself. The necessary will of God is exclusively directed towards his absolute freedom and has freedom itself for its content. This is God's characteristic nature.

But God is free to will (or not to will) something other than God. For example, God can will the world thus or so. However, whatever God wills

31. Cf. John Gerhard, loc. th. T. III, p. 102, ed. Cott.

32. The church had, in the trinitarian controversy, already advanced beyond the deistic concept of the Arians (*agennesia*) and the pantheistic *monas* of the Sabellians to the category of an absolute causality in itself, to the eternal begetting of the Son. But that did not prevent the substantial conception from predominating for a long time in reference to the world. However, the consideration prevails to allow the world to be distinct from God so that God would not constitute its actuality and reality. The world is distinguished from God only as the limitation, or as the nothing that has the appearance of being.

33. Cf. H. Ritter, op. cit. IV, 381ff.; Baur, *Trinität und Menschwerdung II*, 632ff., 642, cf. 634, 667ff., 727f. August Dorner in Herzog's *Real-Encyclopädie* Artikel 2.

is good. God can revoke the world and create another in its place. There is only one thing that such absolute freedom cannot do, namely, make the world equal to itself, or bestow absolute freedom on the world. Thus it appears to be bound by the law of contradiction, even though the latter is supposed to depend on and derive from God and be bound by God's will. However, assuming that God upholds the law of contradiction, the latter has a status not less than God, for otherwise God would not be its absolutely free cause. Since the world has contingent being, contingency must be reflected into God. God is the contingent, that is, arbitrary, effective cause of the determinate being (*Sosein*) of the world. God himself is not thereby altered in his being, for his absolute freedom signifies that he is and remains what he wills to be. But what he wills, that he wills eternally, even though everything is willed eternally in its place and order (*Reihe*). Thus the process and multiplicity of the world are reflected into the will of God. (The latter is unchangeable in itself, since the being of God for itself is to be distinguished from the being of God as the basis of the world.) He assumes there are real distinctions in God in his treatment of Trinity and divine attributes.

But the independence of the world, or its determinate differentiation from God, is achieved by Scotus at a high price. God is for him the absolute causality, but not self-communicating. God is a realm all by himself that has no similarity and nothing in common with our own being. God in himself is transcendent to the world. Although Scotus asserts that knowledge of God is possible, conclusions about God's essence are not possible from the created world. For God's absolute freedom, by which the knowledge of God is present for us, is the ground of the contingent world, and the latter does not have to be what it is, not even in respect to its ethical principles and determinations. For God has not willed the world because it is intrinsically good. Rather everything is good simply because God wills it. The good is understood as whatever corresponds to the will of God, that is, the arbitrary will that Scotus identifies with freedom. The moral law that God ordains for the world could have been otherwise and has no internal connection with God's nature.

From this it follows that the human being is not determined to a free knowledge and love of God, but only constrained to a blind obedience to the empirical positivity of the divine will. There remains for human beings only the freedom of obedience to laws, the free choice of a slave. God can have no historical life in the world, or communicate himself to the world. It is only God's will, this eternal act, that has a relation to the world. God can incite, even require devotion to a magical efficacious grace, but he cannot communicate himself. He can only let his commands be known. By the way, Scotus' teaching is akin to that of Thomas in that for both the world has only a completely accidental position in relation to God. The difference is that for Thomas this position of the world is determined by the nature of divine substance, while for Scotus it is determined by God's absolute freedom, a perfect power that proceeds groundlessly and arbitrarily.

The Reformation in its central doctrine of faith has an original and fundamental insight into the relation between God and the human. It goes beyond the standpoint of substance—for which God is the Being of beings, the life of the living, the nature of all natures—and those standpoints that not only fail to secure human personality but threaten it. For the person justified by faith knows himself to be confirmed in his personhood by God, as eternally favored by God. The Reformation advances beyond the standpoint which regards God to be merely lawgiver and judge and beyond the level of mere rights that remain suspended in the separation between God and man. The believer knows himself as worthy of divine favor only if he stands in a childlike but vital fellowship with God. It is certain that the Reformation principle contains the seed of a new doctrine of God, but it is equally clear that this seed has not yet yielded its fruit. Both main Protestant confessions continue to be dominated by the doctrine of absolute predestination. This culminates in double predestination—the one half glancing at the reality of a continuing number of unbelievers, the other half pointing to the unconditioned grace of God directed at a world of sinners and grounded in the received doctrine of the immutability of God.[34]

34. There remains here a dark remnant of absolute arbitrariness in God that is not determined by ethical motive, and this undermines the Reformation's recognition of the ethical as the highest perfection of the divine will. The double predestination is not consistent with the absolute immutability and self-sameness of God, for God does not remain self-identical vis-à-vis sinners, but rather relates to them unequally: meting out justice to the damned, and mercy to the rest. But this lack in ethical self-identity points to a further defect, namely the loose connection between God's freedom, understood as sheer power, and God's ethical being. We have previously found this defect in both Thomas and Duns Scotus, and it seems to be a common legacy of medieval theology. Nevertheless this same tenuous connection [between the ontological and the ethical] dominates the doctrine of the *decretum absolutum*: at a point where medieval theology allows room for divine mutability, contingency, and variability in the principles of divine action, both evangelical Protestant confessions seek to establish decisively the necessary unity of God's doing with God's immutable being. According to

Also in Lutheran dogmatics the doctrine of unconditional predestination was overcome and an essential role was secured for human freedom in the process of salvation, without which the human personality could not be even a relatively independent magnitude. Thus the Reformation acknowledged and legitimated human personality. But in spite of all this, the doctrine of God remained essentially biased by the limitations of the traditional doctrine, and it was only at later points of systematic theological development—Christology, conversion, and justification of the sinner before God for which a forensic action of God was required—that there emerged traces of a future development of the doctrine of God that corresponded more explicitly with the fundamental principles of the Reformation.

It may suffice to have a brief look at Gerhard and Quenstedt in order to see that while the heart of reformed dogmatics is animated by a new conception of the relation between God and world, the doctrine of God still puts on the same old traditional face that is in no way compatible with the new thinking, namely, the traditional concepts of divine infinity, eternity, omnipresence, omnipotence, omniscience, and blessedness. Although the center of evangelical dogmatics places special emphasis on the ethical, the traditional doctrine of God does not. All divine attributes are coordinated, but the strange coordination of physical and metaphysical attributes with the ethical provokes little reflection on the part of theologians; it is simply taken over uncritically from the past. Thus Quenstedt: *Systema* P.I. S 285: [God's attributes] are contained in him in such a way that nothing precedes and nothing follows (*Nullum ordinem attributa Dei habent a parte rei, quia ita in eo insunt, ut nihil antecedat, nihil subsequatur*).

According to Gerhard the divine attributes are really one among themselves and identical with God's essence. They are predicated of God only anthropomorphically, and Gerhard expressly refers to Pseudo-Dionysius the Areopagite, as well as to Augustine's *De Trinitate*. Neither creation nor preservation nor the affections that Scripture attributes to God imply any change in God. It is not only that time has nothing to do with God's being, but change occurs only in the creatures. This implies that there is

common evangelical doctrine, God must, in the work of reconciliation, demand satisfaction for his justice, while medieval theology remained content with asserting its fitness vis-à-vis justice. Similarly, it is significant that, in contrast to the moral positivism of medieval theology, especially that of Duns Scotus, the dominant assumption of evangelical Protestant doctrine was that the good that God prescribes for us is intrinsically good in itself, and so appropriate both for God and for human nature. The good is not one thing in relation to God, and another in relation to the world. There is assumed here a relation of God's being to God's will which loves the good and hates evil.

no change in God's will. Although God began to be creator, strictly speaking time and alteration do not apply to God, the change of creation refers only to the world.[35] "The relation of the creatures to God is a real relation, but the opposite is not true: there is no real relation between creator and creature, because the work of creation does not add any new perfections to God in time; but God is unmixed and pure act in himself, whose works vary in respect to their effects, but who in his own being is permanent and invariable" (Gerhard, Loc. II c. 7. T III, 86). To be sure, what does not yet exist is incapable of change; but Gerhard reassures himself with the observation that the creatures have come to be out of a nonexisting ontological condition. And such coming to be is an alteration that has befallen them. This implies a preexistence of the creation in God after the model of the Platonic world of Ideas that, through creation, has experienced an alteration, namely, they are translated out of the intelligible realm into actual existence.[36]

However, there is still the appearance of something new because things do not translate themselves from idea into reality. Thus Gerhard's explanation does not suffice. Gerhard can combine the absolute immutability of God with the temporal origin of the world only by assuming the eternal self-sameness of the divine will directed to the actual production of the world, but at first without apparent effect owing to some hindrance that is later removed. And so in place of a change in the world-creating will of God, there appears something else, namely a temporal conditioning, if not an outright passivity in the effective power of God, implying its limitation by something other. But Gerhard adds there can be no real accidents in God; it is only a "human way of speaking" that implies accidents in God. That God created a world does not increase God's perfection, and that God did not create more than one world does not lessen it. Nothing created can add anything to God, only his disposition to create (*habitus ad creaturam adaugetur*) is capable of increase. If God creates something new, he creates it with his eternal will, not with a new will, so that from God's side, not merely God's mode of decreeing matters, but insofar as God wills and acts at all, everything is constantly and equally willed. Even incarnation did not produce any change in God, for the Son of God has not given up his fullness, but only communicated it.

35. Consider the implications this would have for Christology!

36. By the way, Gerhard modifies decisively the principle that God is the essence and life of the world.

But Gerhard does not really dare to assert that incarnation brings nothing new for God. He sticks to the basic position that God is neither diminished by human sin, nor augmented by human conversion; any change occurs only on the human side. For example, the sun remains always the same, standing in the heavens and sending out its rays eternally and equally everywhere. But the earth is illuminated and warmed by the sun only when it is turned towards the sun.

Gerhard demonstrates the impossibility of a change in God in the following way: God is absolutely simple. His attributes, considered as real, are completely one with his essence. Consequently, there can be no synthesis of essence and accidents in God. For such a synthesis can occur only in changeable beings that are in some respect composite. God's eternity implies that, just as God is without beginning or end, he is also without succession or alteration, without even the capacity for alteration in regard to his nature, his ethical attributes, knowledge, and will. For he says with Thomas, God is *actus purus*, but all that changes exists in some mode of potentiality. For whatever changes the general principle holds true, that part changes and part remains the same. Since God's power and being are not really distinct, so his omnipresence is not simply sheer presence, as a result of his power, to the exclusion of his being; rather he makes everything absolutely present. To be sure, there are differences of degree in divine presence. Gerhard distinguishes four levels of divine presence: *praesentia potentiae, gratiae, gloriae, incarnationis*. He also speaks of types of presence. But none of this implies any change or difference in God's presence itself, but only in God's effects. If a difference in the effect implies a difference in the cause, and if the effective divine causality is supposed to be identical with the divine being, we are left in the lurch in reference to the incarnation. For Gerhard's meaning is not that God is related to all things in the mode of self-incarnation, or that God's actual incarnation in Christ alone is due merely to a difference in degree of human receptivity.

Quenstedt, the John of Damascus of orthodox Protestant dogmatics, follows Gerhard on many points and presents the following defense of God's immutability. Immutability designates the constant identity of the divine being with all its perfections and excludes every physical and ethical change.[37] For a spiritual being there are five possible modes of alteration, but none are applicable to God. In reference to existence, change is excluded by God's eternity and necessary being. In reference to space, God is infinite

37. *System*, T. I, p. 288. Thes. XX.

and omnipresent and does not change place. Further, the distinction between contingent accidents and necessary being does not introduce change into God, because such distinctions are excluded by God's simplicity. In reference to God's knowledge, no change can occur in an omniscient being. God not does first learn something in time that he did not already know before. Finally, there is no change possible in God's will or its decrees, for God does not change his mind or repent. Consequently Quenstedt grounds the immutability of God on his eternal and infinite presence, his absolute simplicity and omniscience as well as in the fixed resolve of God's will. However, one can equally reverse this and assert that God's immutability is set forth or exemplified by all these relations and aspects.

Eternity is described by Quenstedt and the Protestant Scholastics not merely as opposed to things that begin and end, but also as opposition to all succession. It is indivisibly one, uninterrupted and incommunicable; it has no past or future; it stands in an eternally fixed, nonfleeting now or in full presence *[Gegenwärtigkeit]*. In this eternity, as if in a full spring or an endless ocean, float those drops of time that carry in themselves the distinctions of past, present, and future, of which the now is not genuinely temporal, but only the end of the past and the beginning of the future. But eternity itself coexists with all of these. Quenstedt characterizes eternity positively as simple duration. This attribute is predicated of God in the sense that it depends neither on an internal nor an external principle, but simply and necessarily belongs to God's nature and to him alone. It should be noted that the immutability of God's being is traced back to his self-sufficiency or aseity.

The Socinians—namely, Crell, the Arminians, and Conrad Vorst—raised the following objections.[38] Every duration has parts that follow each other and so cannot be conceived without succession. The eternal duration could not consist in a moment, nor be comprehended in a moment, for a moment is the opposite of eternity. The latter must comprehend all times within itself. How could it be comprehended within a particular moment, the Now? If in eternity nothing is earlier and nothing is later, then, since everything occurs in eternity, everything must happen in one and the same moment. And so the end of the world must coincide with its beginning. But it is contradictory to conceive the entire infinite duration as coexisting with every particular point of time. For then everything would be and

38. Crellus *de Deo eiusque attrib*. c. XVIII p. 43; Conrad Vorstius, *Tract. de Deo*, S. Episcopius *Instit*. L. IV. Sect. II, c. 14, pp. 294–296.

not-be for God, would happen and not-happen in the presence of God, and God's knowledge of things would not be congruent with the things themselves.

In reply, Quenstedt can only say that the divine duration is undivided, like the divine being, and thus without succession. It is comprehended in every moment, wholly present without temporal change. It is not in a single moment of time, but as the whole comprehends all times. If it contained all times within it as its parts or were it the whole of which the modes of time were its parts, it would indeed not be indivisible. God's eternity is elevated above time and comprehends time without participating in time. If there is no succession in God, nevertheless everything that happens outside of God happens in time. God coexists with time, but not in such a way that he coexists with every time. God cannot coexist with past and future, but only in contrast to such. Eternity in its totality coexists with successive time, like a tree on the river bank coexists with flowing waters without itself flowing or becoming temporal,[39] or, as Gerhard says, like the pole of heaven that remains unperturbed while the world structure keeps to its constant revolution around it. Eternity is here conceived as supra-temporality, as supramundane elevation above time that nevertheless stands in some sort of relation to time. For example, the future is for divine eternity future and not past. So, on the one hand, time has some meaning for God, since God coexists with the future differently than he coexists with the past. On the other hand, the entire significance of time appears to consist only in relation to the world, since for God time does not exist at all.

For Quenstedt, the immeasurability of God is the power to be absolutely and nonlocally present in all places. The actual, efficiacious *Adessenz*, or actual operational ubiquity, is a distant but necessary consequence if the world exists.[40]

God's simplicity is God's absolute opposition to every synthesis. There is no synthesis of universal and particular in God, for God is the *actus*

39. Is this supposed to mean that God's eternity coexists with the future only when it will have become present? He does not mean that. Rather he means that God comprehends the future already in his immutable presence, i.e., knowledge. And what Crell criticizes: *quiquid Deus unquam egit, acturusve est, id eum simul agere,* must be admitted by Quenstedt as following from his own premisses.

40. *Adessenz* is a German rendering of *adessentia*. This is a divine presence which is distinct from omnipresence; *adessentia* is God's presence to the world that is coextensive with divine action.—TRANS.

*purissimus* without the need or capacity to draw together disparate elements; nor is there any synthesis of form and matter, or quantitative parts, for God is an incorporeal spirit. Nor are there subject and accidents, for such distinctions have no place in God. There is no synthesis of essence and existence, because it belongs to God's being to exist necessarily. Nor is there any synthesis of nature and personality or subjectivity, for God's nature is, like his subsistence, an absolute pure act. There is no synthesis of any polar opposites that are essentially relative to each other like potential and actual, nor is his nature potentially his subjectivity, or the latter potentially his nature. Rather, God's act is absolutely pure and simple.

God's omniscience sees everything as present; he does not behold only himself, including all that is possible and impossible, but in his free vision God beholds everything past, present, and future, both as it is in itself and as it is in God, as its immediate cause.[41]

How far this ancient doctrine of God's immutability corresponds to the interests of a vital piety we do not wish to settle here. But it is undeniable that the traditional doctrine combines in itself both acosmic (pantheist) and Deist elements. This will be demonstrated in the following propositions, which dominated the old dogmatics, Reformed and Lutheran alike.

1) There is in God no distinction between before and after. Consequently there is nothing accidental, not merely in God's own being, but also in his decrees and acts of will. The will of God, says Gerhard,[42] is nothing but the willing God. But God's will characterizes God's entire being itself, for with a simple act of will he wills from eternity the unchanging plan he has eternally decided. The simplicity and immutability of the divine will remain unmoved in spite of their many objects, because God wills and decides not through several discrete acts, but through a single simple eternal act, just as God knows everything not discursively through several distinct acts of the understanding, but through a single act. We have already pointed out how such an identification of the divine decrees and acts with God's being threatens an important, otherwise established distinction. For in

41. According to the Areopagite, God comprehends all things in and through his [simple] self-knowledge. God's knowledge of things does not derive from things. This is also the dominant Protestant doctrine. The Socinians are close to the Calvinist view, because both assert that the knowledge of the future is conceptual, since God knows it from his free power to effect all things. But the Socinians believe that, since God wills the freedom of creation, his foreknowledge of free actions that are not produced by his causality must be denied.

42. *Loci Theol*. T. I, 102. Quenstedt makes the same claim: Volitional actions (not merely the faculty of the will), whether in God or directed outwards [towards the world], are not different from God's essence.

analogy with such reduction of the decrees to God's being for the sake of divine simplicity, the objective distinction of the divine attributes from the simple divine being is undermined and threatens to become a merely subjective distinction. Consequently the concept of God retains no more secure determination than indeterminacy and unlimitedness, a diffuse immeasureability or omnipresence, that stands in starkest conflict with the concept of divine personality.

Thus it is easy to see that with such a conception of the absolute simplicity and eternal immutability of the divine decrees, only a Docetic apparent existence is left for the world. If the world is supposed to have something more than a shadow existence, and amount to a reality worthy of God, it must not be conceived without freedom. But such free causes must in turn condition the divine decree. The simple decree would not refer to the concrete world, to the development, guidance, and final destiny of the individual, but would only make such reference in the most vague and general of terms, namely, that there be a realm of freedom, as well as the general laws valid in the world. Gerhard himself teaches elsewhere that the intuition of faith is ingredient in the decree of election. But if that is so, then the immutable divine decree, because it is conditioned by God's perception of the believer's faith, can no longer be a simple act co-eternal with God himself; rather it is synthetic, arising from God's universal graciousness for the sake of Christ, and the consideration of freedom as its necessary condition, although such freedom is not necessarily meritorious and finally from the concrete election of the individual believer.

Our dogmatics stress rightly that divine omnipotence is ordered power. But in the doctrine of God, especially divine immutability, there is a conception of God's idea of the world that has too great a similarity with the Platonic realm of Ideas—a realm that is unhistorical, unfree, in no way conditioned by God's will or doing. It has such a shadowy, eternal, and quiescent existence in God that it never attains a living movement or an independent being outside of God. This realm of Ideas is timeless, in all respects simultaneous and self-coincident, and so it is easily traceable to a simple eternal act of God. However, it is only expression of an eternal beauty; there is no ethical element within it.

In contrast, the Reformation had a deep impression of evil as contradictory to God, and it recognized that the vocation of true personhood cannot be realized by a purely physical "salvation magic" or by power alone, or by a merely natural shaping of the person by the church, but rather only through an interpersonal ethical process. Thus the conception of the world as a Platonic realm of pure Ideas was broken through in principle. Consequently, it became imperative not only to make room for human freedom and its historical action, but to acknowledge that freedom influences and conditions the divine decree, even if that means the simplicity of this decree must be abandoned.[43] The further consequence is that, notwithstanding the unity and fixity of the telos of the world, a plurality of divine actions must be assumed that always correspond to the human condition and are therefore subject to variation. This also rules out a merely simple divine will that is always and eternally the same.[44]

The preceding discussion brought out the acosmic aspect of the system concealed in the traditional doctrine of God's immutability. Traditional theology was also defective in that it did not sufficiently ground the world in God, but assigned it a merely contingent position in reference to God's will. This resulted in the appearance that God was indifferent to the existence or nonexistence of the world. Such a conception is not a secure or adequate foundation for a position that claims God is the ultimate basis and ground of everything. The world can be rescued from such a shadowy existence only if it is not mere indifferent play, but something that is intrinsically good and worthwhile even for God. On this point there is a hidden residue of the Scotist doctrine of God, namely, the conception of free will as arbitrary (i.e., arbitrariness is the highest principle—a point connected with a similar line of thought in Thomas). For it does not matter much whether one says God could make good evil and vice-versa; God's being remains identical and unchangeable in either case and is indifferent to the distinction between good and evil. Nor does it help if one says God is indifferent whether there is a potential ethical world or not. In either case there is an erroneous presupposition that the ethical—whether in the

43. For Dorner's own formulation of this important revision, cf. the third essay below. Human freedom does not only influence, but has an 'impact' (*Einschlag*) on God.—TRANS.

44. A few words about another difficulty for the old dogmaticians in their identification of the divine will with the divine essence. They adhere to the view that creation is accidental, contingent for God. This has the advantage of showing that God's essence is not co-constituted by the world but is rather the logical presupposition of the world. But is this view of the world's contingency compatible with the identification, not merely of the faculty of will, but also acts of willing, with God's essence? Quenstedt saw the problem when he said that in God's will the entire essence wills, but nevertheless the direction of the will remains free. But isn't this direction also willed? If the free will is not one with necessity, but rather opposed to it, then Quenstedt must, like Duns Scotus, recognize at the very least that there is something accidental or contingent in God.

world or in itself—is only of concern for the world and has no significance for God in himself but only for his arbitrary will.

2) A second theme of traditional dogmatics is that all change and succession do not pertain to God, but only to creation. Assuming that the world has a genuine reality and not merely an illusory existence, the preceding assertion has a deistic if not dualistic ring. Accordingly, we would have to imagine that God, in his simple and absolute majesty, is absolutely unmoved and continuously willing the same thing and stands over and against the world in one and the same simple eternal act. We do not wish to make a thorough investigation whether this is consistent with the traditional doctrine of divine omnipresence which, is conceived in the Lutheran doctrine as effective in different places and times and must be found acting differently at different times if free causes are recognized.

But if no succession is supposed to occur in God nor any change in his actions, how can these positions be reconciled with the fact that in humanity God effects a system of actions that he did not create in the very beginning and that God seeks and finds a constantly developing, richer existence and dwelling in humanity? Are we supposed to say in reference to the person of Christ and the kingdom of God that there is no new act of God not previously in existence? That there is no new act that begins with God's appearing and dwelling in the world? That everything remains unchanged as far as God's will and doing are concerned and that change has occurred only on the human side, namely, in human receptivity? If this were so, we would have to infer that while God constantly willed the whole (viz., incarnation, redemption, consummation) with the same power that is eternally at his disposal, nevertheless there are hostile powers that subsequently emerge in the world and oppose God's universal will. But that would clearly be dualistic, Manichean, even if it were understood that among those hostile powers there were some who misused their freedom. For it would imply that God, although constantly exerting his entire power, nevertheless finds in freedom (which after all can only exist through God) an invincible opposition—not merely to God's ethical will, but also to his absolute power! Thus God would be continually struggling against human freedom and frequently fighting a losing battle.

If in each moment God wills the whole with unchanging actuality, it would be inconceivable why the world is not created all at once, yet Scripture attests that the work of creation required six days. Since the divine will actually wills the whole continuously, and since it does not achieve its goal all at once, there must be a recalcitrant principle—perhaps matter—that opposes it. That supposition would take us back to dualism in order to sustain God's simplicity and immutable self-identity such that all succession and change fall entirely on the side of creation.

The only way to avoid these consequences is to say that God attains what he wills at the very outset: he created potentialities in the world from the beginning that are capable of developing further to an ever greater extent and do not require any further help. This would be the authentic Deist view, according to which there are no acts of foreknowledge or providence, and none are needed, since the world is established with the power of self-preservation and development. The most perfect work of art is one that no longer requires its artisan, who may, after creating, withdraw into his sublimity.

However, in this view rebirth would be conceived in Pelagian fashion as the work of freedom—whether as one's own or as a fatalistically predetermined development—or as the work of receptivity for the eternal divine activity streaming into the world. Further, Christ would be merely a quantitative increase in humanity. Implicit here as well is the suggestion that nature once existed without human beings. Hence humanity would be simply a product of nature, and spirit would not merely have nature as the point of mediation of its earthly appearance, but spirit itself would have developed from nature as the plant develops automatically from its seed. For as soon as Deism admits a second creative act on behalf of the creation of human beings, it would have to give up its concept of the absolute self-identity of the highest being and with it the concept of absolute immutability and absence of succession in God's action. It would have forfeited its right to protest against the possibility of further creative actions, for example, the bringing forth of a second Adam. I don't want to spell out further how the apparently noble concept of a world that can manage without God would deny the main point, namely, real community with God that must rest upon God's vital being in the world. It is sufficient to have pointed out how dangerous for genuine religious interests these ideas are—that traditional dogmatics did not invent, but accepted uncritically from the scholastics— because they lead to a false independence from the world and to Deism and Pelagianism.

God should be viewed as a cause always active in producing new changes that result in novelty and goodness. Notwithstanding God's decree, which is not absolutely simple but mediated, God does not always will and do the same thing. That makes it seem as if God wills the whole, but changes originate exclusively through the world, through greater or lesser hindrances and checks on God's activity in nature and history that God could neither foresee nor approve. This would lead to passive changes in God in order to deny that change is grounded in his will.

We will have to teach the following: that not only does humanity change in its relation to God, but the living relations of God to humanity—his being and will—also undergo changes, as both are manifest in the world. And if we establish this point, then the concept of God is not merely the wooden concept of the highest being, but the vital absolute personality that stands in a living relation of mercy and love to the life of the world and its changing needs and conditions. Without reciprocity between God and world such vital relations would have no authentic reality.

The Reformation failed to overcome the tendencies towards Deism and pantheism present in the traditional doctrine of God. These tendencies became explicit in the post-Reformation period. The tradition stripped away the pagan concept of the changeableness of God, but the general pagan concept of God was in no way overcome. Instead dogmatics (as one can see especially on the Catholic side in the case of D. Petavius, *Theol. dogm.*T. I L. I-VII 1730) fell into determinations for which pre-Christian philosophers can be cited as authorities, but which—as we have seen—would lead to the acosmic form of pantheism. This subethical concept of God depends on the pagan concept of being, but, if a real independence were nevertheless ascribed to the world, is compatible with the 'highest being' of Jewish Deism. The highest being imparts to the pagan conception a rigidity and motionlessness as well as a pseudo-sublimity. Thus it might seem that in the traditional concept of God, a higher unity of the pagan and Jewish elements has been worked out. However, such a conception sacrificed everything vital and religiously appealing in the pagan and Old Testament concepts of God. Consequently a higher unity so conceived must dissolve of its own accord, in order that through the unfolding of the errors in Deism and pantheism, a crisis would arise and pave the way for a more satisfactory unity of the two.

Deism—a term that has scarcely been explained—is usually taken only as the theory that separates God and world, while pantheism allegedly confuses them. But in Deism there is a peculiar equating of God with the world that betrays a hidden kinship with pantheism and allows a transformation of Deism into pantheism. Substance pantheism never achieves a world that is actual, but, insofar as it attributes being (reality) to the world, the latter is essentially identified with God. Similarly in Deism there occurs an equation of God with the world, a mundanizing [*Verendlichung*] of God, a loss of God's absoluteness. In short, if "world" means everything finite, then for Deism God belongs, so to speak, in the sphere of the world, albeit as the most powerful, greatest mundane being. Consequently, Deism has only the world, just as substance pantheism or acosmism has only God. To be sure, Deism can be conceived in different ways: some varieties establish and emphasize the immutability of being as constitutive of the divine, while others pass on to think of God as an individual personality. But the common element is the emphasis on the independence of the world, namely, the world is capable of standing on its own. This can be documented especially in the worldview that is peculiar to the legal standpoint [*Rechtstufe*]. But there is a difference: the more the human being—understood as a legal person—takes God to be only the personification of an immutable law—natural or ethical—the more the God of Deism approximates Fate, the Nemesis of the ancient world, even if this god is fitted out with ethical predicates. Or the human being takes God to be a free personal being, to whom the human being stands over and against in a coordinated fashion on the common legal basis.

Let's examine the latter element first. It abandons the concept of absoluteness—like the first version—and approximates the concept of the pagan god. In place of the *Dii minorum gentium* (Gods of the smaller nations), the modern version concedes the human race has a share in the causality of the world, a causality that, as far as it goes, is not supposed to be the causality of the highest being. The religious and ethical interests cannot merely drive human beings to think freely, but also can render God finite, differing only in degree from the human. Owing to such similarity, God is rendered accessible, but too accessible. At least the idea of an unmoved God utterly transcendent by his very nature, or the development of God into a kind of fate, is avoided. This form of Deism, conceiving God as subjectivity, revives something of polytheism, for here God has a relation to human beings similar to that of Zeus.[45]

In contrast, the alternative form of Deism represents God, instead of as a highest divine being, rather as a monistic absolute, an immutable law—be it fatalistic or naturalistic, or moral law. Here God is conceived

45. Judaism also gives God an interpretation reminiscent of polytheism, when the study of the Torah conceives God as similar to the human, and differing only in degree.

as immutable, but as no longer as vital. The predicate of being the supreme cause, which may be attributed to him for the purpose of originating the world, is already past, since the world already exists independently on its own. Consequently, the fundamental enduring significance of God is to be only the law of the world. The personality of God is merely a personification of the law. This conception will not last long, nor will it long allow the assertion of an independent being of God distinct from the world. This kind of Deism will thus pass over into pantheism in the form that the absolute (the law) assumes in the world. This is no longer the acosmic, but the pancosmic form of Deism.

a) In fact the first appearances of Deist modes of thought concerning freedom and self-determination in Socinianism and Arminianism divide God and world from each other. There is an identification of God with the world that renders God finite and mundane and treats God as having the status of a person, standing on the same level as human beings. These movements oppose the immutability and rigidity of the traditional concept of God, as expressed in the *decretum absolutum,* and desire rather to conceive God as changeable out of love for the world. From this it becomes clear that a practical motive rather than a purely philosophical-rational motive was dominant. I shall assume some knowledge of the Socinian doctrine of God. I want to focus upon the thought of someone unknown today, although he was previously renowned, a man of no little acuity and regularly contested by our Lutheran theologians, namely, Conrad Vorst (Vorstius). Alexander Schweizer has recently called attention to him. Vorstius preceded Arminianism and appears to have been of significant influence on the Socinians of the seventeenth century, although he was himself indebted to the older Socinians.

Vorst assumes that human freedom is a faculty of choice. The doctrine of God is shaped from this perspective and in accordance with its requirements.[46] He proceeds from a polemic against the eternal immutability of the divine decree dominant in Calvinism, specifically the view that the divine decree has its basis in the divine nature [*Wesen*] itself. (This position is also widely held by Lutherans.) Against this view Vorst posits a distinction between God's essence—which he regards as immutable, absolute, simple, and necessary—and the divine will that, as contingent (*libera contigentia*), has for its content not everything forever willed, nor that which is presently willed, but rather that which has been always specially

46. Conrad Vorst, *De Deo et attrib. Dei*, Steinf. 1610.

willed. Without a real distinction between the being and the will of God, God's will is not free. The will of God is thus not straightforwardly immutable; on the contrary, it is the principle of a certain kind of mutability and through it some sort of alteration in God. It is therefore not accurate to say that what God does, has, or shall will, he has willed from all eternity in one perpetual act. God's decrees are not simply eternal or co-eternal with God, because the free cause and its reflective consideration of such acts must precede them.[47]

Vorst is quite conscious of violating the traditional concept of God's simplicity and transcendence of time and space. But he does not hesitate to assert that a certain diversity exists in God,[48] and not merely for the sake of the divine decrees that are distinct from each other as well as distinct from God's being. There must eternally and necessarily be in God a distinction between subject and object, between deed and doer, between the living substance and the power through which it lives, between that which possesses and that which is possessed. "How otherwise could God swear by his soul?" (Jer. 51:4; 1 Cor. 2:11). It is therefore false to say that what is in God simply is God, and the traditional axiom that there is no composition in God cannot be valid. Rather there is in God, as a generic feature, a spiritual essence and life (*spiritualis essentia, vita*) and in contrast there are essential attributes in God that, as specific differences or forms, distinguish God from other beings. For example, a genuine body can be predicated of God if 'body' means a true and solid substance.[49] To be sure, he includes eternity among God's essential attributes, but he means by it only being without beginning or end, that is, endless duration (*successio praesentiis et praeteriti et futuri*) but not elevation above time.

It has already been pointed out how he protests especially against the view that for divine eternity all three dimensions of time are simultaneous and are gathered together in the eternal now. On such assumptions, he believes, everything must be eternal like God, for if God continuously coexists with everything, then everything must coexist with God. Therefore, the eternity of God is not simultaneously present in its entire extension. Absolute infinity is not applicable to it. Rather we should remain close to Scripture, which ascribes to God all the dimensions of time (Acts 1:4; Psalm 102:28; Dan. 7:13).[50] If here Vorstius treats time not as a mediate

47. Vorstius, op. cit., 65, 212, 307.
48. Ibid. 209f.; 247. Consequently accidents can be predicated of God.
49. Ibid. 201, 209.
50. Ibid. 221–229.

or immediate product of God, but only reckons it to be God's eternal existence-form, he extends this finitizing even further, since he believes *nihil potest actu infinitum esse in tota natura, ergo nec Deus* (nothing is able to be infinitely actual in all of nature. And so God cannot be infinitely actual). If God were infinite in action (*actu infinitus*) and not finite in himself (*in sese finitus*), he would be without limit, an *aoriston*, an *indefinitum*, nothing determinate. So God's *infinitudo* requires some sort of restriction (*piam quandam restrictionem*). Otherwise there could be no beholding of God.

If God were not delimited, the saints could not conceive God, or else the spirits that behold God would have to be infinite themselves. To be sure, God is infinite with respect to duration, but not immeasurable with respect to his essence. God is great, high, sublime. But Scripture never calls God utterly infinite or simply immense. Therefore we have to say that finitude belongs to God, because God is definable according to his proper nature.[51] According to Scripture, God has genuine magnitude, quality, and he has his palace in heaven, an actual place for his dwelling. Moreover, on earth God is not wholly present everywhere, although God is everywhere active and effective, for he can work through proximate causes, natural or supernatural, like a king works through his servants. Vorstius means that if God were entirely and substantially in things (*totus substantialiter in re qualibet*), he would have to be outside of himself, just as the soul would be outside of itself if it were both in the head as well as in the feet, since head and feet are outside of each other and exclusive. It would also be unworthy of God to conceive him as actual in all places. But the main point is—so Vorstius fears—that the being of things would be excluded by the immeasurability of God if the latter filled all space. Thus Vorstius asserts that place and local presence, as well as a limited sense of quantity, are to be ascribed to God.[52]

Since Vorstius is concerned for human freedom, he demands that God's will or decree not be identified with God's nature. He also rejects the basic proposition of the older dogmatics that God's knowing is identical with God's nature.[53] Thus there can be succession in God's knowledge, a kind of discursive thinking, such that he sees one [thing] after the other.[54] The act of knowing through which God beholds particular things outside of

51. Ibid. 235–238.
52. Ibid. 229–242. The christological significance of this is obvious.
53. Ibid. 269ff.
54. Ibid. 311.

God in their presence, determinacy, and particularity does not belong to God's nature (*Wesen*), that is, is not included in God's necessary self-knowledge. It is an act of divine spirit that, without the mediation of a free act of will, could have no place in God.[55] That God's wisdom comprehends everything simultaneously and foreknows all particulars from eternity through the absolute knowing does not require absolute perfection. God's knowledge in general is certain, but in the beholding of what is present or already past, there are more factors at work than in the beholding of future contingents. Relatively speaking, the latter are uncertain even for God; therefore expectation, hope as well as desire, wishes and concern, also have a place in God. The testing of man would be hypocritical if God already knew the outcome in advance. "In his own way God feared, for example, he justly suspected and wisely conjectured that this or that evil will arise." (*Deus suo modo aliquando metuit, hoc est merito suspicatur et prudenter conjicit hoc vel illud malum oriturum.*)[56] If God had foreknown with absolute certainty that human beings would sin, God would not have had the temerity to create them, for if he had created them with such certainty, God would ultimately be the author of evil.

These extreme assertions—that render God inwardly finite, that portray space and time as primal eternal powers to which even God's life is bound up and subject—are to be sure, comprehensible only as reactions against the pressure of the doctrine of the absolute decrees. Nevertheless they signal significant changes in the doctrine of God, particularly if the *decretum absolutum* is rejected. On the other hand, we can trace in Vorstius the need to have in God something determinate and real, so that it would be possible to enter into a relation with God, such as required by the ethical interest. Vorstius does not want to vaporize the world or its worth, or to allow the concept of God to become a matter of indifference or without genuine significance. He wants to tear apart the old metaphysical skins (to use an expression of Julius Müller) that admit no real distinctions in God, that simply identify God's knowledge with his nature, and that imply that God recognizes the world only through his self-knowledge, no less than those that identify God's decrees and acts of will with his nature. But what this element in God is, that must be distinguished from God's knowing and will, Vorstius does not elaborate.[57]

55. Ibid. 270ff.

56. Ibid. 441; 451.

57. Ibid. p. 340ff. He propounds three levels of divine attributes: 1) those that designate

However, one can readily see that he wants something unchangeable in God next to something changeable. By means of this mutable element, God and world can both stand in correlative and reciprocal relations to each other. But he did not preserve absoluteness for God's being, and, like Duns Scotus, he allows the unchangeable and changeable elements in God to fall apart like two worlds that have no essential or internal connection. For example, he does not grasp God determinately as ethical in his very being. Law and righteousness in reference to the world are not supposed to have any direct reference to God's essence, but depend only on God's free will, which seeks whatever is best.[58]

Arminianism, although it concedes absoluteness to God as Father, nevertheless assumes a variability as well as succession of moments in God with reference to his legislative and vindicative justice.[59] God's omnipresence is for Arminianism only work at a distance; the Arminians, on account of their zeal for the greatest possible human freedom, believe that God's causality must be limited. But its view of the mutability of the divine will does not prevent Arminianism, whenever the well being of humanity requires it, from sometimes allowing divine interventions in the natural course of things through revelation and miracles. Thus God's life is, considered normally, purely supra-historical. In those points where it becomes historical, it appears in the relation of "assistance" to mundane powers, a characteristic expression that clearly signifies a finitizing restriction of God by the creature and its causality. For instead of being mindful of the fact that the creation owes its being and life in every moment to God, Arminian language suggests that God merely comes to the aid of the

God's pure essence without inner or outer energy, and that belong only to the categories of substance and quantity. He reckons among these simplicity, eternity, immensity, but in the sense explained above. 2) The attributes of action, which are principles of operation: *potentia, scientia, voluntas, potestas*. 3) Attributes that express the effects and qualities of God, or his actions and his works: Goodness, piety, justice, truth. The works are contingent. But nevertheless the attributes referring to these works always necessarily inhere in these actions or works. Although he does not reckon the ethical predicates as belonging to the essence of God, he also freely contradicts himself on this point (see p. 342ff.).

58. Ibid. 386, 387.

59. Cf. *Episcop. Amst*. 1650, T. I., 287, 294, 321–330. Following the principle that the first rule of divine action is to seek the best for creation distinguishes Arminianism from Duns Scotus. The world is regarded as a worthwhile good, as the end for which God applies his power, while Scotus still denies that God made the good for sake of the world. Here is some progress. For until both members of a contrast become independent, there can be no talk about the knowledge of their true relation. But the Arminians conceive the good more politically or eudaimonistically than ethically. God makes the well-being of humans his highest norm. This is a good that does not result in the best and, instead of issuing in a community of love, ends in the cultivation of egoism and fails to overcome dualism.

creation. The latter has its own causality independently of God's continuous causality, but its causality is not fully sufficient.[60]

The foregoing account sought to capture the essentials of the supernaturalist mode of thought that prevailed into the nineteenth century. We now pass on to b) the second form of Deism. In order to advance to the rationalism of a Wolffian or Kantian sort, we do not require another or lower concept of God, but rather only a superior conception of the unity, perfection, and self-sufficiency of the world, according to which it requires no assistance. But since this world casts a reference upon its artistic creator, one can, so to speak, say that rationalism places greater emphasis on God as creator than it does on God as preserver and ruler of the world. For rationalism allows the freedom of God to exhaust itself in the act of creation itself, and then allows it to withdraw to an illusory sublimity above the world, into an alien status over and against the world. This concept of divine freedom is not only not ethical, but stands far below the older acosmic conceptions of God's sublimity. For now God is restricted by his own work; God is prevented from acting by his own prior action in creation.

This tendency, originally serving the interest of human freedom and ethical independence, must necessarily turn into its opposite. On the one hand, there is an endless threat to the goodness and unity of the world by the power of human freedom. For, without any restrictions, freedom can set loose chaotic powers and is capable of botching up the world beyond any hope of salvation; it can create situations from which superficial rationalistic optimism offers no way out. Moreover, the presumption of the constant unity and goodness of the world can result in ethical indifference. For only if one abstracts from the ethical powers of the world is it possible to think that without God the world remains eternally by itself the same work of art as it was when originally posited by God's act. However, in that case, all that remains is the mechanism of natural connections, and freedom no longer has any essential place in such a world.[61]

60. The Socinians speak more than did Vorstius about the infinity of the divine *essentia, scientia, potentia*. Cf. Fock, *Der Socinianismus*, Kiel, 1847, Bd. II S. 426ff.; 453ff. "In Socinian determinations of divine attributes there is an undeniable tendency to render God finite. God appears as a finite being posited alongside of the world of finite entities. This finitizing occurs essentially in the interest of creation, particularly in the interest of the independence, spontaneity and ethical life of human beings."

61. This progress from deistic rationalism to a completely mechanical conception of the world is exemplified in Röhr's *Briefen über den Rationalismus* 1813 (61, 73ff.). Röhr is not conscious of the danger his Deism poses for ethical freedom.

God was free, but is free no longer. This mode of thought, if it does not refer to the origin of the world, becomes indifferent to God's existence, and thus only natural necessity remains for it. Naturalism is the consistent result of Deism. Supernaturalism, no matter how wooden it usually conceives God's relation to the world to be, sees neither the exclusive nor the highest act of God in creation. It leaves the path of history open for human beings, and history is more than cyclical patterns of natural processes. Supernaturalism refuses to have God's freedom fettered by its first exercise, but for the sake of religious and ethical interests it holds on to a progressive relation of God to the world. To be sure, this relation is conceived only as one of external assistance or idle examination. Even in momentary revelations and miracles, the relation of God to human beings remains external. Likewise in the work of conversion where everything is reduced to stimulation by doctrine and word, there is no reflection on the community of the Holy Spirit and its inner testimony.[62]

The preceding century generally carries a Deist stamp, as older times with a few exceptions that anticipated Deism, were acosmic. As far as religion is concerned, Deism remains remote, since it grants to the world an independent being and value. As soon as this worth is brought into relation with the ethical Idea, there also appears—insofar as the religious interest finds concurrent expression—a need to assume a reciprocal relation between God and world, instead of the pure eternal self-sameness of God and the simple unalterability of his will. This is necessary even if the reciprocal relation is still conceived as an external relation. Supernaturalism agrees with Deism in allowing God's action to be conditioned by the world. But it does not, as was maintained nearly universally by the older doctrines, want to identify God's action and decree with his unchangeable essence. In stricter Deism the conditioning of God by world occurs once for all *after* the creation. Deism finds the conditioning of the world by God exclusively in the post-creation situation.

In contrast, supernaturalism conceives God's conditioning not as perennially occurring, but as always possible and manifest from time to time. In the older (seventeenth century) doctrine of God the chief emphasis fell on the sublimity and majesty of God, his limitless power and freedom, his total qualitative difference from the world, while God's transcendence and the accompanying acosmism were the unintended by-products. Now, however, the accent falls on the world, which, no less than God, has its own

62. Cf. *Jahrbücher für deutsche Theologie* 1857 I, where Dr. Klaiber sketches more explicitly this aspect of supernaturalism.

being and on the truth of the world's causal connections. In the concept of God the currently emphasized characteristic is a restrictive determination whereby the world is a realm of unhindered free play [*Spielraum*]. In short, the current conception of the transcendence of God no longer emphasizes his sublime elevation above the world. Although language about God as the highest being is retained, this conceptuality no longer conceives the former sublimity. It is rather gladly handed down as a simple mystery, but in such a way that the world that has its end in itself is not disturbed by God. God, although knowing the end (telos) of the world, is alien to it. In contradiction to God's sublimity, such theology does not hesitate to conceive of God as anthropomorphically restricted and only quantitatively different in wisdom and power. The world of free beings is regarded as having an equal standing over and against God.[63] On such premises the validity and absoluteness of the idea of God are watered down. Ethical independence increases at the expense of religion, but with the undermining of the living God, the highest and absolute ethical end is also lost. In the previous century suggestions of a superior doctrine of God are to be found only in Oetinger.

An anti-deistic period in the development of the concept of God begins with Schelling, Hegel, and Schleiermacher. If the doctrine of God had received merely traditional treatment for centuries, or, as in the preceding (eighteenth) century was neglected in comparison with subjectivity, now theological reflection turned to it in the most strenuous labor. The new theological sciences are united in seeking to replace the wooden concept of God and its dualism with a vital inner unity—whether out of philosophical interest, or, as in the case of Schleiermacher, primarily out of religious interest. The chief difference between these three figures as it concerns our present inquiry is that Schelling[64] and Hegel conceive the process of

63. Schleiermacher is right to point out that supernaturalism appears to represent God as a finite free cause. Thus Morus, Mosheim, Reinhard [cf. Schleiermacher, *Glaubenslehre* (ET *The Christian Faith*, tr. H. R. Macintosh et al, Philadelphia: Fortress Press, 1978) §47]. Eternity is for Mosheim and Reinhard only endless duration, no longer elevation above time. Mosheim determines the immensity of God in reference to space. Reinhard ascribes foreknowledge and reminiscence to God in such a way that there is no underlying absoluteness of divine knowledge. Omniscience is designated merely as *cognitio longe perfectissima*. This superlative in place of an absolute unconditional positive is a general characteristic of this doctrine of God.

64. I have abstracted from the more recent form of his system. His investigations in the *Philosophie der Mythologie* 1857, Vorles. 1–3, demonstrate critically the untenability of the classical concept, dominant in theology, of God's unity, simplicity, and uniqueness, that in

the world and the process of the absolute as living and do not essentially get beyond an identification of the divine life with the life of the universe, while Schleiermacher conceives God in eternal perfection while carefully excluding process from God. On the other hand, Schleiermacher seeks to establish the most inward ontological and vital relation of God to the world.

It must be conceded that a God whose distinction from the world is developed no further than it is by Schelling, particularly in his earlier period, or by Hegel, cannot satisfy religion and ethics. These figures are to be viewed as confusing God and world and on a monistic basis. In contrast we must dwell upon Schleiermacher, who develops his doctrine of God with special reference to Augustine, Dionysius the Areopagite, Anselm, and Quenstedt. It seems to be scarcely recognized that he has translated their doctrine of God into the language of our time. The general contemporary reaction against his concept of God shows how opposed we are to the traditional doctrine. Moreover, it is urgent and necessary to continue the work of the Reformation by reconstructing the doctrine of God. The inevitable negative implications [of the traditional doctrine] for the knowledge of God, the personality of God, as well as human freedom, must all contribute to this reconstructive task. Schleiermacher delineates these implications from principles that we have found dominant in the tradition. Therefore we will conclude this historical-critical survey with Schleiermacher.

The force and vitality with which religion lived in Schleiermacher are evident from the original appearance of his *Reden über die Religion* and still more in his *Christian Glaubenslehre*.[65] The latter work arises from his keen conception of forming a dogmatics out of a phenomenological description of Christian religious consciousness. Since, as Schleiermacher often observed, the religious consciousness loves to portray God anthropomorphically, it is all the more remarkable to note the sharp-sighted

---

a variety of ways and respects, excludes internal difference and complexity from God. Concerning Schelling's own positive doctrine, cf. my treatise on *Schelling's Potenzlehre*. [The latter essay follows the Immutability Essay in Dorner's *Gesammelte Schriften aus dem Gebiet der systematischen Theologie, Exegese und Geschichte* (Berlin, 1883). Dorner added this note in the *Gesammelte Schriften*. It reveals that his main source for Schelling's thought at the time he wrote the Immutability Essay was Schelling's *Philosophie der Mythologie*, published in 1857. The third part of Dorner's Immutability Essay appeared in the *Jahrbücher für deutsche Theologie* in 1858.—TRANS.]

65. English translations *On Religion: Speeches to Its Cultured Despisers* (1799), tr. R. Crouter (Cambridge: Cambridge University Press, 1988); *The Christian Faith* 1821, 1830; the translation is of the 1830 edition (Philadelphia: Fortress Press, 1978).—TRANS.

scientific operation with which he seeks to safeguard against the anthropopathic and anthropomorphic representations of God that contribute impurities to religious consciousness as a result of pagan or pantheistic influences.

In the introduction of *The Christian Faith*,[66] he sets forth: the consciousness of absolute dependence can be directed at no particular form (*Gestalt*) in space and time. For everything that appears in the world as a particular is partly active, influencing others, and partly passive, determined by an other. A feeling of dependence that refers to a particular entity in the world can never be absolute or religious, because such dependence is limited by a feeling of partial freedom that is opposed to it. It remains the privilege of piety alone to comprehend the contrast between partial freedom and partial dependence in one and the same absolute dependence, and thereby to overcome their opposition. According to fetishism, God is a finite particular, be it ever so high, next to which other particulars may stand, and thus are placed on the same level. Thus fetishism inevitably confuses God with world.[67] Schleiermacher regards God neither as a simple mundane unity nor mundane power, but rather as a unity in contrast to the world, as that omnipotent, absolute spiritual causality on which everything depends. Although Schleiermacher conceives God as the self-conceiving concept that is eternally and absolutely transparent to itself, he shies away from calling God personal.[68] That on which the world utterly depends cannot itself be or become part of the world; it remains unique by itself. Therefore it is elevated above everything else as that through which the world is limited and finite.

According to the first part of *The Christian Faith*, the world exists by being posited, but it is posited only as something different from God. The more concrete characteristics of its finitude are its divided existence, its plurality, and its divisions. To be sure, the world is a unity, since everything

66. Dorner, like many others, interprets Schleiermacher's doctrine of God out of the introduction and Part One of *The Christian Faith*. This method of interpretation is questionable in view of Schleiermacher's qualifications that these passages do not amount to a doctrine of God, but merely a formal scheme of transcendence. For a critique of this reading of Schleiermacher, see Robert R. Williams, *Schleiermacher the Theologian: The Construction of the Doctrine of God* (Fortress Press, 1978), and Williams, "I. A. Dorner: The Ethical Immutability of God," JAAR LIV/4, Winter 1986. 721–738.—TRANS.

67. The kinship between Deism and pagan polytheism is evident. The preceding analysis confirms Schleiermacher's position.

68. Cf. his *Dialektik* §149–154, 86f.; cf. especially §216, 156ff., and 322. See also his *Philosophische Ethik*, hrsg. von Schweizer, 16, §29 Anmerkung. [Dorner apparently refers to the Jonas edition of Schleiermacher's *Dialektik*. Berlin: G. Reimer, 1833. Trans.]

in it is conditioned by everything else. However, the world is not a simple unity, but rather a unity full of contrasts and oppositions. In contrast, God is the unity that excludes all contrasts, for to God everything is equally related and in the same sense, namely, as absolutely dependent upon his single creative causality.

The plurality of divided being is structured by spatial juxtaposition. To this limitation a second limit of finitude is inferred, namely time, because the many stand in a reciprocal relation of passivity and activity. If therefore we do not want to conceive God in mundane terms, and thereby reduce God to a mundane entity—even if the highest and most powerful—God must be conceived as utterly beyond space and time. So conceived, God obtains his simple self-sameness and self-identity.

The divine attributes are treated according to these principles. The canon of the necessary divine simplicity, or the oppositionlessness of God, as well as his elevation above receptivity or passivity, above space and time, are laid down as the criterion of dogmatic assertions about God, with the following results.

From utter simplicity it follows that in God there is no multiplicity or plurality of attributes, capacities, or powers. There is no real distinction between these in God.[69] Consequently the division of attributes has no speculative significance as a real distinction or objective truth in God, but has only a subjective significance, whose incorrectness we can become aware of, but without any positive recognition of a higher truth and without having any other basis than religious feeling.[70]

In particular, Schleiermacher denies the distinction between the natural or metaphysical attributes, and the ethical attributes. Both must be identical in God; namely, the ethical must also belong to God's nature. He further denies the distinction between quiescent and active attributes, for in a living God everything is activity. The same must hold true for divine capacities or powers. There can be no distinction between God's will and God's knowledge. The following consideration is offered: If there were in God

69. If there were a plurality of divine attributes, each of them must express something in God not expressed by the others. And if the knowledge of an object is appropriate to the object, the latter must, if the knowledge is composite (i.e., a synthesis), also be composite. He says that even the feeling of utter dependence could not be self-identical if there were something different [other] posited in God. For there would then be differences that would not have their basis in the different moments of life, through which they come to expression in religious consciousness.

70. This is the fundamental idea that Schleiermacher's *Dialektik* seeks to establish, particularly in reference to concepts and judgments, the most general form of our thinking.

a knowledge that were not given to him by his own will, we must assume something given to God not posited by his knowledge, and this would imply passivity or receptivity in God. Consequently, God's knowledge is nothing but his omnipotence spiritually conceived, and God's omnipotence is nothing but his almighty spirituality.

For Schleiermacher there is not supposed to be any distinction in God between will and ability. Not simply because such a distinction refers to the distinction between quiescent and active attributes, such that the allegedly quiescent attributes sooner or later can become active, but especially because what is actually possible, that is, is good, is actualized by the will of God, and nothing is held back.[71] But if, in order to distinguish between the will and ability of God, one says that at least in reference to the good of the world, that the good, though not yet actual, will become actual in its appropriate time and place, Schleiermacher protests that what is supposed to be actual, God does not first will at some specific moment, but in an eternal way, just as his ability is likewise eternal. Otherwise we would have a duality in God, namely, a pure inner quiescent life, and an active life directed towards the world, and both of these would be separated from each other.

We cannot even conceive God's willing of himself in separation from God's willing of the world. For if God wills himself, he wills himself as creator and preserver, such that in his self-willing the willing of the world is already included. In willing the world, God also wills his eternal omnipresent omnipotence. God's self-willing, with which the world is also posited, is nothing but God's being itself posited under the form of will. For were it self-preservation, this could not be conceived as an actual will, unless there were something restricting God that must be disposed of. Were it self-approval, this necessarily presupposes a divided consciousness that violates Schleiermacher's criterion of divine simplicity and self-sameness, just as the former violates his elevation above passivity. If therefore God's self-willing and his willing of the world are indivisibly one, the distinction between attributes that are purely inner and attributes that are predicated of God's relation to the world becomes untenable.

It is not merely a question of *not* assuming different relations of God to the world, for then God must be conceived like finite life that subsists in a multiplicity of functions. Since these exist as different and in relative opposition and partially exclude each other, God would be placed in the

71. That is, God does all that God can. God's power is exhausted in the world.—TRANS.

sphere of opposition. According to Schleiermacher, God is the eternal living spiritual cause of the world, but he relates himself eternally to the world in the same fashion. He eternally wills in the world the same things that are included within his self-willing. There is in God no distinction of the almighty presence in so-called "dead forces" or in "free forces." The difference resides not in God, but in the divinely ordained receptivity for the self-identical omnipresence of God. Considered in itself, God's presence is not greater or lesser in different places, for otherwise spatial contrasts would be carried over into God, and his essence would be differently determined in reference to space. God's eternity is to be conceived only as the eternal, everywhere and always the same, self-identical causality.

To be sure, it does not follow that no beginning of the world is conceivable, for God does not need to *begin* willing the world. He could always have willed that the world begin at his appointed time, in the same way that what presently originates in the world has been willed and effected from eternity, that is, in a timeless way. On the other hand, if one assumes that God has eternally willed the world, but has not eternally effected it, then the contrasts of time, as well as the distinction between active and passive, would be carried over to God. And the nonproducing of what has nevertheless been willed would be conceivable only if there had been a hindrance for God to overcome. But this assumes a passivity in God that implies there is something independent of God. Finally, there would be a change in God's omnipresence. First he would at first abide only in himself, but afterwards he would come to be omnipresent omnipotence in the world.

If we sum it all up, Schleiermacher conceives God to be simple self-sameness and self-identical, without opposition. In this simplicity no real distinction between attributes, no distinction between knowledge and will, nor between will and ability are supposed to remain. There is nothing potential in God that does not become eternally actual. Consequently, there cannot be a plurality of different divine decrees or functions and actions, whether or not one wants to construct divine attributes. There cannot first be something, then something other—be it thought, will, or creative causality. God rather comprehends everything eternally and indivisibly with one and the same immutable thought. And this thought is not a moment without the will, or a will without efficaciousness. Consequently, with the being of the world everything is already posited; for example, the world exhausts the actual. To be sure, one may be determined by the other as a causality that becomes actual at a later time. But God adds nothing new to the actualization of the origin. On God's side everything is willed and effected in an eternal manner. Differences in appearance are due solely to the fact that their conditions are not yet present in the vital causal nexus of the world.

If one emphasizes the point that all that originates in a timeless way is not merely thought and willed, but effected, that is, has become actual—as one must if there is no distinction between God's will and ability—then there remains nothing else but to regard temporal succession as merely an illusion. This agrees with Schleiermacher's point that God strives after nothing that he does not already possess, because this would again introduce distinctions into God, if not God's blessedness. But this is equivalent to acosmism and represents a flight to an ideal world apart from this world of temporal distinctions, to an intelligible world standing before God as eternally present, not merely as idea or concept, but as an effected reality. And in order to avoid a Platonic duplication of the actual world, one would have to say that the empirical world is not other than the ideal, but rather is the ideal world existing in successive temporal appearances. But this implies that what we call actuality is reduced to mere appearance. The world no longer consists of a serious, important history of becoming and creation, an actualization of the ideal enriched by opposition and struggle, but is merely a dogmatic repetition and rehearsal of something already eternally accomplished. God's causality would have nothing more to do than preserve this eternal self-sameness for God and from God's point of view, while the successive appearance of what in the ideal world eternally coexists must be traced to the causality of the living natural nexus and its changing receptivity for the ideal.

This world of appearances, like that eternal ideal world, must have its basis and law in God. Schleiermacher, although strictly positing God's transcendence of space and time, nevertheless conceives God as conditioning everything spatial and temporal, as well as space and time themselves. Although the world in its divisions and plurality of contrasts has a unity that is eternally complete and prior to it, it remains true that the contrasts, no less than their connection and unity, must have their basis in God. If nothing can be thought or willed in isolation from God, everything is what it is in distinction from everything else, by virtue of being thought or willed by God. It would then be the case that all real distinctions in the world—these are not to be confused with contradictions and do not disturb its unity—would have no basis in God and so would be merely illusions. Schleiermacher's doctrine is in this respect unsatisfactory. It offers no basis for thinking of God as the cause of what is empirically and historically actual, and thereby fails to secure the actual from the suspicion of being a mere illusion for religious consciousness.

Further, Schleiermacher deprives us of the possibility of conceiving God as the cause of plurality by his claim that God is utterly beyond all contrasts. To be sure, Schleiermacher takes his standpoint in the actual world, not in the idea of God in and for itself;[72] he asserts thereby a "world-wisdom" but no knowledge of God. Thus he appears capable of withdrawing to the position that we must assume an absolute causality that is 'equal in scope' to the natural order but 'opposite in kind' and so fundamentally different from all mundane causality. But this does not justify conceiving the divine causality in such a way that the origination of contrasts out of it becomes impossible. However, such would be the case if real distinctions have no place or basis in God's thinking or willing.

We are instinctively repelled by such a concept of God, just as we are repelled by the old Sabellianism that traced the mundane differences in God's eternally self-identical thinking, willing, and action back to differences in the matter on which God operated. The activity of God reflected differences in his inner history (for this must have matter). Such a result is suggested by Schleiermacher's attempt to ground the appearance of difference in God's omnipresence on differences in receptivity to God. But this can scarcely suffice if these different measures of receptivity must in turn have their basis in God as well as the natural *nexus*. In this way the contrast between matter and form would exist for God. But Schleiermacher is concerned to keep God away from this as well as other contrasts; he is concerned not simply to keep such contrasts away from God's being which no independent matter may restrict or limit, but also to keep such contrasts away from his thinking, willing, and efficaciousness.

More precisely, it is insufficient for Schleiermacher to persist in conceiving God only as a unity that excludes all opposition. For if the world also allows of being conceived as a unity, whose contrasts are for God eternally overcome (acosmism), it is clear that for Schleiermacher God is not the unity of the world. There must be a contrast for God, since the principle and the effect of the principle are not the same. Moreover contrast remains even for the absolute standpoint: God *and* world. It can always

72. Cf. Sigwart, Schleiermachers Erkenntnistheorie, *Jahrb*. II. 268ff.

be said that God, in willing himself, wills himself as creator and so wills the creation. Consequently God's self-willing must include the willing of something other than God, namely, the world. This brings us back to a contrast in divine willing and thinking that is constitutive of the divine nature itself and that must be compatible with God's primordial unity. How this is possible Schleiermacher does not say.

It should be noted that this fundamental contrast between God and world arises out of the truth of the feeling of utter dependence. Without it religion in its characteristic essence would be a mere illusion—something that no student of Schleiermacher would expect as the hidden meaning of his position. For in the religious self-consciousness, the world as a unity stands in contrast to God as the absolute unity, and the feeling of absolute dependence on God is no illusion. Thus the world is for God, something that God is not, namely absolutely dependent, while God remains free. Consequently there is assuredly for eternal omnipotence a contrast between causality and its effect, absolute freedom and absolute dependence. For Schleiermacher the world is no absolute freedom or causality, and God is not the effect of his own causality. Even if one may suspect the latter to be the meaning lurking behind some of Schleiermacher's assertions, unless everything is to be transformed into mere illusion, it is necessary to assume that the distinction between God as cause and God as effect has some reality and validity. Without this contrast, God would no longer be living, but rather conceived in Eleatic terms and so at the farthest remove from the interests of piety.

It is no secret that Schleiermacher's meaning is that God would find only himself in the world and so would be the effect of his own causality. But this has the effect of drawing God into process, time, and space, as well as into motivations, and so draws God into a state of potentiality. This outcome is obviously objectionable. It would be a vain endeavor to seek to carry over his thought to Schelling or Hegel in respect to the concept of God.

The impossibility of Schleiermacher's assertions concerning the absence of distinctions and contrasts in God becomes even more evident if we look at the question of history. For he wants to regard the world—whose center is for him the revelation in Christ—conceived by the divine wisdom as an absolutely harmonious work of art. The wisdom of God is nothing but the highest being in this absolutely simple original and complete self-presentation and self-communication, from which all composition and division, as well as means and end, are supposed to be excluded, since for God every part is the whole (*Gl.* §168). The world is willed by God as a unity; it is willed with a perfect and uniform communication of God or as permeated by God, such that even the nonrational factors are supposed to be brought into living connection with personality, wherein the divine self-communication has its seat. Thus the constitution of persons by the Spirit of God is accomplished through the ethical work of humanity. But with this he also recognizes that the world is not already good, but is developing readiness and receptivity for the good.[73] This suggests a real distinction between the divine decree and its effect, that is, a real distinction, if not between thinking and willing, then between will and its effect. Moreover this shows that God already wills the future and that the future is already woven into the present. This distinction between present and future will cease only when God has become all in all.

There is still more. In opposition to Pelagianism, Schleiermacher insists that the new higher life is not a mere development or unfolding of the old. For the latter a general divine communication would suffice, and without this not even sin could exist. In contrast to Pelagianism, Schleiermacher says that we call the power of the God-consciousness in us grace, "because we are conscious [of grace] not as our own act, but ascribe it to a special divine communication" (*Gl.*§80). "We would go astray into Pelagianism, if all distinctions in the divine causality were abolished, and the divine causality were supposed to be self-identical in both the efficacy of the flesh and the power of the God-consciousness" (ibid.). He continues by observing that if there were in the divine causality no basis for this difference that distinguishes grace from its opposite condition, the related contrast between the original incapacity for God-consciousness and the specially communicated facility for God-consciousness would likewise cease. What is the same in both cases would be merely the human self-activity, or its works. (This implies that the difference between sin and grace would be found only on the side of human beings, in their differing receptivities for the self-identical eternal act of God, while all humans are both in need of redemption and are capable of redemption.) Thus the consciousness of the inability of God-consciousness constitutive of our experience would, on Pelagian assumptions, become a disappearing moment.

73. After he says that the connection of the nonrational with *Geist* is not yet completely actual, he continues that when through us the world is ready for us, this will clearly show that everything is only insofar as it can be the object of divine love (and through the latter is capable of being posited by divine wisdom).

On such premises the concept of redemption has a most insecure position, and the specific difference between the redeemer and the redeemed would be weakened. Consequently, according to Schleiermacher, it is necessary to assume a special act of divine love (*Gl.*§167.2). This act of revelation in Christ is the completion of creation, because God wills it eternally and creates everything in Christ. Christ, or more precisely, the relation to him and the need for him, has been planted in humanity in a timeless way. But he has not always been there as the effect of a general divine will; the relation of everything to Christ does not require such a universal will. Moreover, if no special divine act, but merely the development of humanity were all that was necessary, then humanity would have redeemed itself.

So, we find that when Schleiermacher allows the Christian consciousness to express itself freely, he himself comes back to a distinction in the divine causality, without which there could be no distinction between the redeemer and the redeemed. It is not sufficient to transfer the basis of this distinction to the side of the world. That would be a most precarious situation. Although the divine causality is, in reference to the sphere of pure omnipotence, supposed to allow nothing specific of God's being to be known from its effects—since the effect, despite its reference to the divine causality, cannot be compared with the divine cause—this entire position is reversed when Schleiermacher speaks of the realm of grace. For here we have not merely an act that allows no secure inference to the essence of its author, rather we have an "action of God" motivated by love. Here God is known to be self-communicating, and so he does not remain concealed behind his effects as though behind a curtain, rather God manifests himself in his action. The redeemed person speaks truthfully by virtue of this experienced self-communication of God, that God is love (*Gl.* §167). Consequently it would be easy to show that such a claim assumes an actual knowledge of God on the part of Christian faith; indeed such is not merely possible, but a given. Consequently Christian faith neither must, nor may, remain content with assertions such as divine simplicity or quiescence, or, what leads to the same result, assertions of an eternal and uniform vital causality that always and everywhere produces the same effects.[74]

74. Therefore it seems to me that Dr. Sigwart's exposition of this point of Schleiermacher's position (*Jahrbüch für deutsche Theologie* 1857, p. 323ff.) requires qualification. Schleier-

macher's account of the divine causality can no more be reduced to simple identity than can his account of absolute dependence on God be transformed into a partial dependence on a mundane being, or reduced to our subjective self-consciousness as the oppositionless unity of being and thought. Such assumptions amount to a transformation of utter dependence into a consciousness of absolute freedom. This contradicts Schleiermacher's express declarations against such a concept. I do not deny that if one wants to make Schleiermacher's doctrine of God coherent, it is possible to arrive at a conception like Sigwart's. But if one accepts Schleiermacher's doctrine of God as it lies before us, without the unjustified assumption that part of it has for him merely subjective significance . . . it must be concluded that Schleiermacher failed to achieve a reconciliation between the philosophical and the religious interests. Further, since for Schleiermacher Christianity is not merely a knowing or a doctrine, but above all a matter of life, a life resting upon God's love in Christ, there is no justification for reducing his assertions about God in his *Glaubenslehre* to the level of the merely formal assertions set forth in his *Dialektik*.

## ARTICLE THREE

# The Reconstruction of the Immutability Doctrine

The dogmatic attempt to establish the concept of the immutability of God correctly, and in such a way that it is kept in harmony with the whole system of Christian faith, may be most surely accomplished if we investigate *first*: (A) at what points, in the interest of vitality [*Lebendigkeit*] in the concept of God, a change in the doctrine of the old ecclesiastical dogmatics is required by scientific thought [*Wissenschaft*] and religion; but also recognize (B) that any concept of God's vitality through which his immutability was dissolved would be a false one. It is to be hoped that the foundation will thus be laid for, *second*, exhibiting in a positive dogmatic way the necessary and true union of the immutability and vitality of God in a higher principle, which will contain at the same time the supreme norm for correctly determining the relation of the trans-historical life of God to his historical life, of God's transcendence to his immanence in the world. *Third* and finally, the conclusion should attempt to throw light on the importance and fruitfulness of the result through its application to individual major points of Christian doctrine.

## I

A. If one excludes the brief period in which the pantheistic mode of thought, identifying the life-process of God with the world, prevailed in scientific thought—to the aftereffects of which, to be sure, we are still subjected—

the doctrine of God of ecclesiastical dogmatics has quite predominantly cultivated the concept of God's immutability. Indeed, this concept and those closely connected with it have dominated almost the whole doctrine of God in its narrower sense. In its essentials, this doctrine of God of the old dogmatics was renewed by Schleiermacher, but by virtue of the acuteness of his mind in drawing out the consequences the dangers dormant in it were also uncovered.

In view of the history of our doctrine, as this has been set forth in its chief stages in the second article, one cannot dispute that the ecclesiastical dogmatics, in the justifiable struggle to exclude everything ethnic from the doctrine of God, did too much of a good thing and was drawn on into most dubious doctrines, which can be equally little acceptable to the scientific and the religious interests. To be sure, at other dogmatic points there was already contained in the shape of the Reformation's concrete doctrines of salvation a better, yes, the true concept of God, but only implicitly or in a latent way, that is to say, without benefiting the doctrine of God itself. Alongside its doctrine of salvation, our old dogmatics left standing a doctrine of God which, built up from other principles, was taken over traditionally from the pre-Reformation church and remained essentially consonant with the Roman doctrine, as if the purification from non-Christian conceptions did not have to extend also to this doctrine, whereas in fact the medieval doctrine of God in large part clearly goes back to non-Christian sources. It was beyond the power of individual men, even of a century, to subject all at once the inherited doctrine of God, as well as the doctrine of salvation and the church, to a comprehensive reform. This could have occurred satisfactorily only out of that experience of God that the evangelical consciousness predicates in the so-called material principle of the Reformation, whose proper determination and explication even in only the very nearest and most necessary areas sufficiently took up the really reformatory powers. Meanwhile, until the inherited, heterogeneous doctrine of God cast off its non-Christian metaphysic and replaced it by a formulation more homogeneous with the remaining doctrinal corpus, the life of the church could be nourished on the elements of a better doctrine of God in the foundation of the evangelical confession, all the more so since the evangelical symbols themselves do not treat that doctrine of God consisting of elements of the old metaphysic which penetrated only too much the ecclesiastical dogmatics. But the fact that for long the system of evangelical dogmatics was thus mixed out of heterogeneous ingredients has not merely damaged its consistency, but has also been extremely consequential for the history of Protestantism.[1] On the one hand this provided continuing temptations to a relapse from the Protestant stage of Christian life and cognition to the legal-magical one of Roman Catholicism, which can be maintained theologically only by a medley of deistic and pantheistic concepts. On the other hand, as the attempt to give support to the evangelical doctrine of salvation in a catholicizing authority of ecclesiasticism was shipwrecked, those pre-Christian elements of the doctrine of God were liberated, to flood the entire evangelical doctrine of salvation. Whereby one sins, thereby is he punished. We shall dwell on this briefly.

As defects of the doctrine of God taken over from scholasticism, we have had earlier to specify the apparent contradiction that it exhibits a *deistic* and an *acosmic* strain, both of which are far better suited to the Roman than to the evangelical doctrine of salvation. With us, the deistic strain was effectively opposed at the beginning by the fullness of assurance of living faith. But as this languished, it at once became evident that the inherited doctrine of God of scholasticism became the ally and support for temptations to a relapse to the legalistic standpoint. To the essentially deistic doctrine, that God is eternally the same in his relation to the world, all change falling only on the side of the world, there was joined (far more naturally than by the early evangelical doctrine of salvation) the idea that God represents only the eternal law of salvation—a notion already influential in the Middle Ages. Here the actual dispensation and administration of salvation in its particulars was handed over to the world of intermediate causes, to the church. Thus the admittedly necessary mediation of salvation through word and sacrament, for example, through the church, was set in opposition to the immediate communion with God; at the expense of the latter there was once more posited a false vicarship for Christ, by which the immediacy of his communion with souls was excluded, a false and dividing mediatorship—be it posited through things and institutions or through priestly persons. Christ himself and his Spirit were removed for individuals to a deistic distance. On an essentially deistic basis, a catholicizing doctrine of the means of grace and of the spiritual office sought to erect itself, in order to provide a substitute for the presumed absence of Christ and to provide the support for the validity of evangelical truth.

The *acosmic* strain of this doctrine of God, in contrast, led some Protestants to absolute predestinarianism, and for others it brought the legitimate

1. Cf. Friedrich A. E. Ehrenfeuchter on "Theologische Principienlehre," *Jahrbücher für deutsche Theologie*, I (1856), 53.

element of idealism that is contained in the faith to such a dominance that Protestantism, instead of unfolding its principle on every side, in church and state, in art and science, and so fulfilling its great historical task, again chrysalized itself, almost abandoned the Christianizing and ethicizing of the world, and believed it could lull itself to sleep in self-contentedness if only the pure doctrine of faith were in vogue. Thus the religious interest (and even, increasingly, the dogmatic) was set in opposition to the ethical; and this error joined hands with the deistic strain (in its previous, older form). For the devaluation of the other spheres by the dogmatic had consequently, as in Roman Catholicism, to transform the church with its institutions and offices into a new hierarchy with a doctrinal regency and with a power of the keys possessed solely by it.

However, the danger of relapse into a catholicizing ecclesiasticism could be only transitory among us. The resistance of pietism and the revival by it of the Reformation salvation-faith removed this danger, yet without immediately bearing noteworthy fruit for the doctrine of God. On the contrary, by the powerful manifestation of pietism—because it was not successful in laying hold of the whole church and working itself out ecclesiastically, but on the other hand because the church also did not overcome it completely—the sluices were at the same time opened (contrary to Spener's intention) which till then had held together both the church and its theology in a unity that, to be sure, was more rigidly fixed than it was living and fruitful. And also since pietism, in its overwhelmingly practical direction, neglected to apply the revived Reformation principle to theology, the now liberated and irresistibly insistent elements, which gradually constituted the various forms of rationalism, encountered an unprepared church, one which at that point was no match for them. In its heterogeneous doctrine of God, the church indeed had the enemy in its own house. From it proceeded the neology[2] that was estranged from the evangelical doctrine of salvation and that repelled this salvation doctrine partly by virtue of the doctrine of God. Thus what was concealed in the kernel of the traditional doctrine of God, as it was taken over in the Middle Ages from the pre-Christian time, was to be laid bare, when the surrounding husks and trimmings of a supernatural sort were stripped from it. An essential service was thereby rendered to both the divided churches. To be sure, this was

2. The Neologen or "innovators," late eighteenth-century rationalists, included such thinkers as J. D. Michaelis, J. F. W. Jerusalem, J. A. Ernesti, J. J. Spaulding, and J. S. Semler.—TRANS.

not done in the sense that the subsequent development of philosophy (and of the theology dominated by it) had accomplished the task of working out a Christian doctrine of God, for neglect of which the church has had to pay so severely. On the contrary, at first it was only that the compromise concluded between the non-Christian elements of the received doctrine of God, between the ethnic and the Jewish, was recognized as untenable, and at first with the expulsion of the acosmic clement, there was an attempt to carry through a deistic mode of thought. Thereupon the never-resting power of truth pushed on to acosmism in Fichte. And then followed the pantheistic phase, which by making God and the world one and the same, sought to let the world partake of absolute worth and content, conferring on the God-idea the vitality that was lacking in both Deism and acosmism, till finally under Hegel's loyal disciples and apostate disciples the only remaining alternative presented itself: either evaporation of the world in idealistic illusion, in that only logic is the truth—thus acosmism—or evaporation of the God-idea into an illusion beside and behind the world, which alone is real, thus pancosmism, atheism, and renunciation of all ideal content in knowledge and life. However, if this development of recent philosophy has not directly yielded any doctrine of God which can satisfy scientific thought and religion, it has nonetheless achieved one thing: the uncovering of the untenability of the old doctrine of God, along with its essential detriments not only for the evangelical church but also for the catholic, and the imposing on the church of the unavoidable necessity for a reconstruction of the doctrine in a homogeneous way. If the history of recent philosophy has provided a great example of the fact that the Judaic and ethnic doctrine of God cannot find out of its own resources the reconciliation which it needs, then it will be up to the church to test whether there is not contained *in its resources, as these are comprehended in its doctrine of salvation*, the power of regeneration of the doctrine of God, insofar as this is needed for the present period. That will also correspond to the independence of theology.

But certainly to that end the received doctrine of dogmatics of the *immutability* of God will first and above all need numerous alterations, if God's vitality is to be able to be compatible with it. We shall see that Holy Scripture and the Christian consciousness require this. Just how do matters stand therein with the doctrine of the old dogmatics?

Speaking formally, it was only proper that the old dogmatics, for its conception of God's immutability, should return to the concept of his *simplicity*—to be sure, also referring conversely for the latter back again to the former, because without simplicity God would have to be posited as mutable. Hence the resulting propositions, that God is immutable because simple and simple because immutable, contain no grounds for the one or for the other; immutability is rather only the negative exposition of simplicity, that is, the constant identity of the divine essence in all relations and in all its perfections.

Let us begin then with *simplicity*, to which, ever since Augustine, one has returned for the proof that our various predications about God express no objective distinctions, that none of the divine attributes is anything different from the others, that God does not simply have but is all his attributes. For "that is simple, which is what it has." No distinction of substance and accident, of potentiality and actuality, of matter and form, of universal and particular, or of subordinate and superordinate, is to be posited in God. Thus there is also neither ethical nor physical movement and from this emanates the superiority over time and place. His knowing is therefore also willing, as his willing is knowing, for both are objectively one; they are both God's essence, which would become mutable through a separation of knowing and willing. "But change is a kind of dying." Thus also God's decree, as utterly unchangeable, is identical with his essence. The latter is itself not to be conceived as potentiality, but only as *Actus purissimus*; consequently God eternally, with one and the same pure act, wills and knows himself and the world of his decree.

Now certainly God is not composite; but it does not follow that all those distinctions have no place in God (as Quenstedt[3] in particular thinks). With its assertions of God's simplicity as objective absence of distinction, borrowed from Platonism and neoplatonism, the old dogmatics comes into contradiction with its own trinitarian assertions, especially when the generation of the Son and the procession of the Holy Spirit are conceived (with the orthodox early church) as perennial and not as complete by a once-for-all act. Just as little as it is to be said that God is composite—for whence should the material of this composition come then again from God and in God, just as he would have to be also the compositor—just so certainly is it to be said that while everything outside God is originally only posited, God is the eternally self-positing one. Even God's absolute being is not to be conceived other than as self-positing, as aseity, which as the eternal self-establishment of God yet contains a multiplicity of

3. Johann Andreas Quenstedt, 1617–1688.—TRANS.

moments, whose indissoluble unity (but not identity or mere self-sameness [*Einerleiheit*]) is the divine essence and life. The divine being could not be living, but could only be rigid dead substance or equally lifeless law, if it were motionless in itself, without real distinction of the positing and the posited life, or if there did not inhere in it an eternal going out from itself and an eternal return to itself as its moments of the one divine life. But a similar situation arises in connection with the higher categories of the concept of God. Were God only utterly simple, a unity without distinction and contrast, then he could not know or will himself. Without self-distinction in himself, there would be conceivable no reflection in himself, no transparency for himself and no blessedness. This can be made still clearer for God's ethical being. That is not to be done indeed, as is often attempted in the derivation of the Trinity, with the intent to derive from the—as it were—ready-made divine love two more and other absolute loving personalities; for if the absolute actuality of the divine love is already presupposed apart from the Trinity, then it might be difficult to arrive at trinitarian distinctions without multiplication and self-repetition of God, which always result in subordinationism. Rather, as the absolute life is only eternally constituting itself out of the trinitarian distinctions and has its existence only in them, so is it similarly with the absolute love, whose concept is not one of the merely simple (see below).

Just so, however, an objective truth is also to be conceded to the distinction between *physical* and *spiritual* determinations of the concept of God and, what is more, in such a way that the former are subordinated to the latter, since otherwise even in the world the distinction of physical and spiritual would be untenable and become mere illusion. But by this an analogue from *nature* is to be posited in God himself. Even the distinction of *potentia* and *actus*, if aseity is to be taken seriously, may not be so annulled that God is conceived only as one of the two, as if perfection lay in that one alone, that is, thinking of God simply as *actus purissimus*. Rather, if his trinitarian self-establishment is an enduring one and not something once occurring and now past, then God is to be conceived as eternally both absolute potentiality and absolute actualization by virtue of the eternally self-rejuvenating divine life-process. This, to be sure, will only be possible, figuratively speaking, in that the life of God constitutes an organism and cycle of life, or logically speaking, in that the eternal and absolute self-actualization of God eternally wills and confirms its own ground, just as the latter cannot be apart from the always absolute actuality of existence. From this it certainly also follows that if there were lacking in the divine life even one of the moments out of which it eternally constitutes itself, even for an instant,[4] the other moments would also be no more; for they all exist only as conditioning and conditioned by one another, they stand and fall with one another. Nothing therefore of the distinction between accident and substance is to be permitted in the life of God himself that is to be conceived triunely, in the physical, logical, and ethical.[5] There is nothing in God's essence which does not also exist, and there exists nothing in God which is merely accidental or which need not exist; for the recently expressed idea, that for God himself different, equally perfect modes of existence are conceivable, will not be tenable when one considers that the supposition, that different excellences could not even exist simultaneously in the Godhead, but only the one or the other, betrays something of a polytheistic savor. What is actual perfection for the divine essence must also eternally be immediately actualized in him; there is no place here for option and change. *Essentia Dei involvit existentiam* is valid also for the perfections characterizing the divine essence. If it were not possible for everything that is actually an excellence to be united in one, then there could not be one God; the divine could only be exhausted in a plurality of divine figures. Or again, if there were nothing that is in and through itself good, and therefore also necessarily existing in the necessity of divine being, then God would be only *liberum arbitrium*,[6] and that would be good to which this *arbitrium* in fact willed to determine itself. Thus the good would be only a contingency, based on arbitrariness. For that very reason there would also have to be posited with this supposition a distinction of universal and particular in God, such as we cannot accept. The one, which would include the possibility of all modes of existence that the divine can give itself, would be the generic; to this each form of existence elected by the divine would be related as particularization or species. But since that one [as the mode of all possible existence] would not be species, as are the other chosen modes of existence, which also by their own modes are to predicate excellences, it would follow that the good

4. As the modern kenosis of the Logos proposes. [Cf. Dorner's critique in §98 of his System, translated in Welch, *God and Incarnation*, 191 ff.]

5. In referring here to the "physical, logical and ethical," Dorner has in mind three ways of articulating the trinitarian conception: the "physical" definitions develop the trinitarian character of God's self-originating causality; the "logical" is the analysis in terms of self-consciousness; and the "ethical" derivation relates to the nature of love in God as uniting ethical necessity and freedom (see below). Cf. Dorner's *System of Christian Doctrine*, §31b (Edinburgh, 1880; I, 420 ff.).—TRANS.

6. Free will, in the sense of free choice.—TRANS.

which is possible would be actual either never or only in different species of the divine; whereby we would be led back to the preceding situation. Were God a natural being and nothing more, the distinction of genus and particularization might permit application to his own being. But he is Spirit, and all excellences in the perfect spiritual personality exist immediately in and through each other, thus the actuality of the divine being or his existence is congruent with his essence or his potentiality, and even the latter would not be without the existence or actuality which, directed to itself, serves the self-origination (see above, pp. 136 f.).

But is not the distinction of universal and particular to be applied to God in another respect, viz., *in relation to the world*? For if there is an actual world, God is not all being; rather, God here is in the universality of being that includes God and the world and is indeed a particular being. But on the other hand it would be superficial to stop with this coordination of divine and finite being; for in no way do the being of God and that of the world belong to the same genus of being. God's being is rather, as was shown above, aseity, and the particularization in which he confronts the world is rather the distinction of the *universal* cause of all that is possible and actual from the effects. But if one views God himself apart from the world, then in him all possibility of divine being is at the same time absolute actuality; and God's actuality has eternally embraced not merely a part of the divine and its perfections and brought it to the actuality of existence in God, but has embraced everything that in itself is good and divine. The universal good or the good as such is that with which the absolute divine personality has identified itself, and God is *one* by virtue of the fact that all possibility of divine being is in him also actuality, just as he possesses his uniqueness in his aseity. His *particularity*, his characteristic essence, is his aseity, through which he can be the *universal* ground of all being.

One can therefore only concur with the old Oetinger[7] when, instead of stopping with that rigid simplicity of the divine essence which still played such a large role in the Wolffian philosophy,[8] he speaks rather of a fullness of divine powers, which without prejudice to their diversity are held together by an indestructible bond of unity, whereby the divine life appears not as an endless indeterminate ocean, but as an infinitely determinate and structural organism.

With this absolute eternally perfect existence or actuality of God, which is at the same time a vitality eternally willing and producing itself, we

7. Friedrich C. Oetinger, 1702–1782.—TRANS.
8. I.e., of Christian Wolff, 1679–1754.—TRANS.

have also already expressed, for the concept of God in itself, its superiority over change and over the limits of time and space. For, leaving the world out of account, a change *in* God would be conceivable only if he were to strive from the less perfect to the perfect, since he can change neither into the imperfect nor into another though equal perfection (as has just been pointed out). Likewise, time and space are hardly eternal primordial beings,[9] in which God would exist; rather, since there can be no divine primordial powers above God, which enclose him, time and space must then lie in God, eternally posited and willed by God. So one can say with Augustine: God is (in his eternal being) his own place; he is in himself. The archetype of space, of its dimensions and laws, in the world, is in God as ideal intelligible space. And just so in the inner-divine relation of cause and effect, of the living confirmation of the one moment in the divine life by the other, which naturally is to be conceived as reciprocity in God, there is given a logical and ontological prototype of that which is manifested in the world as *time*. The eternally closed and completed circle of the divine eternity keeps the temporality of succession below itself, because effect in God is just as eternally perfect as cause, by virtue of the absolutely perfect reciprocity in the divine organism, by virtue of the cycle of the divine life returning to itself. In the finite world, in contrast, that circle of eternal life, perfect and rounded in itself, has rather become a straight line; because finite beings are not from the beginning what they should become, their actuality equalizes with their potentiality only in gradual growth. Thus God's eternity is the constantly surmounted possibility of temporality or temporal succession in the inner divine life, which temporality would immediately enter if God's actuality were to lag behind the divine possibility and necessity. Just so, the separation that we see in the world of empirical space, of separateness, is in God a possibility constantly surmounted by his absolute actuality, and his infinity is no diffusion. In the multiplicity of his actual powers each has and preserves its place, the "position" appropriate to it.[10] But they are not broken up into an indifferent separateness or emancipated from one another; rather there is an intelligible order here, by which they are yet also in one another, without dissolution of their

9. As, e.g., is fancied in the curious book, *Gott and seine Schöpfung*, by the author of the *Kritik des Gottesbegriffs in den gegenwärtigen Weltansichten* (cf. article I). Paganism has primordial deities in Uranos and Kronos. [Ed. These two works, *God and His Creation*, and *Critique of the Concept of God in the Present World-Views*, were published anonymously by Friedrich Rohmer (Nördlingen, 1857 and 1856 respectively.]

10. Cf. here F. W. J., *Schelling's Werke*, second division, I, 429 ff. [Ed. *Sammtliche Werke*, Stuttgart, 1856; the *Introduction to the Philosophy of Mythology*.]

difference or their position, so that the *Perichoresis* or *Immanentia* extends not merely to the trinitarian hypostases but also to the actual determinations and powers of God, to his attributes. Even if, for example, one can say figuratively that God as ground is itself the place for God as personality, still the ground would be outside God as the personal and would limit him only if the ground were not also just as eternal as God himself is, if it were not taken up in the actuality of the personal God and illumined as willed by him. Thus in and for God himself the empirical separateness and successiveness of space and time remain eternally only an excluded imperfection, suppressed by his positive and absolute perfections, which cannot remain in mere possibility. This, however, is not in contradiction to the other assertion, that space and time are in God in an intelligible way, namely as possibilities which do not achieve specific actuality. As has already been stated, it is the universal eternal actuality of God, that is, his perfection, through which in him this imperfection, this separateness and successiveness, remains always excluded from the actuality. Nevertheless the possibility, to be conceived *in abstracto*, which would at once become actuality if the power of return to self did not correspond just as eternally to the power of self-positing and of going forth from self, is the foundation upon which it may be understood how there can be for God a knowledge also of separateness and successiveness in the world, yes, a creative conception of these things. Space and time as possibilities, viz., as possibilities suppressed by the inner life of God, are yet eternally thought and willed by God.

The idea of *creation* also is certainly in general not compatible with a doctrine of God's simple, unmoving, rigid essence, which deems it necessary to deny all distinction in this essence and among the divine attributes, for example, between knowledge and will. The assertion that "God thinks and knows himself and the world with one and the same eternal and simple act" does not, as is indeed well known, have a pantheistic meaning. It can rather be given the desirable meaning that God does not come to the creation of the world out of accident or arbitrariness, but that he, thinking himself absolutely, knows himself also as the ground of possibility of a world and that he, willing himself as such, wills and knows himself at the same time as ground of an actual world. But if God is not to be absorbed into being the world-cause, if he is rather above all something in and for himself, then his self-knowledge and self-willing cannot simply be identical with the fact that he knows and wills himself as world-cause. The former is the logical prius of the second, it is the eternal act of his self-positing, an act of necessity of the divine essence, which can never be dissolved or inhibited in his vitality. The second, however, no longer belongs to the eternal self-positing and self-asserting of the divine essence; it does not belong to the completeness of his being, but to the activity of his perfect being. Even the metaphysics of the old dogmatics distinguishes again between the *Actus primus* and *secundus*—though inconsistently on its own premises. Thus (but we shall as yet not draw further conclusions) in one and the same divine thought whereby God thinks himself in his all-sufficiency, freedom, and blessedness and at the same time as creator of the world, there are contained two essentially different thoughts, which indeed may go together in one, but not in one and the same simple thought. It is one thing that God knows and wills himself, and it is another that he knows and wills himself as world-cause. In the former, the condescension of love has no place; in the latter, it must enter as the motive without which God would not conceive himself as cause of an actual world.

However, this argument at once leads further. For how can God will the world as an actual end if he does not will himself as means to this end? Thus God is creator only by the fact that he, the absolutely perfect being in which at first the universe of being was exclusively comprehended (see above, pp. 140-141), became through himself the loving *instrument* for his creative will of love, which determined his wisdom and power for the production of a world. The world is a good, not merely for subjective human contemplation although not for God; rather, it is a good in itself and absolutely, even for God (Gen. 1:31). It is, however, a good in accordance with his love only in that he ordains for it at the same time a participation in his community, in his life and Spirit—in short, in that he wills himself also as the end for the world. Consequently God thinks and wills himself as the beginning, the means and the final goal of the world, and each of these is not the other, not even for God. Thus once more one is not to stop with that notice of simplicity.

If we draw closer to the *world*, however, no one denies that it was eternally in God as world-idea, pre-formed in his wisdom, which is as much as to say that it (as thought) was a determination which God gave himself. For it existed originally only as determination in the divine understanding, that is, as its inwardly produced object. But the world is conceived by God as fluid and changeable, else it would not be thought and willed as that which it is; consequently the divine understanding (even if originally through itself) is also afflicted with the changeable, and indeed not merely as spectator but also as ideationally productive of it. Doubtless it is correct that he comes into relation with the changeable only as an object of his thought; the thought of the changeable is therefore not itself changeable—just as the changeable does not cease to be changeable by its being received by imperishable thought. But the entanglement of the divine thought with the changeable is not on that account any less certain, if God has at all thought the world as it is. Yes, if the changeable owes its existence, however briefly it lasts, only to the divine will as efficacious, then God cannot be thought at all as cause of the changeable, unless—regardless of the unmoved and eternal *knowledge* also of the changeable or the past, and regardless of the unmoved *will* not merely of laws but also of the world—the divine *will* nevertheless ceases to be active in reference to the transient, whereas the knowledge of it remains insofar as it is also knowledge of the past. If this perishing occurs through the production of an other, then this producing is the change in God's activity that requires recognition. If, however, to escape this consequence, one wanted to go back to the efficacy of finite causality, or as was recently attempted, to the angels, then that is the deistic evasion and only pushes back the problem itself. Must one not again say, in general, similarly, that even if God knows and wills eternally what emerges gradually in time, the efficacious, really producing will is in no way as eternal as is the world-idea? Either the effective action of God for the production of novelty in the world must be denied, and the actual emergence of this novelty be traced simply to the productive natural order which God his created once and for all complete and self-sufficient: or else, if one acknowledges that God has also an immediate and not merely the deistic relation to the actual emergence of the new, then it must also be recognized that the efficacious, that is, properly creative, activity of God (to be sure, in unity with the order of the divine decree) proceeds temporally and conditions itself in its action by what is spatially and temporally already given. But with this we already have a change in God's living self-exercise [*Betätigung*].[11]

11. This distinction between the willing of a world as such and the efficacious creative willing is as a rule blurred in the old dogmatics. This was most so when, in respect of the charge that with the acceptance of a noneternal creation God is posited as mutable, and in the antithesis of rest and activity, it sought to dispose of this by appeal to the eternal decree or will of creation, as if it were something new only for the world that it is transposed from nonbeing into being, from being in God's idea into actuality, but is not anything new for God that he began to create. Here the coming of the world to actuality evidently proceeds as if it were no special moment tracing back to God's action, but as if it were already eternally given with the world-idea in itself. Here we would have an intelligible world positing and evolving itself into existence, which would come close enough to pantheism.

The same thing appears to us from a new perspective when we put the word of Scripture, "In him we live and move and have our being" [Acts 17:28] together with that other word designating the goal: "I will live in them and walk among them" [2 Cor. 6:16]. Man is not created in order, after having become a being outside of God, to be independent from God; even the world rests eternally in God as its center. It has an actual being no less than does God, but it has it in that God remains the primal being, the principle willing its being, sustaining and surrounding it. But now man is not destined to rest merely embraced by the divine power, like a child in its mother's lap; he is rather to become a proper causality of a secondary sort. A reality that is purely posited, lacking all powers, absolutely passive, would be only an altogether dead one, a nothingness, and not something actual, so that the divine actuality would be no causality at all, would have effected nothing, if it had not posited something self-maintaining and acting. In the living, God posits a self-positing, an effect which is self-effecting, an act which becomes active. And this is far removed from the notion (held by many, for example, even J. Müller[12]) that God limits his omnipotence when he grants an actual causality also to that which he is not; rather, he first becomes active causality through this alleged self limitation, which in truth is manifestation of his power and extension of his sphere of power.

Only if the finite beings, in particular the free ones, were *given* to him, would the granting of a proper causality for them, that is, their existence, be a limitation for God's creative power. Thus again the now commonly heard expression of God's self-limitation is to be excused only as figurative, whereas in truth God without the free beings would prove himself not more but less in his creative power, as having a smaller rather than a larger sphere of power and government. Yes, in his governing providence also God does not limit himself and his power—unless one supposed there was in God a power which could be and willed to be active not alone at the behest of his will, but which might set forth arbitrarily or according to natural necessity that of which it was capable as power and which would be stayed therefrom by preservation, government, and providence.

The highest causes which are created are those which are *free*, destined to posit themselves ethically and to act freely; they are consequently the highest revelations precisely of the omnipotent causality of God, in the very fact that God endows them richly, allows them to be free and lays

12. Julius Müller (1801–78) of Halle.—TRANS.

claim to their freedom for their self-formation. Now he does not will to stand merely in the relation to them of purely determining power; no more does he will to be in the mere relation of law objective to them. Rather, on the grounds that they live, move, and are *in him* whether they will or not, he wills to dwell and move *in them* as the beings they have themselves actually become, willing and knowing themselves to be what they are recognized [*erkannt*] by God to be, that is, what is God's eternal idea of them. Without participation in God, man cannot attain the concept which God formed of him, and without the developed, actualized receptivity of men for God, God cannot dwell and move in men. Now if God were related to them only as law or only as eternally identical and absolutely determining power, then one might be able to stop with the notion that everything is said with the immutability of this power and holiness. But since, as the Old Testament already says implicitly but as the New Testament actualizes, God wills to make men those in whom he dwells and moves, or since his love has assigned to them even participation in himself, whereby the new, the true humanity comes into being, humanity again is in process and in a history. Thus it is undeniable that God, so far as he dwells in man, also leads an historical life in the world, enters into contact with time; and his life achieves an ever greater extension, not from itself in the manner of a natural process but by continuing deeds, which again are always proportioned and conditioned according to receptivity. The act of God is not to be conceived as something absolutely simple, remaining eternally self-identical, working as it were as constant pressure, to which the diverse results accrue only through the diverse conditions of the world—for that would lead back to the Pelagian thesis. Rather God changes the world, since he works upon it diversely, though to be sure incessantly corresponding to the receptivity present. But in his giving of participation in himself he enters into temporality and the distinctions of the world, so that through the eternal consciousness to be implanted in man, temporality is subjected and all abilities, united harmoniously and in the image of God in simultaneous actuality, are formed into the organized manifestation of man's true essence, that is, of the idea of him as it lives in God.

Were the world to be conceived only as a closed circle of entities, mutually conditioning each other, existing as eternally identical in reciprocal effect, then one might be satisfied to say that God relates himself to the world with a single act which remains continually self-identical. But then there would also have to be no origination and no perishing in the world, or both could be conceived as mere appearance. It might be possible to attempt this from the standpoint that the essence of the world was only in its basic substances—whether one calls them atoms, molecules,[13] or genera, forms (*eide*)—and which is indifferent to everything which first makes the world into *kosmos* (cosmos). But if even the slightest weight is laid on the shaping, and God is not excluded from that in which the main point lies, viz., the meaning of the world and its ideal content, then nothing remains but to acknowledge that from the world as it is, with its progressive becoming, temporality and change are also reflected into God's acting, just as surely as everything still remains held together by the one eternal decree. If this must be valid even for nature, in which temporal progress in the direction of a goal is yet concealed behind an apparently eternal cycle, how much more so in the realm of free causes, of ethical powers! For even in nature (in which surely everything was not created at once, but in successive gradation) the divine activity as productive efficacy is everywhere conditioned by what is temporally already at hand; the one will of creation is here, so to speak, already broken up temporally into a series of teleologically homogeneous acts, which may by no means be traced back to the extent or the form of what is given in the earlier or the first act and its causality, unless mechanism, chemism, and so on, are to be considered as the creator instead of the mere *conditio sine qua non* of the higher levels. If this is so, then how much more is a multiplicity of divine acts, and not a mere one-and-the-same simple eternal act, to be posited in the world of humanity, the crown of creation. For here indeed is the place of the highest earthly causalities, *qua* free powers. But this will surely not imply that they are less in need of the acts of God than nature is; they are, rather, far more in need, and this is a guarantee of their dignity. We have just seen that, according to their idea, they alone are receptive to communion of love with God—which is not to be conceived without an appropriate act of God's love in every case—and thus that they are in need in a way not to be found anywhere else. In the human world there is marked out a second world, the ethical, for which nature (the human included) has only the significance of conditioning presupposition. Humanity can fulfill its commission only in a history of freedom, which

13. In his *Mikrocosmus*, Lotze has strikingly convicted materialism of the charge that if its atoms are to help it explain anything, they must rather become intelligible entities of an infinitely manifold content, with the capacity (even the impulse) to enter infinitely rich combinations, and by these, conformable to the postulated immanent Spiritus rector, i.e. God, to build up Microcosmus. [Rudolph Hermann Lotze, *Microcosmus: An Essay Concerning Man and His Relation to the World*, trans. by E. Hamilton and E. E. C. Jones (2 Vol., New York, 1885), ed.]

(according to the preceding) is essentially conditioned in its successful progression by the fact that the divine self-impartation is increasingly interwoven and intertwined in it. But precisely in this it is again being said that we are to accept also an historical life of God in the world, a life conditioned by human exercise of freedom—in the last analysis, to be sure, what is also a self-conditioning life. Through the world of free powers and their determination it first becomes properly clear that God could not produce the world that he willed with one almighty word, already spoken in the beginning. For what then would be left of freedom, if its deed were completed without it? But that *cannot* occur without freedom; without it, the deed remains undone. Thus if there were nothing more than the almighty word creatively positing the natural order, then henceforth the divine activity (which would now be merely sustaining) would have to coincide with the posited natural order, and *everything* henceforth would be no less the work of the latter than of God. Then, however, freedom would remain without the care which it needs for its realization, if it is not to be wholly eliminated by the natural order. Freedom can have a power which is a match for the whole natural order only, first of all by having its origin not merely from below, in the natural order upheld by God in preservation, but from above, from God, and then by being taken in faithful and constant care by the God who wills to put images of himself in men, to let the power of the whole dwell in them.

Nor is this all. In the relation of *God* to the free powers, although they are in every moment equally dependent in their *being*, that is, absolutely dependent on God's sustaining activity, it cannot suffice to trace everything from God's side to his bare omnipotent will. The relation of love, which is aimed at in the creation of free powers, resists the absolutism of bare power; the place of the latter is taken by the communion of love. And for that measure of love for which the divine omnipotence is only tool and servant, a love of the creature for God which was not freely offered but was only impelled by an utterly irresistible determination would have little worth (if indeed it could be called true love). Thus for the production and preservation of free powers the omnipotent causality of God must have acted and must act, so powerfully that through God the power of possible resistance to God and his love is also present in these, in order that their free devotion to God in self-sacrificing love becomes also a new good, valuable for God himself, which could never be achieved by omnipotence as such. But if we assume a freedom of the creature also in this sense (since this is not the place to work out an argument to that effect), and we lay it down that on the foundation of nature God wills a second world to exist, the free world of love in a family of God, then it is also to be said further that the relation of love between God and man must be a *reciprocal relation*, as this is required by the nature of love. Consequently, it is to be taught that God *himself*, who on the side of generating power remains eternally the sole original principle (see above, p. 137), enters the realm of the ethical or love in a reciprocal relation; yes, *God enters into a relation of mutual and reciprocal influence*.

If to the essence of that second, ethical world, which is built up out of free powers and by the mediation of their act, there did not belong also freedom defined as the ability to resist God's ethical being, and if it were thus possible that the highest good, love, were implanted in man by the bare operation of power of the divine will of love, then it would have to be said: Adam could have come into existence as perfect loving being, complete from the beginning. For why should God not have granted man the best at once? The originally limited condition of man, even a helpless one at the beginning as we observe it, and his poor ethical endowment, as well as the law of gradual development to which he is subjected, is conceivable only because in man we are concerned with a sphere in which God's creative or generally prevenient impartation of love cannot in and of itself alone bring about everything. Rather, a series of human acts of freedom is required, by which the divine love allows its work to be conditioned and according to whose createdness that love proportions and orders the form and mode of its self-impartation. After all, if these divine acts, subject to foreknowledge of the acts of free powers, are eternally conceived and embraced in the one divine decree as moments belonging together, this decree itself is still a decree of temporal production, which is actual as conditioned by human free actions. So surely as God, in willing and knowing, had the whole in view at the outset—just so little is the moment of *effecting* or producing will constantly and equally present for all; rather it advances with the history of the world, and thus itself becomes historical. Accordingly, since in the beginning there is still much which God wills to bring forth in his good time, which remains contained in him as in his potentiality, it cannot be said of the relation of God to the world that there is in God only pure act and nothing of bare potentiality. The ethical determination of the world requires in particular that the divine self-impartation occur first of all (in the law) to man's knowledge in conscience and for its cultivation, so that he, in accordance with his need and receptivity, may freely attain to a higher impartation of the divine will than that of the law, to the impartation of the spirit of love which is the fulfillment of the law. There is a deep truth in the distinction (found in Luther, Calvin, Schleiermacher) between the producing and the commanding will of God, for God does in no way produce forthwith the good which he commands and sets as goal. Yet in the old dogmatics this distinction remains without motive and foundation. But it has its basis in this, that the humanly ethical is not permitted to stop with what is finished all at once by creative production, since the human act of freedom, the willing of self in God and God in self, must enter in between the moral ability and its divine-human actualization. Now to be sure, since God created what is free for the sake of the ethical, he has in a certain way set over against himself a being of the same kind, which can resist him (Gen. 3:15). By the creation he has exposed himself to the creature's possible opposition and defiance, which for him is by no means simply a matter of indifference. He cannot break this opposition inwardly and turn it into devotion by any force, because such a contesting of the opposition outside him would involve him in contradiction with himself as the one who wills man as free ethical being. He can annul man, but he cannot at one and the same time will to preserve man as the free being which he is and annul him as free being. Thus man's great responsibility for the use of the divinely granted freedom which sets him independently over against God. Here the depth of the concept of guilt has its root. The further consequences of this for the conditionedness of the historical life of God in the world will be discussed later.

In the preceding we have also substantiated that the divine *omniscience* has intrinsically an historical side, that is, if there are free powers in the world, then there are free decisions by the creatures, which indeed have their ground of possibility in God but which have their ground of actuality only in the free beings and not in God. But from this it follows that by self-awareness God cannot know these acts as *actual* but only as *possible*. Consequently God cannot have a knowledge of the actual world of free beings by "that same most simple eternal act of his self-knowledge," but only by a *different* act of knowledge, however this may be conceived. For this there must be a receptivity in God, which is not to be confused with passivity. But this also means that the divine decree—insofar as it does not merely indeterminately embrace the world-goal, without fixing on definite persons, but embraces at all that which actually will be—must be not a simple but a composite, even so to say mediated entity. From himself God has only the knowledge of a world of freedom as he intends it, though to be sure with the penetrating, all-embracing overview of all possibilities of the exercise of freedom; however, *the knowledge of the actuality for which freedom will decide comes to him from the world of free beings.* Without this factor, however, the divine decree that becomes actuality cannot have been fixed; the knowledge of the free acts, which actually will take place, forms as it were the creaturely *impact* [*Einschlag*] on the divine decree. It is possible to speak thus of such a decree; for once there is willed the creation of the free world in view of all the possibilities given with it, so that for God nothing unexpected and new can occur and since God provided for the world all the possibilities, also those that here become actual, this is more than mere permission, it is acceptation.

And then in conformity with what he knows as actually developing acts of freedom, God also establishes that which serves for the sure attainment of the world-goal. An interplay thus takes place between the divine and the human, and only out of that does the divine decree result. Certainly this is to be said not merely from the standpoint that God has no foreknowledge of the free but has sight of it only when it has become present; rather, this also holds if one affirms a foreknowledge of the free. Here is hardly the place to discuss in detail the difficult question, which of the two positions is to be preferred.[14] But it will be proved by what has been expounded that the divine decree may not (as for the ancients) be identified with God's essence by the connecting link of the divine will, but rather that in this there is indeed a factor which accrues to God from the world. To be sure, this means that God is related to it not passively, but as sanctioning the actually becoming along with all possibilities. Thus also God's knowledge of the free cannot be compared with our empirical knowledge, which bears a primitively passive character, whereas the divine rests on the divine act of positing the free possibilities and in any case precedes as the sanctioning conception of the possibility of actuality (which without God would not be possible). *Thus if there is to be that which is free, there must be in God a double form of knowledge, one which is unconditioned and created immediately and eternally from himself, and one conditioning itself by free causalities.* Through the latter, however, temporal history is again reflected into the divine knowledge itself.

14. The necessity eternal fixity of the divine world-goal, which has as its content not merely an economy or a law in general, not mere thinghood, but precisely free persons, appears more favorable to the latter. Holy Scripture also speaks for this, especially in its prophecy. As pertaining to persons, the former position cannot accept a pre-temporal decree, but only one gradually established in the course of history. On the other hand, it is not to be denied that we cannot formulate any conception of divine foreknowledge of the free as actually becoming, but only of foreknowledge of all future free events as the possible.

And this is not yet all. We cannot be satisfied with the assertion that for God there can be nothing past and nothing future as such, but that everything exists before him as in an eternal self-identical present. The desired freedom of God from time is not in fact to be found in this way, since eternity as the present or the now would once more be conceived as something temporal, viz., as a contrast to both the other dimensions. But apart from this, if God did not know what is in actuality past as the past, and likewise the future as yet future, but rather both as only equally present, then he would not know each as that which it is, in its truth, but would know both in falsity. Were one yet to say, perhaps, that what is essential in the past is not past but continues into the present and that the eternally self-identical divine knowledge refers only to this, then the scope of the divine knowledge would have had to be suspiciously limited, and it would lie only too close at hand to speak in the same way of the future as well: what is essential in the future is already given in the present, and the divine knowledge of the future refers only to this. And with that we should come not simply to the denial of foreknowledge proper, but also to the essential worthlessness of what is yet to be actualized in the future and is not yet somehow presently at hand, that is, to an anti-teleological Docetism in the conception of the actuality of the world and its value. As the truth of that eternal "presence" of all things before God, therefore, we may assert only this: What is past is as unforgotten (but as past), and what is future is as clear (but as future for him), as if it were present. God's knowledge thus bears also a knowledge of what is past and what is future as such, or as not in itself present. Otherwise the knowledge of human knowledge, in which those dimensions play such an important role, would also elude God.

But now it is to be said: God knows what is present as the present, and thus the divine knowledge of actuality advances as appropriate thereto. What was yet future and known as such moves into the present and from there into the past; but the divine knowledge accompanies it in its course, it assumes a changing shape in the divine knowledge itself; and that presupposes a movement, *a change even in the knowing activity of God himself*. Something new is always passing into the divine knowledge of the past, as into the knowledge of what is present, and thereby other items, previously known only as future, cease to be for God what is still future. Thus God's knowledge is a knowledge conditioned by contemporary history, interwoven and advancing with it. Something enters into that knowledge and is embraced by it which was not previously in it, viz., the knowledge of what, out of the possible and actual content known in itself eternally and immediately, enters from the future into the moment of the present or from this into the past or of what in each moment the present appropriates from the future and the past again from the present.

This can appear to be quite unimportant, and yet the living relation of God to the world depends essentially on it. For it would be equally unsatisfactory for scientific thought and for piety if God were not to have, for example, in relation to man, the stance and attitude appropriate at every point to man's present condition, but only a disposition which would be eternally the same and identical for past, present, and future. For then God's participation would precisely not enter into human contemporary history, in which what is essential of the world goal is nevertheless supposed to be formed or worked out. Then in truth God would remain only the eternal law, which stands immovably over against the world, once and for all condemning the evil and sanctioning the good. But if he were even conceived simply as living law, he would have to be active in the actually present, be it as lawgiving or as judging, and thereby alteration in his deed would already be posited; and if he were related to the present simply as to the past, which cannot be undone, or as to the future, which still has no reality, then the present, insofar as it also is not to be as immovably unalterable as the past, would have to have the principle of its movement purely in itself—and this would be the deistic or Pelagian thesis. Thus the living participation of God in the world, his living communion of love with it, depends in fact upon our positing that God knows continually what is now present and that he does not have to the present simply the relation which he also has to the past and the future, as if these were just as much present for him as the former, since that would lead to a very lifeless and inadequate relation—yes, it would transpose God directly into Deism's false exaltation, which expresses an indifference of God to the world that would be unbearable to science and religion. Rather, aware of the actually present, he acts in it according to his eternal essence, but also according to its condition; and even if his deed is eternally decided, as his knowledge of the present does not at all date only from today, nevertheless the moment of life-filled, efficacious participation, which for God also is something other than mere "intention," takes place only with the incidence of the actual present. Thus what in his decree is eternally present to God in idea, he himself experiences historically only with the world, and he intertwines his acts with the world according to that intention, now also with the appropriate meaning and motive, as conversely in the divine decree the moments of actuality are woven into the world of his loving thoughts.

After all this, it is self-evident that the doctrine of the divine *omnipresence* must also be partly different from that of the old church dogmatics. The latter is indeed correct in positing the presence of God as far as the world extends and in the *adessentia*[15] being united with *operatio*. For an essential and continually effective factor in the actual world is its idea, as this is eternally in God as a determination of the divine understanding. In this sense, the world is eternally in God, and thus God is present with it. But with this eternal conception of the world's idea there is also united the divine will to call it into existence and to maintain it therein; and thereby God's understanding or wisdom is creative. Thus the world rests in this wisdom as its eternal living ground and is embraced by it. This condition is not altered by the fact that the world is posited by the creative wisdom as living and as positing itself; for it still possesses its self-positing eternally only by virtue of God's remaining both the eternal ground of possibility and the ground of actuality of its existence. Nonetheless, we are to affirm a variety in the *presence* of God in the world and an alteration here too. He is one thing in inorganic, another in organic nature, other than both in man, and finally other in the evil than in the good. To be sure, he is in himself always wholly and immutably the same. But his being for the world and in it is something different. If one is not, contrary to what has just been established, to reduce this to a mere long-distance action, or to transform the multiplicity of created things (and therewith the world) into illusion, or finally and dualistically to assume something in itself not posited by God's creative power but originally given to him, that is, a measure of varying receptivity for that divine activity and being which is, intrinsically, identically related to everything—then there is nothing left but to assert a differing being and activity of God in the world. This is possible through the fullness of the divine powers (136), which we held was to be accepted instead of that bare simplicity. This diversity of his presence is already conceived and willed with the divine world-idea and in conformity with that which God wills to reveal and exhibit in each realm of the creature. God's omnipresence in and for the world is thus not that of a uniform extension, but like his activity it is an omnipresence endlessly structured, yes, a changing and varying one in the area of the originating and the perishing also, although constantly embracing all that is in one way or

15. God's "presence to" the world, which is united with his action.—TRANS.

other. But it is structured and preserved in eternal unity by the will of the *polupoikilos theou sophia* (variegated divine wisdom) which embraces the world and directs itself to all individuals in it. Thus not merely does the world live, move, and exist in him, but also he lives in the world in structured revelation of his power and impartation of his fullness of life, without which he would not be for the world and in it—yes, without which the world would not be. Hence even the physical world is nowhere a barrier for him: what for us is spatial limitation of one by another, is for him diversity and structure of what is manifoldly, simultaneously and jointly willed—each of that which it is. Thus, in accordance with his pure divine conception, it does not exclude and is not hostile for God, but only together forms the whole. And this whole is also accessible to that noble creature of which it is said: Everything is yours (1 Cor. 3:21). But although all things form a unity, certainly they are not destined to be an amalgamating unity, and to this extent the structured omnipresence of God participates in space, but not as a barrier. Rather, space becomes a barrier only as it is filled, that is, by things which are barriers for other things. Now God, who sustains all things, indeed is and acts in them in special ways, according to the form in which they are conceived in the world-idea, or not in the same way that he is everywhere in and for the world, and therefore makes them to be the particulars they are. He does not will that any kind of thing should at the same time be the opposite of itself and disposes his omnipresence accordingly (his *adessentia operativa* [active presence to the world], see above). But as nothing whatever can set a boundary to his being and action, so also his being and action in the one is not separated from his being and action in other things. Rather there is in him the undivided coherent unity of all his ways of being and acting in the world, and therefore the rational creature can find in him also the power of all overcoming of space, insofar as space is a dividing barrier; and whereas the diversity and particularization of things remain, the emergence of the (for us) dividing barrier of space and of the mutual exclusiveness of the spatial is always an impossibility for the divine freedom in respect of space.[16] However, with respect to unfilled space, and therewith the question

16. The extent to which the divine omnipresence experiences alterations in its condition through evil in the free creature is evident from the above. Certainly the physical omnipresence of creative and preserving power continues even in the evil; but his ethical being and action in them and for them—what he intended for them—is conditioned and limited by their use of freedom.

of God's *immensity* in distinction from his omnipresence, this is to be said: God is omnipresent in the entire actual world; but empty space is not actual world, as the limit of the real it is never absolutely immeasurable creation; it is in fact nothing but the end of the already real and actual, and just because of this it is the beginning point of the realm of the remaining possibility of continuing creation. Self-evidently, one cannot here talk of omnipresence in the sense hitherto discussed; for in the realm of what is still only possible there cannot yet be an efficacious being of God. Instead of representing God's immensity as an infinite extension in space, since space is no primordial being outside God, we must stop with the inner infinite creative power of God, in which rests an unexhausted fullness of possibilities that have not yet become actuality, nor ever need to be all actual in a given moment (and this realm of possibility is the truth of space, when taken apart from what fills space). On the other hand, the whole actual and everywhere determinate or organized world, which is not infinite but rather is bounded by possibility that is not actuality, is upheld and throughout governed by the divine omnipresence, which is likewise structured but everywhere ruled by the divine will. Thus it is also confusing to represent omnipresence as a necessity of the *physis* of God, viz., as if by virtue of his infinity he could be nothing else than everywhere present. To be sure, it is certain that God is omnipresent in the whole realm of actuality, but only because all actuality cannot be conceived apart from his being and action in it, and thus with actuality God's presence is already asserted. But this actuality exists only by God's *will* and consequently his presence.

The significance or fruitfulness of our conclusions for a series of the most important dogmas is to be pointed out subsequently.

B. In the preceding discussion, it is hoped, we have cleared away a series of assertions that have dragged along only too far in theology and have held the concept of a living God as it were in fetters, which have been fastened on him in the name of a supposed eminence and purity from sensuous admixtures. But the second step is just as important, viz., the rejection of such representations of God's vitality as would injure his immutability and true eminence.

Certainly one must attribute it largely to the thirst for the living God that after the period in which Deism predominated, through generations, pantheism in its manifold forms found so many adherents. But theology has experienced too much of evil from pantheism not to have always to be quite on its guard against its damaging after-effects in the reconstruction of the doctrine of God that is necessary and that is now under way.[17] What then do we have to view as the fault in the system of pantheism and as the reason that the immutable absoluteness and the vitality of God, which doubtless the highest forms of pantheism have sought to unite, again and again have split apart and repelled each other in the sequel?[18]

Does the error lie in pantheism's thinking too highly of the world, since it makes it a moment of the life of the absolute self? But it does not ascribe aseity to the world; this it reserves for God, even if unclearly; and here freedom remains withheld from man. Man is a mere modification of the one all-life or world-spirit; and because of this, that which constitutes the crown and dignity of man and by which he comes to be in the image of God, the ethical, can retain a place only in a stunted way and only together with the necessity of evil. Thus in pantheism it is rather the concept of man that is destroyed and sacrificed to the absolute. Or does the error lie in pantheism's thinking too highly of God or the absolute? Were that not already intrinsically an impossibility in itself, the opposite would necessarily become evident simply because all forms of pantheism conceive the absolute or God egoistically and assign the absolute perfection of the divine life to it in that they identify his life-process with the gradually evolving world. Thus they ascribe even to the absolute a reality which is only

17. To be sure, there is still another way of misconceiving the vitality of God, other than the pantheistic, viz., that which makes him a particular individual, superior to others only in degree, and which forgets that God must in every moment be the universal principle of being and life (see above). This is essentially polytheistic, even supposing that only one highest essence be accepted for which the name "God" is to remain. God is here only the highest in a series of existents essentially like him. It was discussed earlier [in the second article] how this false way of vivifying the concept of God, by particularizing and finitizing, attaches very easily to deistic presuppositions, namely by personification of law or fate or eternal necessity to which the concept of God is reduced) in order to lend to this something of the warmth of life. Thus polytheism has frequently arisen against a background of Deism. But it is not necessary to dwell on this false vitality of the concept of God which arises from the particularization of God, for such a God-concept leaves out the absoluteness of being as universal principle of being and life. In such a particular God, who is merely one individual beside other individuals (be it even as the highest in the series), not even the idea of *theion* (divinity) is conceived, let alone that of *o theos* (God). Much that is instructive at this point is to be found in Schelling's *Einleitung in die Philosophie der Mythologie*, in the section on monotheism. [ed. See F. W. J. Schelling, *Sammtliche Werke*, Pt. II, Vol. I (Stuttgart, 1856).]

18. It is well known that for the most consistent exponents in Hegel's school, the life of God and the world shrank into thought, into the lifeless shadow-realm absolute logic, which was regarded as the only thing that is real, and thereby one was again in acosmism (even if it was now of a logical, and no longer of a substantial sort); whereas others, like Feuerbach, "thirsting for the lifeblood of actuality," renounced every absolute, of whatever form, in order to hold on to life and the living, which they now (despairing of all that is ideal) had to grasp only sensuously and empirically, whereby they became precursors of the now prevalent materialism with its enmity to spirit.

becoming perfect, or else they posit life as entirely immaterial to the actuality of the absolute's self, to its own spiritual reality, but precisely thereby make the advance of the world to the reality of its perfection into something indifferent. And then the properly divine and valuable fall simply into the potence or essence—and with this the whole view has reverted to the substantial form of acosmism. Or does the error lie in the too close connection of the two, God and the world, in this mutual entanglement of the life of God and the life of the world in one another? In Christ and the community sharing in his spirit, Christianity posits a far more intimate connection than pantheism ever achieves; for as the reverse side of the pantheistic homogenizing there becomes manifest again and again (as our time in particular can not yet have forgotten) the exclusiveness now of the divine against the human (for example, in logical acosmism), now of the human against the divine (in anthropologism). Finally, the error of pantheistic systems cannot be found in their speaking of an inner-historical life of God and of its alteration; for the preceding section has shown the necessity of this supposition.

The error lies rather in that God himself, in respect of any kind of inner perfection, is conceived by pantheism only as *potence* and not at the same time as eternal actuality of this potence. God is therefore not recognized as that being whose absolute actuality in all his perfections belongs to his concept just as does the eternal being from itself. The supposition that the absolute actuality of perfections does not belong to the necessary concept of God is the premise under which that homogenizing of the divine and the human life-process seem possible, even inviting; but it is also the reason why the supposed intimate unity of God and world turns out again finally to be exclusiveness. In that one life-process embracing God and world, man becomes deprived of all independence; whereas with this unselfishness of the world, not only is nothing gained for God, the all-life and all-spirit, but he (so that he can thus devalue and depotentiate the world) is himself essentially reduced to mere potence. The actuality of the divine perfections is changed into something indifferent and accidental for the concept of God, and thus is robbed of absolute character. These perfections are there as something thought, which can be actual or not, so that their absence would not prejudice the reality of the concept of God, and their existence would not constitute that concept.

But now if we may not grant this thesis of pantheism, that in God the potence is not necessarily, eternally actual in himself,[19] but above all hold fast the eternal and absolute self-actualization of God in himself, that is indeed in no way to say, as the older theology supposed, that the distinction between potence and act has no meaning at all for God's being and activity; the preceding section has shown the opposite. But it surely is to say that an inner-worldly and an inner-historical life of God and an alteration in this life are to be spoken of only on the basis of the eternally actualized and immutable perfection of God.

It is true that recent theology generally accepts this, but in such fashion, if I see rightly, that much obscurity still prevails, and therefore the pure working out of the Christian concept of God is still often beclouded by pantheistic thinking, in part mixed with deistic. Some think they have done enough when they suppose that prior to the world the personal God once existed as absolute actuality; but they think that for the world God strips himself of this absoluteness and becomes finite in himself, ceasing to be absolutely actualized God, in order to associate with the finite world and to lead an intra-historical life. This is supposed to be the prelude to the further step of the self-limitation of God (the Son), by which for the sake of sin he who has become extra-divine ceases to be God and becomes mere potence of God, in order to become man in Christ.[20] Thus we would have here a theistic beginning; but only in order to enter from that point into the line of that pantheistic doctrine according to which God is to be conceived as mere potence, more or less stripped of absolute divine actuality. The difference is simply that the pantheistic God seeks eternally to exalt himself to actual being in absolute reality, but is hindered from reaching it (by what, one does not know); whereas here God himself, to the concept of whom (as we saw) belongs the absolute actuality of his potence, is

19. The conception of God as absolute being and life, which in respect of spirit is only potence and advances to infinite self-perfection in continual labor thereat and in growing clarity of self-consciousness, is expressed in the boldest, even the crudest, form by the author of the above-mentioned *Kritik des Gottesbegriffs*, in the work *Gott und seine Schöpfung*, 80f. (ed. See above, 124.) God must even relapse into his origin and sleep, in order to awaken again strengthened; he must in himself be able to rest and sleep because he is certain of his awakening again. There can be, yes, there must be, in him an alternation of night and day, and so on (149ff.). On a pantheistic basis, the author mounts a deistically limited individual essence which he calls God. Similarly in the case of E. von Hartmann. [ed. The last sentence is added in the republication of this essay in the *Gesammelte Schriften*. The reference is presumably to philosopher Karl Robert Eduard von Hartmann, 1842–1906.]

20. Cf. the critique of kenoticism in Dorner's *System*, §98 in Welch, *God and Incarnation*, pp. 181–205.—TRANS.

supposed more or less to strip himself of this his actuality, so that he can lead an intra-worldly and intra-historical life. Dominant here also is the presupposition that God can come into living fellowship with the creature only by self-finitizing. But that is surely to say that as long as the world continues, that is, eternally, God is not absolutely actualized God, unless it be that this finitized God, the Son and his limitation, does not concern the essence of God. But then there no longer exists any right to speak, in contrast to pantheism, of God as the eternally and absolutely actualized—all the less so since, on this view at any rate, the absolute God retreats into a deistic background and we never enter into immediate relation with him nor he with us, because all real fellowship is supposed to take place with the God who is turned into other-being, limited and thus subordinated, with the Son and the Holy Spirit.

Others have sought to correct this, in the interest of the vitality of God and his inner-historical life, by appearing to accept a kind of doubling of God. They posit a God eternally and absolutely actualized in himself, whom they (with the church) conceive triunely; but the old distinction between the immanent and the economic Trinity works out for them to a doubling of God. They intend particularly to bring the christological problem closer to solution by assuming the following: The Logos of the immanent Trinity exists in the eternal and absolute actuality of the divine life, and thus shares without disturbance in the clarity and perfection of the absolute self-consciousness of God (to which also belongs indispensably the knowledge of all the possible) and in the divine love. The Logos of the economic Trinity on the contrary can abandon himself to the lot of finitude, and thus strip himself of actual divinity. And what he can do he also does according to his love, for the sake of the incarnation, by so receiving finitude into himself that as economic he ceases to be genuinely actualized God. But the pantheistic thesis, that actuality or perfect reality is not requisite for the existence and concept of God, is not adequate as the key word of Christology. On the contrary, if the economic Logos had taken on himself that kenosis, whereas as immanent in God he remained undisturbed by that act and persisted in his absolute actuality, we would have two Logoi instead of one, and he who alone is the absolute reality of the divine would not have become man at all; the incarnate Logos, however, would be an extra-divine subordinate being, over which the *ano Christos* (higher Christ) hovered until the consummation of the God-man.

Consequently, the solution of the problem here in question must now be attempted by welding theistic and pantheistic tenets to one another and presenting them alternately, as it were putting a theistic head on an essentially pantheistic body of doctrine of God's vitality in the world. It cannot help to speak now of God as necessarily and eternally actual, immutable and absolutely real, and then again of God as a mere potence. Rather, the speculative task is precisely to apprehend the *reality* of God in itself—immovable and eternally remaining absolute, never reducing itself to mere potence—as the source and ground of possibility (consequently as the potence) of the creation of the world and of the vitality of God within history; and conversely to see in God as intra-historical and self-revealing him who makes good the capacity and freedom for world-creation, world-redemption, and fulfillment, precisely as the one who is eternally perfect in himself and affirms himself as such. The point must be this, that instead of God's reducing himself to mere potence for the sake of the world and his being changed into it, it is rather the actual divine perfection itself and nothing less (and indeed as perennially as immovably affirming itself) which is to be apprehended as the potence for the world. The whole historical life of God in the world takes place, not at the expense of the eternal perfection of God himself, but precisely by virtue of this permanent perfection. Only so does his eternal freedom also remain in its place vis-à-vis the never absolutely closed natural order.

Christology presents the archetype, the utterly perfect form of union between God and humanity in general. The way in which the uniting of the divine and the human is conceived in Christology is at the same time decisive and typical for a series of other dogmas. How could it be supposed to be true and worthy of God that Christianity should have conquered the heathen religions and philosophies by a piece of the doctrine that is at home in the pantheistic schools and religions, by the doctrine of a God who is potential, growing and only gradually working up to self-consciousness or to spiritual actuality in general? If this were the foundation of the chief objective Christian truth, then heathenism, in the myths of the God who sacrifices himself on behalf of the world, would contain more prophecy of Christ than the Old Testament; to them especially the idea is not so foreign, that God has thus given and sacrificed himself on behalf of the world.[21] Against such ideas, the Old Testament sets with utter seriousness the inviolable majesty and holiness of God, which is not even violated in love.

21. Cf. (Karl Friedrich) Adolph Wuttke, *Geschichte des Heidenthums* (Breslau, 1852–53), II, 292, 323, etc.

But now if, like pantheism, the doctrine of a self-transformation, such as the self-duplication in a limited God alongside the absolute and actual God, is also objectionable, if this way to apprehension of the vitality of God and his participation in the historical life of the world is thus altogether untenable: are we not thereby forced once again to accept the view with which the majority are content, that we distinguish between an eternally immutable but also permanently transcendent God and a God who is living and related to the world but in no way immutable, and we try to hold the two apart without being able to assert anything about the manner of the uniting of the two? But such a rending asunder and external juxtaposition of the immutability and the vitality of God would already be in partial discord with the theses arrived at above (A). Thus we are driven to the attempt *to establish dogmatically the necessary and true union of the immutability and the vitality of God*, to which will then be joined some of its most important applications.

## II

Certainly recent theology, following the school which lasted about a century and a half, does very well to repudiate Deism and pantheism; both of them, inimical as they are to religion, lead to impossibilities for scientific thought, the one to atheism, the other to acosmism, as well as to denial of the absoluteness of precisely the higher determination of the concept of God. All but unanimously, recent theology postulates both God's immutability, which is often confused with transcendence, and God's vitality, which is often identified with his immanence in the world—the former against pantheism, the latter against Deism.[22] Yet as these two still seem contrary to each other, the temptation to one or another one-sidedness is always necessarily involved, so long as the compatibility and inner homogeneity of the two are not apprehended and demonstrated. It is still Deism that professes God's immutability and transcendence, as pantheism does the vitality and immanence of God, so that the wedding or adding of those two contraries does not promise any liberation from the one-sidedness of Deism and pantheism, but rather opens the door to a pure contradiction, thus to a nothingness. To be sure, each still has truth in itself, but just this

22. The task is rather to apprehend God's immutability as intrinsically also living and God's vitality in itself and in the world as intrinsically also immutable—yes to derive precisely from God's immutable but living essence the alterations in his activity and being in the world, and through this to see that immutability of God confirmed.

truth is denied by the counterpart and its concept of God. Further, the history of philosophy surely shows that each of these theories is in a state of constant unrest, because it remains a scientific impossibility to stop entirely with the one, and by a continuing process each restlessly passes into the other. Thus is made known not merely their inner affinity, but also the power of truth, which drives them irresistibly to pass at least successively through the essentially homogeneous moments of the truth that they rend apart. But if by their methods they do not find a way out of this vicious circle (as is evident), it is nevertheless quite manifest that not only the concept of immutability but that of vitality, both transcendence and immanence, must be conceived *quite differently* than by Deism and pantheism (which may well mutually negate and generate, but can never bring into union the true elements which lie in them). There is thus needed a new, a *higher* principle than that which the two represent, and this will have to possess the clear and certain norm for the elimination of what is erroneous in both, as well as the power of uniting the moments of truth in them.

Religion and science have to take an equally vital interest in solving satisfactorily this problem of the union of God's immutability and vitality. For, to glance at the tendencies of the present, if the union of the two does not occur and appears unattainable for the consciousness of our time, what is the consequence? As matters now stand with us, obviously this: At best God is placed in the unknown, as immutable indeed but also as lifeless, and life and movement are located only in the world. If God is not conceived as in himself living, as also historically living, without prejudice to his immutability, then (as we saw) his significance is absorbed into being the fate or the law of the life-movement of the world. Or, how can an eclectic seesawing between two such contrary standpoints, a mutual tempering of each by the other, be trusted for revival or fruitfulness?

Even with the best intentions, one cannot here appeal to ecclesiastical authority and to tenets which were already to have brought the innermost experiences of the church to doctrinal expression. The confessions do not cover this question, and as we have seen, ecclesiastical dogmatics lays down articles of belief which can only lead us to perplexed astonishment as to how such a doctrine of God could have coexisted with the rest of the body of doctrine, if each religion and each system is after all to be defined and characterized by its concept of God. Here if anywhere the church has left us the heritage of a great task to be done.

Or are we now to fall back somehow on *religious feeling*, with the conceptions which appear involuntarily and as of themselves corresponding to those feelings, and to say that no solution of the problem is possible which at once satisfies the religious need and scientific thought; therefore let each one go its own way? Many now subscribe to a dualism between understanding or science and feeling, and look for salvation in a renewal of doctrines of a double truth. But how can religious feelings themselves, flexible and mutable as they are—yes, open as they are to passionate excitations of an elevating and a depressing sort—be directive and decisive even within religion alone? They indeed do not fail to call forth living conceptions of God; but the amount of impure admixture from sense-consciousness that can accompany the "vitality of God" is most patently set forth in paganism—and Christianity also, even the evangelical church, contains examples enough. Thus if one does not want to accept a standpoint so subjective that everything in the religious realm appears equally valuable and justified, if one still wants to speak of a difference between religious health and sickness, it is incontestable that only in the true objective doctrine of God is there given the measure and norm by which both are to be measured. And since the progress of true piety is also essentially conditioned by God's being represented neither as simply immutable nor in such a fashion that the sensuous pollutions of the God-consciousness (of an anthropomorphic or an anthropopathic sort) remain without corrective, it is patently no less in the interest of religion than of science to find the principle according to which the elimination of the false, of that which is unworthy of God, has to proceed. The religious interest demands adherence both to the immutability and to the vitality of God. That scientific thought also points and presses towards the union of these two sides is shown by the whole of recent history. In mere acosmism, as in atheism, science comes to an end. Instead of allowing one of the two, God and world, to be negated by the other, it therefore requires the recognition of the two distinguished but related to each other, the acknowledgment of a God who is not merely dependent in his being on nothing outside himself but who is also absolute as spirit, and of a world conditioned by God. In quite the same way, however, piety also wants to have to do with a God who in elevation over the world still governs its course and change and directs these toward the proper goal. Accordingly, the same demands arise from scientific thought and from religion; in the attempt at a solution we cannot satisfy the one without also achieving for the other what it essentially desires, just as we cannot injure the one without striking the other along with it.

There is a widespread prejudice, to be sure, that inadequate and even incorrect images of God are necessary and as it were inborn to man, since he cannot think of God, at least in religious communion, as other than limited and man-like; and if in thought he casts this off, then the vitality and the sheen of the picture of God which piety forms are necessarily wiped away, and what is left, in comparison with the God of religion, is the *caput mortuum* [dead rubric] of an abstract concept. But if one were seriously to believe in an essential contradiction between the true God and the God of piety, between cognition and disposition, to do so would be destructive not only of religion but also of science, whose activity would have to remain an empty and circumscribed one if it were found to be in necessary contradiction to that which occupies not merely essential, but the central position in the spiritual organization of mankind. For that reason the immovable confidence in the essential concurrence of disposition and cognition, of God's vitality and truth, and thus the trust that considers the dissonances as accidental and surmountable because connected with sin, belongs to the basic moral obligation. But this is already to have said that these dissonances are to be counted among those things from which, intrinsically, Christianity already has brought deliverance. Such confidence is especially becoming to every Christian man and to Christian theology.

The objective fundamental fact of Christianity, the incarnation of God, is the factual solution of the problem of the uniting of God's immutability and vitality. By the God-man, man's nature as image of God is not simply confirmed but brought to full actualization and to this actualization also belongs the cognition of God. As in Christ's person the humanity has apprehended God truly, so Christ wills to have his knowledge for others also; he longs for those to whom he can reveal it through his Spirit (Matt. 11:27). And since in him Christendom knows not simply a new and higher revelation of God himself, but the conclusive and perfect revelation of God—for everything that remains is henceforth only further revelation of Christ—it also becomes Christendom to make its cognition of Christ fruitful for the doctrine of God and to test whether there is not also to be found in him who reveals the Father's heart the key word to break through that enchanted circle of natural life which moves in Deism and pantheism. The depths of God are unfathomable, and it belongs essentially to the cognition of God to become ever more vitally conscious of this. A healthy theology may never be forgetful of the continuing difference between seeing and believing. But this does not hinder Christianity from requiring belief in a reconciliation of disposition and cognition; for the apostle sees this as being already posited and brought to pass germinally in all Christians when he speaks of the eyes of the heart (Eph. 1:18) which faith opens. The question must thus be simply one of ever purer expression, and in language determined by science, of that which faith already bears in itself in principle and which the eye of the believing heart apprehends, in order that an evermore harmonious doctrine of God, growing in height and depth, may also in its way become the victory over the world, that is, in order that the non-Christian conceptions of God may be judged as spiritual idols and laid in the dust before the only true living God. The Spirit of the Son that faith receives will make it possible to free even the world of ideas and conceptions from all false anthropomorphism and thereby to expose obstructions and disturbances of the truly godly life. No less, however, does this make it possible to establish in its due place of honor that from which religious disposition can and may not depart, however anthropomorphic it sounds to some, and therein to permit apprehension of a portion of divine reason in the suggestion of that worthy philosopher when, reaching far beyond his own system, he says: "God formed man theomorphically, therefore man anthropomorphizes God."

As we have found, God is not immutable in his relation to space and time, nor immutable in his knowing and willing of the world and in his decree. On the contrary, in all these respects there takes place also on his side change, alteration, a permitting of himself to be determined—though to be sure without there being called into question that immutability which matters, for the concept of God, in the interest of piety and science. What is the nature [*Wesen*], the center, as it were, of the immutability that we have to ascribe to God and that is the norm, yes, even the source of the alterations which are reflected back into God from the world? Conversely, God's *vitality* cannot consist in his taking on himself negation, the "destiny of finitude," in his being or becoming mere potence,[23] and thus restlessly disposing of himself. For a vitality bought by such self-finitizing would be partially dormant. In what then does the center and the essence of the divine vitality consist?

We answer: in the same thing in which the center of his immutability also consists, namely, not in his being [*Sein*] and life as such—for these categories, which in themselves are still physical, lead us forever to Deism or pantheism in restless interplay—but in his ethical being [*Wesen*].[24] By

23. *Potenz* probably means 'potential' or 'potentiality' in this passage.—TRANS.

24. The distinction between *Sein* and *Wesen* is difficult to capture in English. It is customary to translate *Sein* with 'being,' but *Wesen* is sometimes equivalent to 'being' and sometimes

this there is given in God himself the true copula of eternal rest and movement, of immutable self-identity and most intensive vitality. In this we have both the supreme and immovable norm for the eternally steadfast and constant, and the principle for that sort of change which can be reflected into God's spiritual life; no less therefore do we have the principle generally for the relation between God's super-historical and historical life.

That the ethical is the utterly valuable, with which nothing could be coordinate but to which all else is subordinate, and which assigns to everything its value and its place, we shall not discuss here, any more than the other point, that this must necessarily be conceived and acknowledged by the rational essence of man as such.

But then is God also actually to be conceived as *ethical in himself*?— and if so, to what extent are the true immutability and vitality of God established conjointly in the ethical concept of God?

Nothing is more common now than to lay it down as simply an axiom that God is love—to which on the opposite side it is customary to reply that this is a popular representation, derived from feeling, but in fact unworthy of scientific thought and the concept of God. However, the matter is rather to be put this way: The idea of the ethical generally does indeed have a kind of ontological necessity; it cannot be thought unless the mind which thinks it becomes aware at the same time of the inner truth and absolute excellence of the ethical. But this idea of the ethical is still in need of and accessible to closer scientific treatment. The ethical in general

---

equivalent to 'essence.' The former is general yet concrete, while the latter involves abstraction. Dorner does not mean that the ethical is God's abstract nature (or essence); rather the ethical contrasts with nature, or is a 'second nature.' This means that the ethical good, in contrast to natural good, must be brought about by will. Consequently, Dorner's thesis, advanced subsequently, is that God's being (*Wesen*) is complex, having multiple modes of being (*mehrfache Daseinsweisen*). Dorner identifies these modes of being as the ethically necessary (what ought to be) and the ethically free. His thesis is that the ethically necessary—what ought to be—can only come to existence through the mediation of freedom. Only such a complex ontological conception can do justice to the fundamental concept that God is love, and involved in reciprocity with the world. Dorner's use of the term ethical being (*ethische Wesen*) reflects the deontological tradition in ethics, which distinguishes between nature (*Sein*) and freedom, and understands freedom not as an 'is' but a value that 'ought to be.' Love is an ethical concept, and according to Dorner, constitutes God's ethical *Wesen*. Here Dorner follows Schleiermacher, whose analysis of love as a distinctive divine attribute breaks down the traditional distinction between God's essence and attributes. According to Schleiermacher, love is distinctive in that it is the sole attribute identical with God's being (*Wesen*) (Schleiermacher, *The Christian Faith*, §167). Dorner observes that Schleiermacher's analysis implies the supremacy of the ethical in God, i.e, the priority of the ethical over the physical or metaphysical attributes. Dorner appropriates these distinctions, but formulates Schleiermacher's argument in Hegelian-triadic concepts.—TRANS.

is at first still something very indefinite; it is far from being scientifically allowable to lay down immediately as an axiom that God is love; rather, to the cognition of this belongs a mediation, one that is not merely subjective but also objective, one that must eternally have a place in God himself, whereby he is love. Only with this will the true immutability and the vitality of God also be apprehended in their unity. It must thus appear very hasty, to start from love in God as a simple ready-made entity, as if it could come into being without mediation, and then in order to achieve something of God's ethical vitality in itself, to proceed to a threefold self-repetition of this ready-made love and to derive from the love, not in order that the love should eternally become and be, but in order that it should be active, a triad of divine egos.

It was Plato who posed the subsequently oft-repeated question, to which the answer will lead us deeper into our task, whether the good is good because God wills it, or whether God wills it because it is good. As is well known, Duns Scotus opted for the first alternative; the second is in accord with Thomas Aquinas. The first answer does not mean simply that the good which is to have validity for us as good is known to us by God's revealing will. With this one could indeed only be in agreement. Rather, the meaning is also that the cause of the good's being good does not lie in its inner essence and concept, so that it would have to hold as the good just as much for God as for the humanity which becomes aware of it through God; instead, it is only God's *beneplacitum* [good pleasure] or absolute power, his supreme *dominium* [lordship] through which the good bears in itself the character of good. God's omnipotence is the source of the ethical, but in such a way that the opposite would have also been validly good if God had desired to elevate it to this dignity by the stamp of his power, as he could have done without self-contradiction. Here God in himself is in no way defined ethically or by the ethical, but in the presumed interest of the unrestrained absolute power of God all the weight is laid on God's free will; here the ethical does not belong to the original powers, as the Greeks had already partially apprehended it, but to the created; it falls outside the divine being.[25] The absolute perfection thus lies in omnipotence, and the ethical that is valid for the world has its origin only in the physical category of power.

25. How much better is the *Formula of Concord* [T. G. Tappert, ed., *The Book of Concord* (Philadelphia, 1959), 478 (Art. V, 3); 561 (Art. V, 17: ". . . Strictly speaking, the law is a divine doctrine which reveals the righteous and immutable will of God . . .")].

It is out of our way here to pursue the consequence of this opinion and to expose its close connection with the legal standpoint of a purely external authority, in that there an insight into the inner goodness of the good, and the evangelical freedom in general, would be impossible—for that which has to be valued as good would then have no inner goodness at all, but only a formal authority owing to omnipotence, which could just as well have arrived at the opposite if it had so pleased the divine *liberum arbitrium*. Who does not perceive how this seeming eminence of God over the ethical through his absolute power turns over into the opposite? How in this view God, in order to be exalted over the world into the absolutely incomparable, is degraded to a merely physical essence of power; and the ethical itself in part (as obedience) is only for man and in part, according to its inner and absolute value, is treated skeptically? An all-decisive will, which is yet utterly undefined and indeterminate, can only be called arbitrariness; how it decides is thus absolute accident. In the last analysis, what the good is and what its opposite is, is thus pure accident: at heart God behaves indifferently toward the good and the evil. In his absolute power as in the dark womb both lie together as equally possible—except after God had decided to hold as good the one which would have been evil if God had decided for the opposite. For the heart of the good resides here only in the validity of the divine absolute power.

But should we now say, conversely, that God wills the good because it is the good? We would thus secure the inner goodness and necessity of the good, that is, that it is not arbitrariness which first makes it to be the good, but that it is established through itself. God is here no longer merely indifferent power, and the good is apprehended absolutely in itself. But when one says that God wills it because it is the good, then it seems already to possess its goodness independently of God, and God seems to be God even without involving the good, and by both of these the good once again obtains its original position outside God. Indeed, when the second consequence is taken seriously, and God is God even without willing the good, then we lapse back again to the standpoint of Scotus. The good is nothing essential for the concept of God itself; rather, because of existing outside God or above him, it remains something accidental for him, of puzzling derivation, concerning which Scotus tried to give us information which certainly we cannot call sufficient.

Thus evidently nothing remains but to posit the good originally *in God* himself, neither to give it the position of a mere law above God nor to let it be simply sanctioned for the world by the divine *power*, but to assign it its place in the center of the concept of God itself, to think of the good as constitutive for himself. The ethical is to be posited as primal power *[Urmacht]* in God himself, without which God would not be God; God is to be defined as the ethical in itself, as the primal ethical [*Urethische*].

This also follows simply from the concept of the ethical as that which is valuable in itself and unconditionally, which is the way it must be conceived (see p. 175 f.) if it is actually conceived. For it is self-evident that the unconditionally valuable cannot have its original place outside the divine being.

But now *how* is the ethical in God, and *how* is God to be conceived ethically? Because he *wills* it, or again because it is his *nature*? Here the previous antithesis returns in a new form: Is God good because he wills the good, or does he will the good because he is already good according to his nature?

This much must be certain at the outset: the ethical as the unconditionally highest and valuable lays claim to reality in God, thus to the being of God, and has to be the all-determining in him. The good cannot have the existence which is due it in God merely in the divine understanding, which thinks it as that which is in itself true. For surely mathematical propositions have their truth so purely in themselves that it is for them wholly indifferent whether the circle of which they speak, for example, exists also in actuality. But the ethical, although likewise true in itself, is not indifferent toward its reality; rather, it is essential to the ethical to become actual, to be *willed to be*. Toward this it is unconditionally directed. Thus also in the divine being it must unconditionally have the actuality which it seeks; in the absolute sphere there can be no question of a hostile resistance to the ethical, as is found in the creaturely world. Since the ethical, as has been indicated, belongs to the nature of God himself, God would be divided against himself if he were at variance with the ethical, if something in him offered resistance to the good. Accordingly, it appears that God has to be called good simply because it is his nature to be good and because this his nature defines him directly.

But against this there rightly arises once more an objection. It is just as essential to the ethical in itself not to be simply immediate being, but always to become and to be only by a *positing of will*—only as willed to reach the existence that it seeks. Accordingly, there can surely be no question simply of an immediate absolute actuality of the ethical in God, but only of an eternal self-actualization of God as the good through his will. Innate virtue in the strict sense of the word is inconceivable in man; but even the divine goodness cannot be a matter of simply good *nature*. For if we excluded the idea that God is actual ethical essence through his will, we would again not be outside the physical standpoint. There we would have an immutable being; God would be the substantial unfree necessity of the ethical, his being would be fatalistically determined by the good, without freedom and act of will—but that would not be the God of love, the archetype whose image we are to become.

And yet the former approach can still retain its claim over against this second one. For if, on the other hand, we rest the ethical in God purely on the will, if we allow the ethical in no way to be presupposed by the will but rather only to be posited by it, then we fall back again into the error of Scotus, and thus simply in another way back into the physical standpoint once more. For a will, a freedom, which the ethical in no way decisively precedes, is again itself something merely physical, mere will to power, and thus we would again have in God only the natural character of capriciousness, as in the former postulation we had that of mere natural necessity. An absolute divine will to power that has no essential relation to the ethical in itself, but wills to determine itself ethically only through its absolutely free choice, could also never maintain ethical character, because it could will the good itself only out of capriciousness.

Justified as it is, therefore, to think of God not merely as an ethical nature or substance, we may still not lay such a weight on the willing of the ethical that only by this does the ethical come into being at all. To think of God only as ethical being or as ethical substance and to think of God only as actualized ethical will—these lead to the same result: either way, we stay in the circle of the physical instead of achieving the ethical level itself. Consequently it is equally necessary to declare both that the good becomes constantly or eternally actual through the active divine will, but also that the ethical cannot have its actuality in God simply through God's will; rather the ethical must be an eternal actuality in God's being and essence.

But how is this apparently direct contradiction to be squared? We cannot conclude with what has so far been found, for what we have indeed attained is this: Deity is to be conceived as the absolute actuality of the ethical, but the question of the *how* has brought us only to the insight that a merely ethical nature would be a *contradictio in adjecto* and that it would contradict the essence and concept of the ethical no less if everything were to rest simply on the will. And this drove us to the postulate: The ethical becomes constantly or eternally actual through the actualized divine will, but it must no less also possess an actuality in the being and essence of God. This is unified, however, only if we say: God is the absolute actuality of the ethical only by the fact that *the one ethical actuality has in him a multiple and yet inwardly coherent mode of existence.*[26]

God is to be conceived *first* as the ethically necessary being or as the holy, *second* as the ethically free; through both of these, God actualizes himself eternally as self-conscious, holy, and free love. The necessity of this diremption or eternal self-distinction of God in the ethically necessary and in its opposite, the free, in order that God may give himself absolutely ethical reality and be absolute ethical personality, is amply established in the foregoing discussion.

The ethical in the character of necessity cannot lie outside God, but lies in the divine compass itself; since there can be no law of the good above God, God is himself the law. Also, this ethical necessity in God cannot occupy merely the position of an ought, of a law that lacks being, of a necessary idea without a holder thereof; the ethical in the character of the necessary is rather a necessary *mode of being* of God and indeed the primary one. We cannot begin[27] with the divine will as free if God is to be conceived ethically. For had we only the free, without any kind of conditionality and determination by the ethically necessary, so that we never arrived at all at a good in itself, a truly necessary, and at its being willed, then we would be left eternally in capriciousness, because out of capriciousness only the capricious can come, whereas the will can only be good by willing the good because it is the good and not its opposite, the good which is in itself the ethically necessary and utterly valuable in its worth and not dependent on capriciousness. Thus it is indispensable to begin with the ethically necessary (but as a *mode of being* of God); this must lie in God himself and must be God himself. The ethical in God is thus once present in the form of *that which cannot not be*, as the holy and necessary power which neither will nor can renounce itself, but which must be and which must be willed to be valid as the holy necessity of the good. This first mode of being of the ethical God we call *Father*, by the analogy of ecclesiastical

26. This passage shows Dorner's triadic conception of God, or the immanent ontological Trinity.—TRANS.

27. As the *Revue chrétienne* has attempted in several articles, likewise the work of Charles Sécrétan, *Philosophie de la Liberté* (Paris, 1849), etc.

usage and the New Testament. In Scripture the Father is so conceived even for the world of revelation. All the ethically necessary is grounded in him; the law in conscience and on Sinai points back to him, and even the Son sees in him his ethical *dei* [obligation].

But this ethically necessary being is not a fate inimical to freedom, nor is it by itself the description of God as such. Rather, it is ethical necessity which demands that the good be actualized; it therefore tends just as eternally through itself to *freedom*, as the adequate form of actualization of the ethical. God does not will to be merely an ethical being which he in no way posits, which operates only as natural necessity, as it were fatalistically; rather, the ethical necessity which he is must in itself necessarily will the free, through which alone can what is necessarily good for its own sake find the mode of being it seeks. The ethically necessary is the lover of freedom, for the good wills to be for the free and by the same; that is its desire and glory. The naturalism which posits the actualized will of God as only simply and immediately determined by a nature not posited by God would be the death of the ethical, as one would quite clearly visualize if he tried to say: God must be love and must love by natural necessity. Be it thus certain that without the presupposition of the ethically necessary in God the ethical would not appear at all: it is equally certain that God as himself ethical does not will to be merely a *given*, viz., the good which is necessary in itself. Rather, he wills also to be the one eternally and vitally positing his love, and consequently he also wills, just as eternally as he is the ethically necessary being, the principle of the ethically free in itself, as the instrument for his eternal self-actualization into absolute ethical personality. For without freedom there is no love.[28] This second mode of being, the ethical in the form of freedom, we assign to the Son, according to the New Testament and ecclesiastical analogy, so that the Son is the divine principle of the realm of freedom and history, the principle of movement on the ground of a given basis. For the ethically necessary, in the world as in God, is the conditioning presupposition of

28. If one wanted to think of God as the good being, but this good being as power which determined its will indifferently, that would lead to the denial that there is even in God a free positing of the good, a willing of the same out of love for the good as such. Still less could there be free ethical personality in the world. A God in whom there was not free love also could not reveal and implant it. On the contrary, by the equally eternal and essential factor of the free, God gains this eternally: that even his absolute, necessary, holy being is not merely a *Natura*, but even within himself and by himself, it is that which is eternally posited, willed. And this is his ethical aseity, which must be added to the ontological and the logical.

all that is free. The incarnate Son calls himself the one who makes free (John 8:32) and the Son of the house in distinction from the unfree.[29]

It having been established that the ethical in God must have the designated double mode of being, it still remains to be considered, how are these contraries united without being obliterated?

God's primary being as ethically necessary does not suffice for the ethical in him; because it is essentially distinguished from nature as the ethical, it seeks a second mediated form of existence. It wills to be for the free and freely willed thereby; it seeks its adequate form, the stamp of its essence (Heb. 1:3), precisely in its apparent opposite. The free in itself and as such, however, is nothing more than the real possibility for the eternal self-generation of the ethical into actuality. The free cannot exist in order to have the good as its content by physical necessity; rather, it exists in order to mediate the good by its conscious will; it is not physically necessitated, but is the producing, spiritually willing principle of actualization of the good. The free in God certainly cannot be unethical arbitrariness; but the eternal result, which is the point, would be just as little secured if we conceived this free reality as defined simply by the knowledge of the ethically necessary. *Were the good and the necessary merely a given for the free and not also something freely posited by it, or if the free did not rather know and will in the necessary its own true essence, its own self, then the good would still remain for the free only an other, something alien, to which the free voluntarily subordinated itself.* Only when the free has found itself in the unshakable objective, so that in the depths of the ethically necessary the free is also something willed, is the absolute actualization of the ethically necessary achieved in freedom's own desire and love. This occurs by the Spirit of God, who ruling in the depths of deity is the bond of unity between the ethically necessary and the free, who shows in the one only the reverse side of the other and who mediates these antitheses into the eternal absolute actuality of the ethical divine personality.

This explication can suffice for what needs to be established here, that the ethical, far from leaving us with an either/or of immutability and vitality, has in itself the inner character of laying claim to both for itself, of willing and having to be both, in order to correspond to the proper concept which must be absolutely and eternally real in God. If one admits this, and likewise that which is no less necessarily and eternally to be posited, viz., the union

29. Presumably no reminder is needed that in this context a full treatment of the doctrine of the Trinity is not intended.

of these two necessarily conceived modes of being of the ethical in God, then a firm point is won beyond the sphere in which pantheism and Deism must lie in eternal conflict with each other. Then both pantheism with its aimless vitality and Deism with the rigid lifelessness of its God-concept are definitively surpassed, since in the truly ethical concept of God, the truths that are present in both, the vitality and immutability, attain union.

In the pre-Reformation period we see a vacillation, now a preponderance of the ethically necessary, which leads to legalism, now a preponderance of the free as such, not merely in the form of sensuousness but also of *opera supererogatoria* [works of supererogation] not only in the doctrinal form which establishes a sub-legality but also in that which establishes supra-legality. Nomism as well as antinomianism come to their highest, that is, theological, expression in those two theses, of Thomas on the one hand and of Duns Scotus on the other. The Reformation did indeed attain anthropologically or soteriologically the union of the necessary and the free in the principle of faith, in which arbitrariness and legalism, paganism and Judaism are excluded. But there is still the question of developing ethically the received doctrine of God (which was still not able definitively to overcome Deism and pantheism), so that there is apprehended in God the archetypal eternal union of the necessary and the free, simply in order that the ectypal union of the two which is given in faith may also receive its absolute foundation. The two theses of that old controversy only *seem* to be in contradiction. They are united in the truly ethical concept of God; for, to look at the essential moments through which he eternally constitutes himself, each of these thus represents an essential side of the truth. If God were only eternally given to himself as good, and did not eternally will and posit himself as ethical, he would not be the eternally living goodness and freedom, but only a good nature; and in the same way it would be only apparent eminence, if God were simply above the ethically necessary, as it were *exlex* [lawless], if the ethical were for him only an effluence of his will to power and not also holy necessity in him. However, the absolute union of the ethically necessary and the ethically free, in which the two confirm one another, is *love*; and thus the primal good is *love* only because in him the ethical has a threefold and yet indissolubly coherent mode of being.[30]

30. On the other hand, it is not permissible to deny that there is freedom in God because a contradiction to the ethically necessary cannot be conceived in him. The possibility of this contradiction does not belong to the concept of perfect freedom; even the perfected finite spirits will exist in the impossibility of this contradiction, yet not on that account merely in a legal or physical and fatalistic necessity of the good, but rather in the life of free love, which never forsakes itself but eternally posits itself anew.

The analysis of the ethical in its perfection shows us, therefore, that God in himself is to be conceived both as immutable, viz., in respect of the ethical, and as living and free, but these two are not simply left existing alongside one another. Rather, the ethical immutability that is in God requires also for itself the vitality that is just as eternal; the ethically necessary points of itself to freedom as its means of actualization. The vitality of God, the principle of which lies in his freedom, is no less bound up with the ethically necessary through itself, through its inner essence; the free is for the ethically necessary. We must say, therefore, that there is in God not a fixed but a living immutability; but just as little is there in him a restless or unsteady vitality by which he could forsake himself; rather, God's vitality has also taken the ethical immutability up eternally into itself.

We shall consider this somewhat more closely still, in order to satisfy ourselves that the ethical concept of God (1) is able to guarantee that *immutability* of God on which alone it depends, and (2) that it can do no less for the *vitality* of God.

(1) God is love (1 John 4:8). The ethical in God is God in his divinity. All so-called proofs for the existence of God are, rightly apprehended, only preludes to the ontological, which attains its truth, however, only by the ethical. And the ethical does not have merely physical or cosmological or logical necessity; rather, it must be conceived, and when conceived, it is conceived as existing because it is the absolutely valuable in itself, which alone has its basis and goal in itself, and alone is absolute end in itself. Only in the ethical concept of God, therefore, does even aseity achieve its true meaning and its absolute foundation. God wills and posits himself eternally, because as love he eternally takes up what is in the highest sense the necessary, the ethical, into his will so completely that his freedom is wholly identified with the ethical. And everything else that is or may be conceived in God exists for this his love, is willed by God for it and as it requires. Thus not merely (to speak with Plato) does everything outside of God have the guarantee of existence and harmony in God's goodness; rather, the love of God also contains the supreme, absolute guarantee for everything which may be designated as a divine attribute. The so-called physical attributes of God do not exist for themselves, as if they had in themselves the absolute necessity of being and actuality; rather, there is in God the subordinate and the superordinate, and the physical attributes serve the ethical essence of God, which is the power over them. Similarly,

the so-called logical attributes do not exist for their own sake or in themselves, they exist for the absolute love of God and its eternal self-generation.[31] In a word, all the divine powers and attributes do not in the last analysis exist for themselves, as if they were for themselves absolutely valuable and necessary; they exist for absolute love.

Thus the ethical concept of God leaves room for vitality and movement in God—yes, it may well permit even change and alteration to be reflected into God (to be sure, this must always be only ethically motivated), if only one thing continues to be preserved, the *ethical self-identity* and *immutability* of God. This must remain inviolate; according to the argument above, it must also be eternal actuality in God, it cannot in God himself be at any time merely or even partially potentiality; the inner personal reality of the ethical, which is God himself, can have no intermittent existence, but only one which is constant and self-identical. God in himself can never be mere potence of love, nor become that, nor reduce himself to it. Neither God's nature nor his logical essence can introduce such self-depotentiation into him. That would have to take place by his love itself.

But how could the absolute actuality of the love of God, which constitutes the absolute concept of God and expresses the utterly highest good, arrive in itself at the point of turning against itself? How can actual love be able to determine itself so that out of love, love surrenders the utterly highest? How can it, in a kind of *ecstasis* (displacement) from itself, be able to fall out of its absolute actuality in order to serve love? Love would here be involved in the sheerest contradiction with itself. For this would mean on the one hand that love, which is to be conceived only as actual, is the unconditionally valuable good, that end which *sensu eminenti* is the end-in-itself and without which everything else would totter, but on the other hand that it is conceivable for love not to view itself as the highest end, but at least momentarily to give itself up in order to become a means and to serve love. "But if I tear down again what I have built, then I condemn myself."[32] Rather, that surrender of the love which is absolute and in itself actual, even if one may seek to regard the surrender as a superabundance of love, is unethical. A love which out of love gave up loving even for a

31. By "physical" attributes, Dorner means such attributes as infinity of being, simplicity, omnipotence, and also beauty and harmony. The "logical" attributes, which he also sometimes calls "intellectual," refer to consciousness and knowledge in God. Cf. Dorner's *System of Christian Doctrine*, §§31b, 32; also 136f. above.—TRANS.

32. Cf. Gal. 2:18.—TRANS.

moment would be no love; this has its place only in the systems of pantheism. Pantheism knows a potential love, a sleep of love, a self-forfeiture of love, because it knows no true love.

Instead of that, the God of the Old and New Testaments is not without eternal self-affirmation of his ethical essence, not without *justice*, which is concerned with and guards the absolutely valuable as such. Self-affirmation or self-love is not egoism, but it must be and remain immanently self-giving and self-impartation, and this negative is decisive for the ethical character of the latter. This righteous self-affirmation belongs in its unconditional necessity to the honor of God, therefore the religion which has the idea of justice as its center accents the honor of Jehovah in such a wholly special measure. The burning zeal of Jehovah for his holiness and honor, at the service of which stand all his power and strength (Exod 20:5), is not egoistic, because it is not of a particular sort. As Jehovah affirms himself by virtue of his ethical aseity, even in judgment and punishment, and loves his honor jealously, he thereby gives the honor due it to the holy and the good *generally*, for he is himself originally *the holy*, the ethically necessary. That is not to say that this could exist only in him; on the contrary, according to its universal form the holy and good desires to be and to prevail wherever there is a place for it. But God's will and freedom have eternally grasped the good and holy with its universal tendency so absolutely and are so identified with it that his self-love and self-affirmation are at the same time nothing else than the self-affirmation of the majesty of the holy and the good generally.

Accordingly, the absolute divine love is above all directed to itself; it is reflected in itself, conscious of itself, having and willing itself. Giving is preceded by having, ethical giving or loving impartation by self-possession. Only the personal, the self-conscious, can love;[33] as indeed perfect love exists only where the good is willed in the self-willing. The divine personality in itself is in no way a finitizing of God, but is only the divine life of love itself, willing and affirming itself; it is the adequate form of the universal, the good in itself, its impress in will and consciousness.

(2) But for that very reason this immovable self-affirmation or justice, *the true (i.e., ethical) immutability of God*, does not exclude but includes

33. Therefore the suspending of self-consciousness would be identical with the cessation of love, by which fact a kenosis in which the Logos even momentarily surrendered his self-consciousness, be it for the purpose of creation or of incarnation, is proved to be an ethical impossibility.

the movement to self-impartation (which one commonly identifies with love generally) and thereby includes vitality. We have seen that he in himself, as ethical absolutely spiritual vitality, is neither mere law nor mere ethical substance or nature. But the same thing can be apprehended in his relation to the idea of the world. By absolute ethical self-possession, God is indeed eternally distinguished from everything which he is not; the justice of God is the point of divergence from pantheism. But his self-possession and self-willing also refer to him as love which wills to impart. Since his self-love embraces the holy and good as such or in general, and not as it were only as *his* good, as a particular possession, there is in God nothing of an exclusive jealousy (*Pthonos*) toward a being and life or an entity outside him, as the pagan world thought of him, not knowing or believing God's self-sufficiency and certainty of himself. The divine jealousy is one that is holy and not one that is envious; this holds for the universal good or holy which God is, it holds for the divine personality simply because this is the absolute form of actuality of this good. It is for this universal good that the holy life of love also wills to be the divine personality; thus also in its self-love, by virtue of which the divine personality can never be lost, it wills at the same time universal acceptance and honor of that good, and for that very reason it wills the giving of a share in itself and its blessedness. Precisely by reason of the self-love or self-affirmation of God, the love of the personal God also wills objects for its self-impartation, a world of personal beings. This willing of objects is included in God's self-love because within and for the divine sphere itself the self-impartation of pure love cannot yet, in the proper sense, reach manifestation. It is to be insisted that love, as imparting, does not yet find the proper place of its manifestation in God himself, but only where purely free original giving takes place, only where there is pure want in the recipient. Its unselfish purity first reveals itself precisely where there is the possibility that it will not receive back what it gives (Luke 6:30-32). However, the self-impartation to the actual other, the creature, is in no way a loss of self, a giving up of self by God; it is rather the power of love to be in the other itself and to be itself in the other.

Let us now attempt briefly to consider the conformity to Scripture of the basic ideas of the foregoing. However, since it is usually in concrete terms that Holy Scripture speaks of God's immutability and vitality, other elements, especially from the New Testament, will be reserved for the conclusion.

Even the old covenant, however highly the immutability of God is exalted in it, does not accord at all with those doctrines of the old dogmatics, which see in God as it were only the unmoving utterly simple Neoplatonic *on* [being] or the *estos* [substance] of certain ancient religious systems. The Old Testament also accentuates the contrary aspect, the vitality of God, which brings him near the world through his historical deeds and treats the course of the world as something very closely concerning him and his honor. He is not merely the immutable in the stream of time, he is also the one who passes through the times of the world and acts in them.[34] Even the word *Jehovah* gathers up in itself, along with the meaning earlier discussed, the living connection with men and their history; he possesses not merely eminence over space and time, but also a positive relation to both.

Even this world in general, which he called into existence, possesses a value in his eyes; after it is, the created is for him something very "good" (Gen. 1:31), which it had not been previously. God is related differently to the world as created than to the world as to-be-created; also, his action and demeanor are one thing in creation and another in preservation (Gen. 2:1-4). He has given the earth to the human family, and the center of its pre-Christian history is the history of Israel. But this history does not exist apart from a history of his deeds, which are directed to the end that whereas (without prejudice to a constantly existing presence of God) the earth is first of all his footstool, and his throne and his sanctuary are in heaven, heaven and his sanctuary are to be planted in the earth, that is, within humanity (Isa. 51:16). In the Old Testament these divine acts do not at all give the impression that God, for his part, has willed and done always and only the same in every moment and that through the varying conditions of men this one eternally identical beam simply undergoes varying refractions. Rather, as it is unmistakable that the unity of the goal surely pervades the coherence of the divine acts, so a flexibility and as it were an elasticity are unmistakable in them; the divine facts of salvation are conditioned according to the specific need. The divine consistency is not that of a mechanism of nature, of a blind natural law that eternally works identically, but rather one that moves through apparent inconsistency and through a pliability (Ps. 18:27 vv. 25 ff.) which allows to human freedom an influence conditioning the divine activity. This vitality of the participation of God in the world, which everywhere is joined fully and wholly

34. 1 Tim. 1–17: *Basileus ton ainon* [king of the ages].

to the specific moment—and which does not prematurely cause something from the future, which is for his knowledge, to be of decisive influence—is so strongly marked in the Old Testament that one can find there even an anthropomorphic and anthropopathic movability in the divine action with just as much validity (or invalidity) as a rigid immutability (e.g., Gen. 6:6; Amos 7:3,6; Gen. 18; Exod. 32:10-14; Num. 1 ff., 10 ff.; Zech. 10:3; 1 Sam. 15:11; Joel 2:13; Jon. 3:9,10, 4:2; Pss. 5:7, 106:40, 18:27; Song 11:20, 12:22, 16:5; Jer. 4:28, 18:8,10, 26:3,19, 36:3, 42:10; Isa. 1:11-15, 43:24, 44:22). But even where God alters his action and, for example, prophecies do not come to pass, which for the moment, since they were pronounced, were wholly serious or on the point of being fulfilled, but subsequently were not fulfilled because the presupposition on which and in connection with which they were given was altered—and this may be far more frequent in the prophetic literature than is often assumed—even there, according to the Old Testament, God remains eternally self-identical in the ethical respect. *This self-identity and ethical immutability are precisely the reason that he does not always behave in a simply identical way toward mutable humankind*, but that change enters both into his act and even into his attitude toward humanity. According to the Old Testament (as well as to the New Testament), it is not that through sin only the relation of men to God is altered while God's relation to men remains simply the same. To be sure, the latter has a self-identity in that it contains the purely ethical character; but this ethical immutability, in its living relation to each moment of creaturely life, to its value or disvalue, is the basis of continual alterations in the way in which God is disposed toward mutable man.

In the New Testament all this receives its confirmation in still more concrete application (see III).

The preceding explication forbids us to be so hasty in the recognition of so-called anthropomorphisms and anthropopathisms in Holy Scripture; rather it warrants allowing an important place to what has been called biblical realism. If only the ethical immutability of God is protected and strictly preserved, then we have enough to allow movement and alteration also to be reflected into God, into the world of his thoughts and his will, without any danger for the concept of God and for the divine eminence (which itself is above all to be adjudged ethically); yes, in the ethical concept of God we have the principle that requires this, and establishes a living, historico-temporal relation of God to the world.

## III

Now it is time to test the fruitfulness of our result by applying it to some of the chief points of Christian doctrine.[35]

In regard to the creation of the world as a divine act, after what has been mentioned in the first essay,[36] there is little still to be noted, since it is as good as agreed that the world is to be derived from the free divided love. Only this can now no longer be understood by us in the sense of any kind of arbitrariness, for that leads inescapably to an unallowable mutability of the ethical God. The meaning can only be that God has not created out of superabundance, which would be imperfection and disharmony or suffering, nor for the completion of himself, nor finally as necessitated by the creative intelligence and its world-idea, but out of the blessedness and perfection of his love and out of the self-identity of its free being [*Wesen*], in which lives the desire of self-impartation. For example, out of purely conceptual being, out of possibility, he has launched what was not into actuality. The world is a good goal, corresponding to the love of God, not an accident: for God makes the world his goal, even treats it as an end-in-itself—which is united with his necessary self-love only through the fact that for his part God does not merely love the world but he also does not cease to love love and to affirm himself. The two are so united that the world is created for its blessedness and for God's glory. The ethical God remains unaltered in self-identity, even as he posits the world as the end-in-itself of his love, for he affirms himself therein as love for the life of love which has its primal reality in him; but he manifests this joy in the life of love by establishing the possibility of the new life of love along with his. Be that held fast, then there is no danger at all in *not* introducing a *time* between the world as possible and the world as actual; it is on the other hand even necessary. Between God and the actual creation is to be introduced only the conception of the world as a possible, which conception of the world God as it were appropriates in his heart and his will. But again it would be inconceivable that God should bear in himself the conception of a world conforming to his love but at first decline its actualization,

35. It is self-evident, surely, that in what follows no elaboration of the dogmas which come into consideration can be intended, but only a look at the import of the definitions arrived at, and, since dogmatics must for us be a whole harmonizing in its parts, indirectly a confirmation or testing of them.

36. Especially, Dorner's critique of the notion that creation itself involves a *kenosis*, particularly in the sense of a reduction or limitation of the being of God in the Son, an interpretation offered in support of some of the more extreme doctrines of *kenosis* (in the incarnation) that Dorner opposed.—TRANS.

or that there was first a hindrance in himself to be removed, whereupon he first proceeded to the actualization. Both would again mean sacrificing the ethical unchangeability of God to physical concepts of God's absolute power and freedom. For arbitrariness is not ethical, but physical.

Conversely, it would mean limiting the ethical *vitality* of God in just as inadmissible a way if one supposed that with the first act of creation the creative activity of God were also altogether done with, or as it were exhausted (1 Cor. 15:45; 2 Cor. 5:17). The divine love gives us no right to think of the natural order as closed with the first creative act of God, to think of the universe in a given moment as already a whole which rounded-off in itself would permit endurance to nothing else, and thus, for example, would exclude miracles, however admirably they too fit into the proper world-goal, that is, however essentially they were incorporated into God's eternal world-idea, which reaches out over every given time and its world-form. The world shows abundantly that it is still no whole, that it still had a history before it and that God is at all times at his work, even on the Sabbath (John 5:17).[37] But the creative activity of God is intermittent in accord with the divine plan and goal for the world, although the individual acts thereof are held together by the unity of this world-plan and immutable love; and thus the relative rest of God, the not-creating, also has its time (Gen. 2:2 f.), whereas the sustaining activity is perennial.

God thus intervenes in the world as it pleases the wisdom of his love, in order to make the natural order increasingly a perfect whole. It is creaturely freedom in particular, this movable entity with its vocation for history—history whose center is precisely religion, or the communion between God and the free creature—for whose sake God, in order to be immutable but living love, determines himself to enter into alteration and change, not in respect to his being, but in respect to the exercise of his constantly self-identical love.

As we have seen, the will of creation is not joined with God's being accidentally, as a theology ill advised and ill understanding its interests often supposes it necessary to profess; therefore such a view will also not do for the world of *preservation* and *providence*. Rather, because the world coheres with God's ethical essence in its being, according to the goal toward which it is set, and cannot be said to be an arbitrary product, indifferent

37. I excuse myself from more detailed elaboration of this point, since reference can be made here to the admirable essay by Richard Rothe concerning the concept of revelation and miracle in his essays "Zur Dogmatik" [*Theologische Studien und Kritiken*, 1858, 1].

for God, therefore its empirical condition, and indeed in every moment, must be for God himself of the highest significance for his justice and his love. In it the honor of God himself is involved, not merely figuratively but in fullest seriousness, as the Old Testament has it. For a living ethical concept of God does not allow God's cause *[Sache]* and the affairs of the world to be separated.[38] Even a man would not be sufficiently zealous for the good if he thought only of his own good but was indifferent to the victory or defeat of the good outside him. How much more in God must it belong to his ethical self-affirmation that he will the good outside himself with the same holy zeal as he wills it in himself. For there is only one ethical reality, in God and in the world, however manifold its forms of appearance may be. To be sure, the world adds nothing to the perfection of God himself, but this perfection has its exercise in the world. God is blessed in himself, in his love, but by virtue of that perfection which is also love arising to create and creatively imparting itself; he is not merely a resting perfection and blessedness, reflecting in itself and enjoying itself, but rather he is *blessed* as love which is operative, directed to self-impartation. Nor can we say of him that he first becomes blessed by his act of love, for he rather acts out of his blessedness, which permits no disturbance, thus he is yet blessed as the love which he is, that is, as living love, and his products are not mere imaginations or shadows, but move in freedom and independence. His love allows them to be children to him as Father. By this love he deems it gain and joy for himself when the creature freely returns his love and presents himself to God as a living sacrifice of love, which does not lose the love in the sacrifice, does not annihilate itself, but actualizes itself as an end-in-itself, as loving personality which is valuable in itself. For the union of self-love and loving abandon must take place ectypally in man as archetypally in God. Thus out of the realm of historical time and the free creature there results for God something valuable according to his, the absolute judgment, a satisfaction for the divine consciousness which it did not previously have, a joy which he could not have from himself and without the world. And this joy of his consciousness, a consciousness which accompanies historical time, we have to think of as one which grows as the world of his children becomes richer and purer, in which world he extends his holy, wise, and blessed life in

38. We have followed Josiah Royce in translating *Sache* as cause. The term cause is not intended here in scientific cause-effect sense, but used in a practical-social-political sense. Royce translates Sache as cause in his *Lectures on Modern Idealism* (New Haven: Yale University Press, 1922) and extends its practical sense in his *Philosophy of Loyalty*.—TRANS.

an ever less limited way. If the hymns of praise are one day actually to ring out, "The kingdom of the world has become the kingdom of our Lord and of his Christ; the dwelling of God is with men" (Rev. 19:6; cf. 11:15; 21:3), that will be an actually new song even for God, a song which has not sounded from eternity for God, by his foreknowledge or decree, just as it does in the blessed celebration of world-fulfillment; as the gain of historical time is one that is real and valuable in itself, so will it also be for God, by virtue of the immutability of his living love.

But for this very reason it is also to be said: The sins of the world and the enmity toward God which slumbers in it touch him to the heart (Gen. 6:6), and we need not hesitate to teach a holy wrath of God against the evil and against men insofar as they are evil. God is not related in the same way to the evil and to the good, as concerns neither his disposition nor his acts. That is not the meaning of Matt. 5:45. For if so, precisely then would the holy God be mutable. Evil calls forth in him a movement of displeasure and disfavor, which would not arise without evil, as it ceases with it, and which is the motive of his righteous judgment. In this respect there is nothing at all of so-called anthropopathism to be stripped off, which in any way serves simply to declare with all power the vitality of the holy ethical demeanor of God; rather, the whole is well established by scientific thought and only secures the true concept of God. No expression, however strong, of this vitality can ever exhaust the objective truth entirely, and if only it is actually of an ethical sort, it is the direct opposite of moral admixture and pollution in the vitality.

Here a further point is to be made. God's grace, not in spite of but by virtue of his ethical immutability and vitality, condescends to a *real reciprocal relation* with free beings, not merely possibly to the race as a unity—that would be at once deistic and would invite the introduction of intermediate entities—but also directly and in particularity to every individual. For the ethical has its place only in persons; the race is not personal. The ethical condition of each individual touches God directly. What is aimed at is a personal, actualized communion of love with the free creature, and thus one consisting in acts. The exercise of the power with which the ethical God is endowed therefore remains excluded from the moral-religious process of man, but not by means of a self-limitation of God, if we are to speak exactly. For the power of God is not its own Lord, not its own impetus; in it there is no necessity at all to effectuate what it can. It serves the good, but works by mediation for the ethical goals of the freedom which is willed and upheld by God. But thereby the divine work and self-impartation are determined as being historico-temporal. The perfect self-impartation therefore cannot collapse into identity with creation. For the perfection of man must be mediated through his freedom, and the highest receiving can only come to receptivity that is perfected throughout a rich historical reciprocal relation of divine imparting and human willing to receive. In this process, God does in no way always give just the same, as in the physical realm the sun shines alike on the just and the unjust. So long as the preconditions are not yet present, he will not even always give the highest, although that remains the goal; rather, he deals always with man just as he is, he requires of man and grants to him that which is appropriate to his actual level. Thus the one divine will of grace as it were scatters itself in many temporal acts—in a word, *precisely in order to hold fast the unity and immutability of the ethical goal and of himself*, God conditions his action toward free, mutable mankind exactly as the actual condition of man requires. If he cannot posit the evil by his productive will, nor allow it to exist by a lingering of the productive will behind the commanding, no more can he even by his power make it impossible or simply will to crush it. Either event is forbidden by his ethical nature. Yet on the other hand God's ethical nature requires the holding fast of his living connection to the world in general, just as to men, inasmuch as they are entangled with evil. Thus originates that reciprocal relation between God and the free creature by virtue of which God condescends, instead of willing to annihilate the evil and compel the good, rather to exercise forbearance and not to deliver it up at once to the punishment of almighty justice. He woos their souls and their devotion, that at least atoning and forgiving love may perhaps break the hard heart and kindle love in response. Through his wisdom and holy love he engages sinners in combat, as if they were an equal power, in a struggle for their souls (Luke 18:1ff.; Gen. 32:28); and in such combat there is in him a *compassion* [*Mitleid*], a holy inner participation, a living tender mercy, an analogue of affliction (Eph. 4:30)—not of a passive sort but active, posited by his love, until the soul which is still to be saved is drawn to him. And something similar also takes place in the very life of the faithful; for the withdrawal of consolation and of the feeling of grace, though certainly connected with our unfaithfulness, is yet by no means merely a—so to speak—physical effect of the sin that still remains; nor is the withdrawal affected simply by a new unreceptivity to God's favor and grace, as if the latter appeared wholly of itself and ever the same when one turned again to its beams. Rather, faith has to learn that the appearance of the divine favor is not something merely physical, a natural necessity, but in each moment is the free act of God's love; therefore also the lack of consolation and of grace is not simply a natural consequence of our condition, but also has its basis in a withdrawing or a willing not to grant on God's part, which by the refusal prepares a higher granting. For when at the outset God's prevenient love struggles with sin for man, he so preserves the ethical character in such activity that thereafter a struggle of man with God must begin, in order that from the side of man there may come a serious, firm affirmation of the divine message and imparting, a grasping for the being-grasped, and thus a completion of the reciprocal communion, as the living fellowship of love requires (Luke 18:1ff.; Gen. 32:38; Phil. 3:12).

But that concept of God in which vitality and immutability are indissolubly united is also of the most far-reaching significance for the Christian facts and dogmas in the stricter sense. Thus for the *incarnation* and *reconciliation* in Christ. If, as we saw above (in the second article) the life-filled efficacious participation of God in the real world is something quite other than bare "intention," and if his intention embraces rather only the decision that what is eternally present to him in idea is to be experienced historically only with the world, then indeed the center of history, the appearance of Christ, stood constantly before God as certainly as if it were eternally present, but not in the same way as if it were actual. Before Christ, God did not yet know the world as actually united with himself, not yet in reconciled presence, but simply as that which was to be reconciled and was being reconciled. Cocceius was quite right when, for the pre-Christian period, he allowed the Son to be only the *Fidejussor* and not yet the *Expromissor* of salvation.[39] In this temporally diverse divine knowing, this alteration in itself, nothing of an inadequacy in God is asserted, according to the preceding discussion; it is rather the contrary which would annul the divine knowing as true. Thus it is not that God views the world in the same way before and after Christ, and that only the relation of the *world* to God has been changed by Christ, but not the relation of *God to the world*. It is even unallowable to suppose that God, for his part, sought equally, in every period since the fall, to accomplish the incarnation, and already willed to call the God-man into existence in the devout, the prophets

39. Johannes Cocceius (1603–69), the federal theologian. The legal distinction was between one who gives security, is bail or surety for another, and one who promises to pay a debt or judgment for another.—TRANS.

and the kings of the Old Testament—this act being delayed and thwarted only by sin in the holy men of the Old Testament, who thereby really become types of Christ by having exhibited elements of the God-man, even though imperfectly. For if the activity from God's side in this relationship had been constantly one and the same in invariable identity, the incarnation would first have undergone a continual miscarrying, until finally success came about through human freedom. Here the uniqueness of Christ would be threatened, as also the divine eternal idea of the personality of devout individuals would be altered. For they would all have been destined to be God-men, those who by sin now have become ruins, but who by redemption can still be brought to the point of becoming God-men. Instead of that we shall thus say: By reason of his grace, God has indeed willed the incarnation eternally; he has not, however, willed *to effect* it in every moment, but only when the time was fulfilled (to this, of course, belongs also the maturity of human receptivity); what he willed to effect and did effect before Christ is the preparation of this receptivity for his deed, which is unique of its kind and only *once* willed efficaciously on his part.

Christ's appearance denotes something new in God's *activity* in the world, and is also a new actuality for God's *knowledge*. As surely as the real reuniting of God and humanity is first given in Christ, so surely is the origin of this new beginning found in a new deed of God, one not previously existent, though constantly belonging to the divine intention. The main point here does not lie in the decree as such, nor is the decree immediately identical with the effecting and immediate willing to effect what is decided; it is, rather, in history and actuality that the main point lies, and for this even the decree is only a means. To the distinction that exists in us between intention and execution, there is an analogue in the divine sphere too, all the more surely as the divine intention for effectuation takes into itself conditionality or self-conditioning by "the fullness of time," and thus it determines itself to an entering into the form of temporality. Therefore the doctrine of the eternal divine intention may not be misused, as so often happens in the concept of God of the old dogmatics, in such a way as to make the living connection of God to the world (which is at every moment present and suited to the need of the world) into something that on his part is only eternally the same, that is, pallid.

Nor is this all. The idea of the incarnation is not merely a *deed* of God like any other; rather, it comprehends what has by God's deed become a *new being of God himself* in the world, which previously existed only according to potence or decree, and first achieves actuality in Christ. *Mansit, quod erat, factus est, quod non erat* [remaining what he was, he was made what he was not]. To say that in the incarnation God did not become anything which he previously was not would be Nihilianism.[40] By the incarnation there is posited a being, a being of God joined with the world, which previously did not exist; and thus this new *actuality* is also something new for God's knowledge of himself and of the world, although the decree to this end was eternally in him. If this actuality involved for him only as much as and no more than his eternal decree, then the former would itself have only a Docetic significance. History would bring nothing new, would have no real product, but would at most be an exhibition of what is eternally and identically present; it would not be something to be distinguished by this doctrine. But where then would love be? For it is the essence of love, and thus the requirement of the ethical concept of God, not to stop with mere ideas or doctrines but to participate in a living way in historico-temporal humanity, sharing in it in order to give a share in itself.

This participation of God in historical time is further of special importance for the inner sanctum of the Christian religion, *reconciliation*. It is an essential ingredient of Christian faith that through Christ God has revealed not just some eternal being-reconciled to sin on the part of God—for there is no such thing; instead there is a real, serious tension, the divine disfavor toward sin and the sinner. The Christian faith is—and this does not offend the immutability of God but rather confirms it as ethical—that henceforth God looks upon humanity in another way than before, because in Christ's person, work, and passion, the objective and all-sufficient potence [*Potenz*] of the reconciliation of all sinners is implanted in our race and has become truly proper to it, or because Christ has gained and actualized something which did not previously exist but first became possible in him, namely satisfaction of the divine justice. For since God views humanity as it now is but previously was not, he views it not without the real efficacious potence of the reconciliation of all individuals, which belongs to the whole race. And thus humanity, as a unity for God and his

40. A view, with which Peter Lombard was charged, according to which the human nature was only the garment in which God clothed himself in order to appear as a man. The person of the Son (not the divine nature) assumed human nature (not human personhood), and no compound of nature or person results; therefore, it is inferred, the incarnation (in which God does not become anything he was not before) is no more than a simple relation of God to humanity, a permanent theophany. See Dorner, *Development of the Doctrine of the Person of Christ,* II/1, 309ff.—TRANS.

contemplation, is no longer merely an object of the divine *Anoche* [forbearance] for the sake of the future reconciler. Rather, he now sees it equipped with the power [*Kraft*] of reconciliation which it previously lacked, but which it now has in him who is destined to be its head. The disfavor and the displeasure with the sinful race of men are now not without the good pleasure in the Son of man, who belongs to it and standing in whose fellowship all can become objects of the divine good pleasure, yes, for whose sake God *preveniently* can offer grace to sinners. For he died not merely for those who become faithful, but for all, though not all must come to actual enjoyment of that which stands open to all; they can put unbelief in Christ squarely between themselves and reconciliation in him. If they do this, they replace the atoned and forgiven sin by a new one for which Christ cannot have interceded atoningly—the despising of Christ.

Again, however, the passion of Christ requires no self-loss of the Logos or of consciousness; rather, the significance of his work depends here too on the most intimate and living participation of the whole person of Christ in humanity. Far from being that the divine life in him underwent a troubling or even a disturbance in his self-sacrifice, it was rather the power and deed of his indissoluble life, it was Christ's conscious life of love (Heb. 7:16; 9:14) that was engaged in his sacrifice. Love was not given up by him, nor put out of actuality for a moment, nor consumed in the flame of suffering; rather his divine-human love had to affirm itself and did affirm itself even as he was enveloped by the night of death. By death he does not turn "into the condition of complete unconsciousness and impotence, his self-consciousness lost to him";[41] the shrouding of the sentient side of his consciousness in darkness wrenches from him neither the consciousness of the Father and of himself nor the actuality of his love.

But our conclusions also show themselves fruitful for the doctrine of the justification of individuals. This is not identical with election. Even the certainty of election is not merely knowledge of the status of the person-embracing decree (though it is also this); for otherwise it would be without

41. As, e.g., Frédéric Godet would have it, *Revue chrétienne*, 1858, no. III, 158, 160. Associating himself with the modern kenotics, he says: "Will it not be with a similar cry, 'Father, into thy hands I commit my spirit' [Lk. 23:46] that the Word plunges into that voluntary annihilation which was the condition of his incarnation?" In this the Logos is supposed to have maintained the "germ" of a conscious and free personality, for this is presumed to be "precisely the common element between the divine and human existence, and this divine ray became the principle of his human existence." Thus out of the Son is made a ray, a germ. Against those who, with the church, cannot reconcile themselves to these assertions, M. Godet contends somewhat too resolutely that to him they are rationalists.

any historico-temporal act of God's love toward the individual and would be nothing else than the knowledge of the divine law for the form which our personal consciousness should have. There would still be nothing said of a participation in the graciousness of the livingly present God. The knowledge of an immovable gracious decree is one thing, and the actually present but not previously existing encounter of love is something else. The heart of the Christian needs and experiences the greeting of the fatherly kindness and grace which enters into time, for we human children live in time and can only be lifted up into the eternal consciousness by God's act of love making itself temporal. In the strict sense of the word, only those are elected whose faith in justifying grace God has recognized; but justification or reconciliation is offered not to the believer but to all sinners, in order that they may believe. The justification of the sinner *precedes* faith as the divine announcement of peace on the basis of the sacrifice of Christ (as *actus declaratorius*), and is nevertheless a genuinely valid act of God. But the forgiveness of sin is proclaimed to the individual as something which from God's side has already occurred, in order that he may believe it and have as his own, not merely the fact of being loved by God but the belief and knowledge that he is loved by God. The justification of the sinner is not a result materializing of itself for the sake of his future faith or his sanctification; it is this so little that, as the objective divine act of announcing or declaring that God looks upon the sinner as reconciled in Christ, it must precede even faith. On the other hand, the justification of the individual is not identical with the universal and eternal decree of salvation, nor is everything already given with Christ's work on earth; so little is this so, that for the eternal act of the decree of grace concerning the world and for Christ's once-for-all eternally valid sacrifice, there is yet required, even on God's side, an historico-temporal act concerning the individual and revealing or applying to him the forgiving love of God, an act which proceeds from the heavenly high priest. To be sure, this reveals not merely a present or momentary graciousness, but God's loving will that reaches forward and backward into all the depths of eternity (Rom. 5:8-10). God "deals" with men historico-temporally; in the encounters with human life whose conjunction is ordered by him, he does not let power alone affect our souls; he does not make the encounters and everything external into substitutes that might intrude between the soul and himself or his own dealing with souls; rather, he deals with us himself and immediately, that is, primally, through external things as his instruments—yes, he even uses us ourselves (for example, our apprehension) as such instruments of his action on us. Thus by a present act in a given moment God knows how to bring to individuals the temporal revelation of an eternal love, in order that man, apprehending his being-loved, may *will* to be loved and out of the blessedness of knowing himself to be loved may attain the blessedness of love. These are continuing temporal and time-overcoming acts of God's love, conditioned partly by the freedom of man, but a dealing of God directly out of his eternity into the world, although this *his* dealing is performed through the mode of appearance of external media for the sake of individuals. In the preaching of the word of God, along with the sacraments, there is an historico-temporal dealing of God with man, ever anew entering into the present, for word and sacrament are his means of grace. They do not work magically, substituting in place of God, as if God had relinquished his activity to them; he remains the living love. Behind word and sacrament, as it were behind a thin veil, there stands God himself with the fullness of his Spirit, which he distributes as he wills, and the word of God is never at work unless he is there and allows it to work what pleases his wise love.

From this it can become evident how, by the right conception of the relation of God to the historico-temporal, the right mean between two extremes can also be found for the doctrine of the *means of grace*. For the one view emphasizes only the immediacy of the relation of God to the individual spirit, and allows no essential place to the external means of grace which bring us in contact with the historical world, the salvation-history. But this view does not attain, in the purely internal realm of spirit, a secure distinction between what is of God and what is of man; nor does it any more attain a real connection with the salvation-history which took place and takes place on earth, or an incorporation of personality into the coherence of this continuing history. But that distinction between what is of God and what is of one's own spirit is the precondition for the mutual reciprocal relation and the communion of love between God and man; and that incorporation into the real world of the saving acts of God on earth binds the new personality, even in its origins, with the historical life-circle which is the propitious place for its ethical development, that is, with the church. The other view indeed holds on to the world of the means of grace, but treats them magically as substitutes for God, as though he had relinquished his saving power to them and no longer worked immediately through them as instruments by which he acted; or, in still more openly deistic fashion, it treats them as entities which refer back to God in their origin but which have only a purely natural operation, the so-called logical-moral, beside which there is no operation of the Holy Spirit. The right mean between the two extremes is this: The immediate presence of God is not repressed by the means of grace, his loving actuosity is not brought to a stop; but on the other hand this love, which in eternal wakefulness is directed also to individuals, maintains in the means of grace the ordered expression of itself which is historico-temporal and temporally impinging.[42] We shall only mention in a word how, by the same mode of consideration, a standpoint is also gained for the doctrine of *ecclesiastical office*, in particular for that which from the evangelical point of view is the chief issue, the function, divinely instituted for humanity, of the sermon and the administration of the sacraments—a standpoint that sets aside anarchistic spiritualism as well as the hierarchicalism that rests on deistic representations, because in the sermon and in the administration of the sacraments, insofar as they occur in conformity with the gospel, there is rather to be seen an instrumentally mediated dealing of God himself with man.

The participation of Christians in the Holy Spirit also takes place, not through participation's being reproduced of itself by a good contagion or by the act of will of office or community, but repeatedly by a new free act of God which sends the Spirit into hearts, as also the Son was sent in time. So also, the illumining of subjective justification with the feeling of the peace of God and the rebirth of each individual are described in Holy Scripture as a special divine act of love, which impinges in time and actuality by the Holy Spirit, and not as something already finished with the eternal decree in itself, nor as a consequence necessary of itself to faith, without an inner act of God (Rom. 5:5).[43]

42. Cf. the fine explication in Julius Müller's essays on the relation between the Holy Spirit and the means of grace. *Theologische Studien und Kritiken*, 1856, 297ff., 493ff.

43. How our findings may also be made fruitful for the doctrine of miracles and of inspiration, I pass over the more readily since Richard Rothe, in *Theologische Studien und Kritiken*, 1858, 1 [art. "*Offenbarung*"] has given us such a fine discussion of these. I add only a word or two concerning inspiration. In general, I would say that the more we have satisfied ourselves as to how God himself treats and associates with humanity humanly or anthropomorphically in the good sense, the less right or occasion we can have to deny or disguise the human side in the sacred words of Scripture. In particular, however, I would note that the particularity and variety, in levels and kinds, of doctrinal types in Holy Scripture, are among the most important and most enriching apprehensions of recent theology. Yet this gain is threatened once again by an opposition which seeks its justification in the pure divinity of the Word of God, and intends thereby to represent the interests of Christian faith. Such a position might be correct, if individuality were identical with subjectivity and if the concept of God in the old dogmatics were the right one. For us, on the contrary, the matter stands thus: Precisely because God truly and actually has the will of love to reveal himself, he does

So also the true *concept of worship* can emerge only from the stated conception of the relation of God to time, from the assumption of an actually historical life of God, which nevertheless affirms his ethical immutability because it takes place by virtue thereof. For as that could not be a worship in spirit and in truth in which the object of adoration had been transformed or lost in finite individuality, in order to be as near as possible and as it were palpable, so also that would not yet be Christian worship in which, even though it was not lacking in subjective devotion to God, there took place no actual, temporally ingredient act of the devotion of God to the community, in order to impart himself to it and to celebrate even in its midst the act of wedding with the spirit of the community (Matt. 18:20; John 14:21,23; 1 Cor. 3:16; Rev. 21:22).

Is it still necessary to point out the importance of the above assertions for the life of prayer of the individual as well?[44] The realism of the Bible concerning the hearing of prayer corresponds throughout to the true and scientific concept of God, as well as to the need of the praying Christian. The one who prays always enters into this conception of God and his living relation to the world when he communes with God in prayer (Luke 18:1ff.; Gen. 32); there he needs a present testimony of God, there he needs the assurance, on the basis of the divine will, of being able to influence God and the disposition of God toward him. There, even in the particulars to

---

not speak through organs which are unconscious or displaced in unethical ecstasy; and also he does not, for his part, reveal everything in the same way to individuals, as the sun shines alike on all, so that the difference would stem only from the subjective condition of the organs, which would then grasp only fragmentarily the whole divine truth that is presented, and which would thus presumably have blurred it by their subjectivity, with the result that God had not actually achieved his purpose of revelation to them. Instead of saying that it is holy men who have intermixed the individuality, we are rather to say, according to the relation of God to men which we have found, that in the divine act of revelation in men there takes place a self-individualizing of the divine revelation, and only thereby is the revelation living, powerful, and corresponding to God's will of love. Thus the recognition of individual types of doctrine hardly produces a weakening of inspiration; it rather involves an enhancement; only it is now all the more necessary to consider the individual scripture once again as a member of the whole, i.e., of the canon—and this is a further gain. On this occasion I cannot refrain from calling attention to the splendid words on this subject by the late Adolphe Monod, in his *Adieux*, 1857 [Farewell to His Friends and to the Church (New York, 1858)]

44. Cf. Richard Rothe, *Theologiscbe Ethik* (Wittenberg, 1st ed., 1848), I, 124ff. The pious man, in his immediate and absolute certainty of the reality of prayer which is actual and properly so called, will and must with bold confidence, even in spite of an apparently incontrovertible science, rebut as nugatory every representation of the divine world government which allows prayer no free play, i.e. by which there is excluded the possibility of an actually determinative influence from our side on the will of God and on his guidance of the direction of the world (pp. 263, 368–73). See also Gottfried Thomasius, *Dogmatik* [Christi Person und Werk] II, 572–74.

which his prayer may be directed, he does not have to await in mere submission, to say nothing of resignation, that which a necessity written in the stars commands. Rather, in prayer he must maintain that God in all his sovereignty and majesty is a God who yields to entreaty by the voice of the least of his children—save that this flexibility of God, without which a living, intimate communion of the child with the Father would not be possible, has its inner limit in the ethical immutability of God, from which on the other hand this flexibility flows with necessity. Only so is it possible, again properly through the prayer of the individual and the community (Matt. 18:18-20) in the name of Jesus, for there to be granted to the faithful a *symbasileuein*, a co-rule [*Mitregiment*], about which Schleiermacher has said many a fine word, though without acknowledging the necessary presuppositions for it. To be sure, God does not hand over the reins of government to the faithful; but neither does he want to make of them automatons, beings resigned to a determined will. From the very beginning he has preferred to give his friends a joint knowing [*Mitwissen*] of what he wills to do (Gen. 18:17ff.), and to deal historico-temporally through them as his instruments, which as personalities may even co-determine his will and counsel. No less does he seal to them, through an inner but historico-temporal act, the certainty of the hearing of prayer, and fill them with the courage which is certain of the victory before the victory. Here is the innermost point where servitude and sonship part. The servant does not know what his master is doing (John 15:15); at most he knows the Lord's law, but neither its reason nor the result and goal which the Lord wants to attain; therefore fatalism has so readily been joined with the legalistic standpoint of servitude. But those who are his the Savior has called friends (John 15:15), children and free in the Father's house (Matt. 17:26; John 8:32).

I add only one further point. From the time of the Roman emperors it is reported to us that many stood and prayed before the statues of their gods, struggling in vain with the fleeing faith in the gods' hearing their prayers, and that they finally withdrew from their temples, in despair and without higher support for their life. How many have fared similarly in these our days, as a fault of the prevailing unclear concepts of God with which dogmatics has been encumbered! For if they have not lapsed into pantheistic representations [*Vorstellungen*] of a vitality of God which destroys his concept [*Begriff*], then deistic representations of a false eminence cling all the more and are thrown in their way when they seek to pray and to grasp such a representation of God as is needed by the one who prays, and without whose objective truth, prayer, and faith in God's hearing it would be folly. Others do not go as far as to desist from prayer. But in ordinary life their thinking is ruled by a mechanical deistic outlook which has clothed itself for them, without thoroughgoing domination, in the appearance of a scientific nature, and which condemns the concept of God that asserts itself in their prayer. The consequence of this is that their prayer to God can be only halfhearted—even that prayer, by some self-reflection, is dissolved for them into something which has only subjective meaning, so that it is indifferent whether God hears and therefore whether he is or not. For this reason it is of the profoundest importance that theology finally come to the point of bringing concept of God into true scientific balance with the religious interests, in order that the gap between the life of thought and that of religion may more and more be closed, and the unhappy conflict between the immutability and the vitality of God may end in the ethical concept of God, grasping both in their truth for the first time, but therefore also unifying them.[45]

45. We omit here a three-page appended note in which Dorner replies briefly to several criticisms recently made against his Christology, in particular the charge of Nestorianism. What is said there adds nothing to the argument of the present essay, and Dorner's developed christological position is fully presented in the sections of his *System* translated in Welch, *God and Incarnation*, pp. 205ff.—TRANS.

# Bibliography

## I. Dorner's Major Writings

*Entwicklungsgeschichte der Lehre von der Person Christi.* Stuttgart, 1839. 2nd ed. 4 vols. Stuttgart, 1846–56. Translation from the second edition, *History of the Development of the Doctrine of the Person of Christ,* 5 vols. Edinburgh, 1861–63.

*Geschichte der protestantische Theologie.* Munich, 1867. Translation, *History of Protestant Theology,* 2 vols. Edinburgh, 1871.

*System der christlichen Glaubenslehre.* 2 vols. Berlin, 1879–81. 2nd ed. 1886–87. *A System of Christian Doctrine.* 4 vols. Edinburgh, 1880–82.

*System der christlichen Sittenlehre.* Edited by August Dorner, Berlin, 1885. Translation, *System of Christian Ethics.* Edinburgh, 1887.

*Gesammelte Schriften aus dem Gebiet der systematischen Theologie.* Berlin: Verlag Wilhelm Hertz, 1883.

## II. Secondary Literature

Axt-Piscalar, Christine. *Der Grund des Glaubens: Eine theologiegeschichtliche Untersuchung zum Verhältnis von Glaube und Trinität in der Theologie Isaak August Dorners. Beiträge zur Historischen Theologie*. Tübingen: J.C.B. Mohr (Paul Siebeck), 1990.

Barth, Karl, *Church Dogmatics: The Doctrine of God II/1*. Translated by Parker, Johnson, Knight & Haire. Edinburgh: T & T Clark, 1957.

———. *Protestant Thought in the 19th Century.* Valley Forge: Judson Press, 1973.

Bobertag, J. *I. A. Dorner, seine Leben und Lehre*. Gütersloh, 1906.

Brown, Robert F. "Schelling and Dorner On Divine Immutability. *Journal of the American Academy of Religion* LIII/2 (June 1985): 237–50.

Jaeschke, Walter. *Reason in Religion.* Translated by J. Michael Stewart and Peter C. Hodgson. Berkeley: University of California Press, 1990.

Liebner, Theodore. *Christliche Dogmatik aus dem christologischen Prinzip dargestellt*. I/1: *Christologie, oder die christologische Einheit des dogmatischen Systems*. Göttingen, 1849.

Mehring, G. *"Die immanente Wesens-Trinität." In Zeitschrift für Philosophie und spekulative Theologie*. I/9. Edited by I. H. Fichte. Bonn, 1842, 157–95.

Welch, Claude, *God and Incarnation. In A Library of Protestant Thought*. New York: Oxford University Press, 1965.

Welch, Claude, *Protestant Thought in the 19th Century.* Vol. 1. New Haven: Yale University Press, 1972.

Williams, Robert R., "I. A. Domer: The Ethical Immutability of God." *Journal of the American Academy of Religion* LIV/4 (Winter 1986): 721–38.

Williams, Robert R. *Recognition: Fichte and Hegel on the Other.* Albany, NY: State University of New York Press, 1992.

Williams, Robert R. *Schleiermacher The Theologian: The Construction of the Doctrine of God*. Philadelphia: Fortress Press, 1978.

# INDEX